Voices:
Tapping the Child's Voice

Pamela E. Watkins
Compton Community College

Alliance Press

Printed in the United States of America.

ISBN: 1-58316-025-6
00-256

 Alliance Press

3151 Skylane Drive, Suite 102B • Carrollton, TX 75006 • (800) 970-1883

Address all correspondence and order information to the above address.

Contents

Themes

Some Voice Categories

Humor
Salvation
Daisy Fay and the Miracle Man
Toussaint
Chicken Tetrazzini
The Sharkskin Suit
Butch
"What Means Switch?"

Anger
What is White?, A Dollar a Day
Momma
The House on Mango Street
Impressions of an Indian Childhood
The Sky is Gray

Pain
The Sky is Gray
The House on Mango Street
When I Was Puerto Rican
Pat and Pan
Impressions of an Indian Childhood
Salvation

Happiness
Toussaint
Daisy Fay and the Miracle Man

Innocence
Pat and Pan
Salvation
The House on Mango Street
My Sharkskin Suit
"Dear Friend . . ."
"What Means Switch?"
Daisy Fay and the Miracle Man

Rhetorical Table of Contents

INTRODUCTION

What is voice? That illusive, vague creation we often hear about, refer to and try to capture. Some call it tone, some call it atmosphere, even style, but voice is much more complex than the above euphemisms indicate because it's more difficult to find and define. Voice, however, is not tone, atmosphere, or style. These words merely describe the result of the writer's voice. Voice is created from within and style, tone, and atmosphere are the products of that inner voice.

Voice has two masters—listening and writing. One cannot be accomplished without the other. Eudora Welty, who won the Pulitzer Prize for *The Optimist's Daughter*, is a superb writer with provocative thoughts on voice. Welty writes in her essay "Listening to Words,"

> Ever since I was first read to, then started reading to myself, there has never been a line read that I didn't hear. As my eyes followed the sentence, a voice was saying it silently to me. It isn't my mother's voice, or the voice of any person I can identify, certainly not my own. It is human, but inward, and it is inwardly that I listen to it. It is to me the voice of the story or the poem itself. The cadence, whatever it is that asks you to believe, the feeling that resides in the printed word, reaches me through the reader-voice. I have supposed, but never found out, that this is the case with all readers—to read as listeners and with all writers, to write as listeners. (qtd. in Dunbar, Dunbar Rorabacher 66-67)

I am like Eudora Welty; I hear everything I read. Although voice is often equated with narrative fiction, it is also prevalent in the non-fiction narrative. "Salvation," "Momma," What Is White?" and "A Dollar a Day," "When I Was Puerto Rican," "Toussaint," and "Impressions of an Indian Childhood," as well as the student essays, are all evidence of writing from the child's voice in the non-fiction format. This text explores different types of voices and the different strategies used to portray those voices. For example, notice how the dialogue in "Toussaint" by Gus Lee captures the essence of survival and longing; while the rhetorical modes of definition and description punctuate the depth of Anne Moody's pain in "What Is White?" and "A Dollar a Day." In "Dear Friend . . . ," William LaValle epitomizes the quintessential child's voice of innocence using the flashback technique. Therefore, the reader must listen to the child's voice in the essays as preparation to write from that voice.

Listening

The first step is to listen to the author's words and sentences in order to grasp the true meaning of the work. Voice, then, comes from within the writer; it's the moment we've tucked away, it's the trauma we've buried; it's the longing we've suppressed; it's the anger, sadness, and happiness we've controlled. Read the words and listen to the feelings of the author/character. In this text, the authors have listened to the sounds and words of their childhood. For instance, in "Lessons" by Robert Hilton, I can hear the wonder and curiosity of a child as he describes the intricacies of insects, especially ants; I can hear the pain and disappointment of Esperanza Cordero in Sandra Cisneros' "The House on Mango Street" as she explores her new home; I can hear the little boy in Gaines' "The Sky Is Gray" as he endeavors to learn all the secrets and lessons of manhood. Listening to the writer's words enables the reader to transcend his own reality and enter that of the author. If that reality is a childhood adventure, a painful memory, a happy event, the reader becomes a part of the happening, the adventure. In "Butch" by Josef Pinckney, it is easy to feel and understand the author's excitement and fear because the reader hears it in the words. In *On Writing Well* William Zinsser states, ". . . an ear that can hear the difference between a sentence that limps and a sentence that lilts . . . will not only sound right but will seem to be the inevitable choice" (237-238).

Writing

"The sound of what falls on the page begins the process of testing it for truth . . ." continues Welty (67).

Now it's time to transfer the sounds and feelings of childhood onto the blank page. Looking back on our childhood may be difficult, but so enlightening. At this point, I often tell my students about my experience in the Writing Program at the University of San Francisco. Before we could even embark upon writing the "great American novel or short story or poem," we had to take a course called "Autobiographical and Narrative Writing" where we were expected to write our autobiographies. This meant we had to look back and remember incidents both fun and painful. We had to remember events that revealed the vulnerabilities we had stored in a "Do Not Disturb" drawer. In order to write our autobiography, we had to become vulnerable enough to hear the truth, and courageous enough to write it down. Writing in the voice of a child requires the same openness to the truth as well as the courage to write about that truth.

But when you look back on your childhood whose voice is heard? Is it the voice of the adult looking back through tinted glasses, or an adult looking through the lens of a child's reality and truth, hearing a child's voice? Let's select the latter option and step further inward to hear the truth of the moment as the event, situation, incident occurred.

Questions will abound. Will I expose too much if I crawl inside my secret place and unlatch the door of my childhood traumas, pains, happiness, sadness, longing? Will the light shine too brightly on a period I've tried to leave behind? Or will I fight the childhood demons to give clarity to the stilled once clear voice of the child inside? Tapping that child's voice and seeing the words flow across the page is sometimes painful, and sometimes a struggle. I remember one writing instructor telling me "that writing isn't therapy." Maybe not, but I always feel exhilarated after a good listening and writing session. ". . . I write and the sound of it comes back to my ears," states Welty (67).

Creating

I've explained my perception of voice, especially the child's voice. It is those emotions deep down in our soul; it is that true inner feeling you have about events, situations that you should strive to capture.

In order to tap the child's voice, let's go on a meditative roller coaster. I call it a roller coaster because of all the emotions you will encounter along the way.

1.   **Place.** Find a place where you were comforted by a parent, a place where your fears disappeared, a place where you felt secure. It could be a corner of the sofa where you and your mom cuddled, a garage where you and your dad built things or just puttered around, or it could be a favorite chair. Go to that place even if it isn't the same house, apartment, or garage.

2.   **Meditate.** Sit quietly in a meditative state and listen to the childhood you left behind. Touch, smell, taste, see, and hear your childhood. Many events will trip over themselves, but one will have prominence. Relive that event from the perspective of a child.

3.   **Moment.** Continue to listen and meditate and stay in the moment. Gradually begin to write. Let the feeling, and then the words, and then let the child's voice direct you.

4. **Finish.** Don't stop until the story is finished. Put the essay down and go back to it in two days to revise. Remember to listen to the voice when you make your revisions.

Eudora Welty ends her essay with, "I have always trusted this voice" (67). You, too, can trust your child's voice because it will be the voice that captures truth and clarity, and therefore, deserves to be heard.

Remember to read, listen, and write, and most of all *Trust the Voice Within*.

Pamela E. Watkins
English Instructor
Compton Community College

WORKS CITED

Welty, Eudora. "Listening to Words." *Assignments in Exposition.* Ed. Georgia Dunbar, Clement Dunbar, and Louise E. Rorabacher. 10th ed. New York: HarperCollins, 1991. 64-67.

Zinsser, William. *On Writing Well.* 6th ed. New York: HarperPerennial, 1998.

Ernest J. Gaines

THE SKY IS GRAY

ERNEST J. GAINES (b. 1933) was born on a plantation in Pointe Coupee Parish, New Roads, Louisiana. Gaines' fiction captures the thoughts, fears, and humanity of poor people who live in rural environments. In his stories, including "The SkyIs Gray," Gaines uses the town Bayonne to represent his birthplace. His previous works are *Catherine Carimer* (1964), *Of Love and Dust* (1967), *The Autobiography of Miss Jane Pittman* (1971), *In My Father's House* (1978), *A Gathering of Old Men* (1983), and *A Lesson Before Dying* (1993). In 1976 "The Sky Is Gray" was published in Gaines' only book of short stories, *Bloodline*. Currently, Ernest J. Gaines teaches at Louisiana State University and San Francisco State University.

An eight-year-old boy provides insight into his world and the lessons he must learn.

1:     Go'n be coming in a few minutes. Coming round that bend down there full speed. And I'm go'n get out my handkerchief and wave it down, and we go'n get on it and go.

I keep on looking for it, but Mama don't look that way no more. She's looking down the road where we just come from. It's a long old road, and far 's you can see you don't see nothing but gravel. You got dry weeds on both sides, and you got trees on both sides, and fences on both sides, too. And you got cows in the pastures and they standing close together. And when we was coming out here to catch the bus I seen the smoke coming out of the cows's noses.

I look at my mama and I know what she's thinking. I been with Mama so much, just me and her, I know what she's thinking all the time. Right now it's home—Auntie and them. She's thinking if they got enough wood—if she left enough there to keep them warm till we get back. She's thinking if it go'n rain and if any of them go'n have to go out in the rain. She's thinking 'bout the hog—if he go'n get out, and if Ty and Val be able to get him back in. She always worry like that when she leaves the house. She don't worry too much if she leave

1

me there with the smaller ones, 'cause she know I'm go'n look after them and look after Auntie and everything else. I'm the oldest and she say I'm the man.

I look at my mama and I love my mama. She's wearing that black coat and that black hat and she's looking sad. I love my mama and I want put my arm round her and tell her. But I'm not supposed to do that. She say that's weakness and that's crybaby stuff, and she don't want no crybaby round her. She don't want you to be scared, either. 'Cause Ty's scared of ghosts and she's always whipping him. I'm scared of the dark, too, but I make 'tend I ain't. I make 'tend I ain't 'cause I'm the oldest, and I got to set a good sample for the rest. I can't ever be scared and I can't ever cry. And that's why I never said nothing 'bout my teeth. It's been hurting me and hurting me close to a month now, but I never said it. I didn't say it 'cause I didn't want act like a crybaby, and 'cause I know we didn't have enough money to go have it pulled. But, Lord, it been hurting me. And look like it wouldn't start till at night when you was trying to get yourself little sleep. Then soon 's you shut your eyes—ummm-ummm, Lord, look like it go right down to your heartstring.

"Hurting, hanh?" Ty'd say.

I'd shake my head, but I wouldn't open my mouth for nothing. You open your mouth and let that wind in, and it almost kill you.

I'd just lay there and listen to them snore. Ty there, right 'side me, and Auntie and Val over by the fireplace. Val younger than me and Ty, and he sleeps with Auntie. Mama sleeps round the other side with Louis and Walker.

I'd just lay there and listen to them, and listen to that wind out there, and listen to that fire in the fireplace. Sometimes it'd stop long enough to let me get little rest. Sometimes it just hurt, hurt, hurt. Lord, have mercy.

2:       Auntie knowed it was hurting me. I didn't tell nobody but Ty, 'cause we
        buddies and he ain't go'n tell nobody. But some kind of way
Auntie found out. When she asked me, I told her no, nothing was wrong. But she knowed it all the time. She told me to mash up a piece of aspirin and wrap it in some cotton and jugg it down in that hole. I did it, but it didn't do no good. It stopped for a little while, and started right back again. Auntie wanted to tell Mama, but I told her, "Un-un." 'Cause I knowed we didn't have any money, and it was go'n make her mad again. So Auntie told Monsieur Bayonne, and Monsieur Bayonne came over to the house and told me to kneel down 'side him on the fireplace. He put his finger in his mouth and made the Sign of the Cross on my jaw. The tip of Monsieur Bayonne's finger is some hard, 'cause he's always playing on that guitar. If we sit outside at night we can always hear Monsieur Bayonne playing on his guitar. Sometimes we leave him out there playing on the guitar.

Monsieur Bayonne made the Sign of the Cross over and over on my jaw, but that didn't do no good. Even when he prayed and told me to pray some, too, that tooth still hurt me.

"How you feeling?" he say.

"Same," I say.

He kept on praying and making the Sign of the Cross and I kept on praying, too.

"Still hurting?" he say.

"Yes, sir."

Monsieur Bayonne mashed harder and harder on my jaw. He mashed so hard he almost pushed me over on Ty. But then he stopped.

"What kind of prayers you praying, boy?" he say.

"Baptist," I say.

"Well, I'll be—no wonder that tooth still killing him. I'm going one way and he pulling the other. Boy, don't you know any Catholic prayers?"

"I know 'Hail Mary,' " I say.

"Then you better start saying it."

"Yes, sir."

He started mashing on my jaw again, and I could hear him praying at the same time. And, sure enough, after while it stopped hurting me.

Me and Ty went outside where Monsieur Bayonne's two hounds was and we started playing with them. "Let's go hunting," Ty say. "All right," I say; and we went on back in the pasture. Soon the hounds got on a trail, and me and Ty followed them all 'cross the pasture and then back in the woods, too. And then they cornered this little old rabbit and killed him, and me and Ty made them get back, and we picked up the rabbit and started on back home. But my tooth had started hurting me again. It was hurting me plenty now, but I wouldn't tell Monsieur Bayonne. That night I didn't sleep a bit, and first thing in the morning Auntie told me to go back and let Monsieur Bayonne pray over me some more. Monsieur Bayonne was in his kitchen making coffee when I got there. Soon 's he seen me he knowed what was wrong.

"All right, kneel down there 'side that stove," he say. "And this time make sure you pray Catholic. I don't know nothing 'bout that Baptist, and I don't want know nothing 'bout him."

3:     Last night Mama say, "Tomorrow we going to town." "It ain't hurting me no more," I say. "I can eat anything on it."

"Tomorrow we going to town," she say.

And after she finished eating, she got up and went to bed. She always go to bed early now. 'Fore Daddy went in the Army, she used to stay up late. All of us sitting out on the gallery or round the fire. But now, look like soon 's she finish eating she go to bed.

This morning when I woke up, her and Auntie was standing 'fore the fireplace. She say: "Enough to get there and get back. Dollar and a half to have it pulled. Twenty-five for me to go, Twenty-five for him. Twenty-five for me to come back, twenty-five for him. Fifty cents left. Guess I get little piece of salt meat with that."

"Sure can use it," Auntie say. "White beans and no salt meat ain't white beans."

"I do the best I can," Mama say.

They was quiet after that, and I made 'tend I was still asleep.

"James, hit the floor," Auntie say.

I still made 'tend I was asleep. I didn't want them to know I was listening.

"All right," Auntie say, shaking me by the shoulder. "Come on. Today's the day."

I pushed the cover down to get out, and Ty grabbed it and pulled it back.

"You, too, Ty," Auntie say.

"I ain't getting no teef pulled," Ty say.

"Don't mean it ain't time to get up," Auntie say. "Hit it, Ty."

Ty got up grumbling.

"James, you hurry up and get in your clothes and eat your food," Auntie say. "What time y'all coming back?" she say to Mama.

"That 'leven o'clock bus," Mama say. "Got to get back in that field this evening."

"Get a move on you, James," Auntie say.

I went in the kitchen and washed my face, then I ate my breakfast. I was having bread and syrup. The bread was warm and hard and tasted good. And I tried to make it last a long time.

Ty came back there grumbling and mad at me.

"Got to get up," he say. "I ain't having no teefes pulled. What I got to be getting up for?"

Ty poured some syrup in his pan and got a piece of bread. He didn't wash his hands, neither his face, and I could see that white stuff in his eyes.

"You the one getting your teef pulled," he say. "What I got to get up for. I bet if I was getting a teef pulled, you wouldn't be getting up. Shucks; syrup again. I'm getting tired of this old syrup. Syrup, syrup, syrup. I'm go'n take with the sugar diabetes. I want me some bacon sometime."

"Go out in the field and work and you can have your bacon," Auntie say. She stood in the middle door looking at Ty. "You better be glad you got syrup. Some people ain't got that—hard 's time is."

"Shucks," Ty say. "How can I be strong."

"I don't know too much 'bout your strength," Auntie say; "but I know where you go'n be hot at, you keep that grumbling up. James, get a move on you; your mama waiting."

I ate my last piece of bread and went in the front room. Mama was standing 'fore the fireplace warming her hands. I put on my coat and my cap, and we left the house.

4:      I look down there again, but it still ain't coming. I almost say, "It ain't coming yet," but I keep my mouth shut. 'Cause that's something else she don't like. She don't like for you to say something just for nothing. She can see it ain't coming, I can see it ain't coming, so why say it ain't coming. I don't say it, I turn and look at the river that's back of us. It's so cold the smoke's just raising up from the water. I see a bunch of pool-doos not too far out—just on the other side the lilies. I'm wondering if you can eat pool-doos. I ain't too sure, 'cause I ain't never ate none. But I done ate owls and blackbirds, and I done ate redbirds, too. I didn't want kill the redbirds, but she made me kill them. They had two of them back there. One in my trap, one in Ty's trap. Me and Ty was go'n play with them and let them go, but she made me kill them 'cause we needed the food.

"I can't," I say. "I can't."

"Here," she say. "Take it."

"I can't," I say. "I can't. I can't kill him, Mama, please."

"Here," she say. Take this fork, James."

"Please, Mama, I can't kill him," I say.

I could tell she was go'n hit me. I jerked back, but I didn't jerk back soon enough.

"Take it," she say.

I took it and reached in for him, but he kept on hopping to the back.

"I can't, Mama," I say. The water just kept on running down my face. "I can't," I say.

"Get him out of there," she say.

I reached in for him and he kept on hopping to the back. Then I reached in farther, and he pecked me on the hand.

"I can't, Mama," I say.

She slapped me again.

I reached in again, but he kept on hopping out my way. Then he hopped to one side and I reached there. The fork got him on the leg and I heard his leg pop. I pulled my hand out 'cause I had hurt him.

"Give it here," she say, and jerked the fork out my hand.

5

She reached in and got the little bird right in the neck. I heard the fork go in his neck, and I heard it go in the ground. She brought him out and helt him right in front of me.

"That's one," she say. She shook him off and gived me the fork. "Get the other one."

"I can't, Mama," I say. "I'll do anything, but don't make me do that."

She went to the corner of the fence and broke the biggest switch over there she could find. I knelt 'side the trap, crying.

"Get him out of there," she say.

"I can't, Mama."

She started hitting me 'cross the back. I went down on the ground, crying.

"Get him," she say.

"Octavia?" Auntie say.

'Cause she had come out of the house and she was standing by the tree looking at us.

"Get him out of there," Mama say.

"Octavia," Auntie say, "explain to him. Explain to him. Just don't beat him. Explain to him."

But she hit me and hit me and hit me.

I'm still young—I ain't no more than eight; but I know now; I know why I had to do it. (They was so little, though. They was so little. I 'member how I picked the feathers off them and cleaned them and helt them over the fire. Then we all ate them. Ain't had but a little bitty piece each, but we all had a little bitty piece, and everybody just looked at me 'cause they was so proud.) Suppose she had to go away? That's why I had to do it. Suppose she had to go away like Daddy went away? Then who was go'n look after us? They had to be somebody left to carry on. I didn't know it then, but I know it now. Auntie and Monsieur Bayonne talked to me and made me see.

5:      Time I see it I get out my handkerchief and start waving. It's still 'way down there, but I keep waving anyhow. Then it come up and stop and me and Mama get on. Mama tell me go sit in the back while she pay. I do like she say, and the people look at me. When I pass the little sign that say "White" and "Colored," I start looking for a seat. I just see one of them back there, but I don't take it, 'cause I want my mama to sit down herself. She comes in the back and sit down, and I lean on the seat. They got seats in the front, but I know I can't sit there, 'cause I have to sit back of the sign. Anyhow, I don't want sit there if my mama go'n sit back there.

They got a lady sitting 'side my mama and she looks at me and smiles little bit. I smile back, but I don't open my mouth, 'cause the wind'll get in and make that tooth ache. The lady take out a pack of gum and reach me a slice, but I shake my head. The lady just can't understand why a little boy'll turn down gum, and she reach me a slice again. This time I point to my jaw. The lady understands and smiles little bit, and I smile little bit, but I don't open my mouth, though.

They got a girl sitting 'cross from me. She got on a red overcoat and her hair's plaited in one big plait. First, I make 'tend I don't see her over there, but then I start looking at her little bit. She make 'tend she don't see me, either, but I catch her looking that way. She got a cold, and every now and then she h'ist that little handkerchief to her nose. She ought to blow it, but she don't. Must think she's too much a lady or something.

Every time she h'ist that little handkerchief, the lady 'side her say something in her ear. She shakes her head and lays her hands in her lap again. Then I catch her kind of looking where I'm at. I smile at her little bit. But think she'll smile back? Uh-uh. She just turn up her little old nose and turn her head. Well, I show her both of us can turn us head. I turn mine too and look out at the river.

The river is gray. The sky is gray. They have pool-doos on the water. The water is wavy, and the pool-doos go up and down. The bus go round a turn, and you got plenty trees hiding the river. Then the bus go round another turn, and I can see the river again.

I look toward the front where all the white people sitting. Then I look at the little old gal again. I don't look right at her, 'cause I don't want all them people to know I love her. I just look at her little bit, like I'm looking out that window over there. But she knows I'm looking that way, and she kind of look at me, too. The lady sitting 'side her catch her this time, and she leans over and says something in her ear.

"I don't love him nothing," that little old gal says out loud.

Everybody back there hear her mouth, and all of them look at us and laugh.

"I don't love you, either," I say. "So you don't have to turn up your nose, Miss."

"You the one looking," she say.

"I wasn't looking at you," I say. "I was looking out that window, there."

"Out that window, my foot," she say. "I seen you. Everytime I turned round you was looking at me."

"You must of been looking yourself if you seen me all them times," I say.

"Shucks," she say, "I got me all kind of boyfriends."

"I got girlfriends, too," I say.

"Well, I just don't want you getting your hopes up," she say.

I don't say no more to that little old gal 'cause I don't want have to bust her in the mouth. I lean on the seat where Mama sitting, and I don't even look that way no more. When we get to Bayonne, she jugg her little old tongue out at me. I make 'tend I'm go'n hit her, and she duck down 'side her mama. And all the people laugh at us again.

6:     Me and Mama get off and start walking in town. Bayonne is a little bitty
       town. Baton Rouge is a hundred times bigger than Bayonne. I
went to Baton Rouge once—me, Ty, Mama, and Daddy. But that was 'way back yonder, 'fore Daddy went in the Army. I wonder when we go'n see him again. I wonder when. Look like he ain't ever coming back home. . . . Even the pavement all cracked in Bayonne. Got grass shooting right out the sidewalk. Got weeds in the ditch, too; just like they got at home.

It's some cold in Bayonne. Look like it's colder than it is home. The wind blows in my face, and I feel that stuff running down my nose. I sniff. Mama says use that handkerchief. I blow my nose and put it back.

We pass a school and I see them white children playing in the yard. Big old red school, and them children just running and playing. Then we pass a cafe´, and I see a bunch of people in there eating. I wish I was in there 'cause I'm cold. Mama tells me keep my eyes in front where they belong.

We pass stores that's got dummies, and we pass another cafe´, and then we pass a shoe shop, and that bald-head man in there fixing on a shoe. I look at him and I butt into that white lady, and Mama jerks me in front and tells me stay there.

We come up to the courthouse, and I see the flag waving there. This flag ain't like the one we got at school. This one here ain't got but a handful of stars. One at school got a big pile of stars—one for every state. We pass it and we turn and there it is—the dentist office. Me and Mama go in, and they got people sitting everywhere you look. They even got a little boy in there younger than me.

Me and Mama sit on that bench, and a white lady come in there and ask me what my name is. Mama tells her and the white lady goes on back. Then I hear somebody hollering in there. Soon 's that little boy hear him hollering, he starts hollering, too. His mama pats him and pats him, trying to make him hush up, but he ain't thinking 'bout his mama.

The man that was hollering in there comes out holding his jaw. He is a big old man and he's wearing overalls and a jumper.

"Got it, hanh?" another man asks him.

The man shakes his head—don't want open his mouth.

"Man, I thought they was killing you in there," the other man says. "Hollering like a pig under a gate."

The man don't say nothing. He just heads for the door, and the other man follows him.

"John Lee," the white lady says. "John Lee Williams."

The little boy juggs his head down in his mama's lap and holler more now. His mama tells him go with the nurse, but he ain't thinking 'bout his mama. His mama tells him again, but he don't even hear her. His mama picks him up and takes him in there, and even when the white lady shuts the door I can still hear little old John Lee.

"I often wonder why the Lord let a child like that suffer," a lady says to my mama. The lady's sitting right in front of us on another bench. She's got on a white dress and a black sweater. She must be a nurse or something herself, I reckon.

"Not us to question," a man says.

"Sometimes I don't know if we shouldn't," the lady says.

"I know definitely we shouldn't," the man says. The man looks like a preacher. He's big and fat and he's got on a black suit. He's got a gold chain, too.

"Why?" the lady says.

"Why anything?" the preacher says.

"Yes," the lady says. "Why anything?"

"Not us to question," the preacher says.

The lady looks at the preacher a little while and looks at Mama again.

"And look like it's the poor who suffers the most," she says. "I don't understand it."

"Best not to even try," the preacher says. "He works in mysterious ways—wonders to perform."

Right then little John Lee bust out hollering, and everybody turn they head to listen.

"He's not a good dentist," the lady says. "Dr. Robillard is much better. But more expensive. That's why most of the colored people come here. The white people go to Dr. Robillard. Y'all from Bayonne?"

"Down the river," my mama says. And that's all she go'n say, 'cause she don't talk much. But the lady keeps on looking at her, and so she says, "Near Morgan."

"I see," the lady says.

7:     "That's the trouble with the black people in this country today," somebody else says. This one here's sitting on the same side me and Mama's sitting, and he is kind of sitting in front of that preacher. He looks like a teacher or somebody that goes to college. He's got on a suit, and he's got a book that he's been reading. "We don't question is exactly our problem," he says. We should question and question and question—question everything."

The preacher just looks at him a long time. He done put a toothpick or something in his mouth, and he just keeps on turning it and turning it. You can see he don't like that boy with that book.

"Maybe you can explain what you mean," he says.

"I said what I meant," the boy says. "Question everything. Every stripe, every star, every word spoken. Everything."

"It 'pears to me that this young lady and I was talking 'bout God, young man," the preacher says.

"Question Him, too," the boy says.

"Wait," the preacher says. "Wait now."

"You heard me right," the boy says. "His existence as well as everything else. Everything."

The preacher just looks across the room at the boy. You can see he's getting madder and madder. But mad or no mad, the boy ain't thinking 'bout him. He looks at that preacher just 's hard 's the preacher looks at him.

"Is this what they coming to?" The preacher says. "Is this what we educating them for?"

"You're not educating me," the boy says. I wash dishes at night so that I can go to school in the day. So even the words you spoke need questioning."

The preacher just looks at him and shakes his head.

"When I come in this room and seen you there with your book. I said to myself. 'There's an intelligent man.' How wrong a person can be."

"Show me one reason to believe in the existence of a God," the boy says.

"My heart tells me," the preacher says.

" 'My heart tells me,' " the boy says. " 'My heart tells me.' Sure, 'My heart tells me.' And as long as you listen to what your heart tells you, you will have only what the white man gives you and nothing more. Me, I don't listen to my heart. The purpose of the heart is to pump blood throughout the body, and nothing else."

"Who's your paw, boy?" the preacher says.

"Why?"

"Who is he?"

"He's dead."

"And your Mom?"

"She's in Charity Hospital with pneumonia. Half killed herself, working for nothing."

"And 'cause he's dead and she's sick, you mad at the world?"

"I'm not mad at the world. I'm questioning the world. I'm questioning it with cold logic, sir. What do words like Freedom, Liberty, God, White, Colored mean? I want to know. That's why *you* are sending us to school, to read and to ask questions. And because we ask these questions, you call us mad. No sir, it is not us who are mad."

"You keep saying 'us'?"

" 'Us.' Yes—us. I'm not alone."

The preacher just shakes his head. Then he looks at everybody in the room—everybody. Some of the people look down at the floor, keep from looking at him. I kind of look 'way myself, but soon 's I know he done turn his head, I look that way again.

"I'm sorry for you," he says to the boy.

"Why?" the boy says. "Why not be sorry for yourself? Why are you so much better off than I am? Why aren't you sorry for these other people in here? Why not be sorry for the lady who had to drag her child into the dentist office? Why not be sorry for the lady sitting on that bench over there? Be sorry for them. Not for me. Some way or the other I'm going to make it."

"No, I'm sorry for you," the preacher says.

"Of course, of course," the boy says, nodding his head. "You're sorry for me because I rock that pillar you're leaning on."

"You can't ever rock the pillar I'm leaning on, young man. It's stronger than anything man can ever do."

"You believe in God because a man told you to believe in God," the boy says. "A white man told you to believe in God. And why? To keep you ignorant so he can keep his feet on your neck."

"So now we the ignorant?" the preacher says.

"Yes," the boy says. "Yes." And he opens his book again.

The preacher just looks at him sitting there. The boy done forgot all about him. Everybody else make 'tend they done forgot the squabble, too.

Then I see that preacher getting up real slow. Preacher's a great big old man and he got to brace himself to get up. He comes over where the boy is sitting. He just stands there a little while looking down at him, but the boy don't raise his head.

"Get up, boy," preacher says.

The boy looks up at him, then he shuts his book real slow and stands up. Preacher just hauls back and hit him in the face. The boy falls back 'gainst the wall, but he straightens himself up and looks right back at that preacher.

"You forgot the other cheek," he says.

The preacher hauls back and hit him again on the other side. But this time the boy braces himself and don't fall.

"That hasn't changed a thing," he says.

The preacher just looks at the boy. The preacher's breathing real hard like he just run up a big hill. The boy sits down and opens his book again.

11

"I feel sorry for you," the preacher says. "I never felt so sorry for a man before."

The boy makes 'tend he don't even hear that preacher. He keeps on reading his book. The preacher goes back and gets his hat off the chair.

"Excuse me," he says to us. "I'll come back some other time. Y'all, please excuse me."

And he looks at the boy and goes out the room. The boy h'ist his hand up to his mouth one time to wipe 'way some blood. All the rest of the time he keeps on reading. And nobody else in there say a word.

8:     Little John Lee and his mama come out the dentist office, and the nurse calls somebody else in. Then little bit later they come out, and the nurse calls another name. But fast 's she calls somebody in there, somebody else come in the place where we sitting, and the room stays full.

The people coming in now, all of them wearing big coats. One of them says something 'bout sleeting, another one says he hope not. Another one says he think it ain't nothing but rain. 'Cause, he says, rain can get awful cold this time of year.

All round the room they talking. Some of them talking to people right by them, some of them talking to people clear 'cross the room, some of them talking to anybody'll listen. It's a little bitty room, no bigger than us kitchen, and I can see everybody in there. The little old room's full of smoke, 'cause you got two old men smoking pipes over by that side door. I think I feel my tooth thumping me some, and I hold my breath and wait. I wait and wait, but it don't thump me no more. Thank God for that.

I feel like going to sleep, and I lean back 'gainst the wall. But I'm scared to go to sleep. Scared 'cause the nurse might call my name and I won't hear her. And Mama might go to sleep, too, and she'll be mad if neither one of us heard the nurse.

I look up at Mama. I love my mama. I love my mama. And when cotton come I'm go'n get her a new coat. And I ain't go'n get a black one, either. I think I'm go'n get her a red one.

"They got some books over there," I say. "Want read one of them?"

Mama looks at the books, but she don't answer me.

"You got yourself a little man there," the lady says.

Mama don't say nothing to the lady, but she must've smiled, 'cause I seen the lady smiling back. The lady looks at me a little while, like she's feeling sorry for me.

"You sure got that preacher out here in a hurry," she says to that boy.

The boy looks up at her and looks in his book again. When I grow up I want be just like him. I want clothes like that and I want keep a book with me, too.

"You really don't believe in God?" the lady says.

"No," he says.

"But why?" the lady says.

"Because the wind is pink," he says.

"What?" the lady says.

The boy don't answer her no more. He just reads in his book.

"Talking 'bout the wind is pink," that old lady says. She's sitting on the same bench with the boy and she's trying to look in his face. The boy makes 'tend the old lady ain't even there. He just keeps on reading. "Wind is pink," she says again. "Eh, Lord, what children go'n be saying next?"

The lady 'cross from us bust out laughing.

"That's a good one," she says. "The wind is pink. Yes sir, that's a good one."

"Don't you believe the wind is pink?" the boy says. He keeps his head down in the book.

"Course I believe it, honey," the lady says. "Course I do." She looks at us and winks her eye. "And what color is grass, honey?"

"Grass? Grass is black."

She bust out laughing again. The boy looks at her.

"Don't you believe grass is black?" he says.

The lady quits her laughing and looks at him. Everybody else looking at him, too. The place quiet, quiet.

"Grass is green, honey," the lady says. "It was green yesterday, it's green today, and it's go'n be green tomorrow."

"How do you know it's green?"

"I know because I know."

"You don't know it's green," the boy says. "You believe it's green because someone told you it was green. If someone had told you it was black you'd believe it was black."

"It's green," the lady says. "I know green when I see green."

"Prove it's green," the boy says.

"Sure, now," the lady says. "Don't tell me it's coming to that."

"It's coming to just that," the boy says. "Words mean nothing. One means no more than the other."

"That's what it all coming to?" that old lady says. That old lady got on a turban and she got on two sweaters. She got a green sweater under a black sweater. I can see the green sweater 'cause some of the buttons on the other sweater's missing.

13

"Yes ma'am," the boy says. "Words mean nothing. Action is the only thing. Doing. That's the only thing."

"Other words, you want the Lord to come down here and show Hisself to you?" she says.

"Exactly, ma'am," he says.

"You don't mean that, I'm sure?" she says.

"I do, ma'am," he says.

"Done, Jesus," the old lady says, shaking her head.

"I didn't go 'long with that preacher at first," the other lady says; "but now—I don't know. When a person say the grass is black, he's either a lunatic or something's wrong."

"Prove to me that it's green," the boy says.

"It's green because the people say it's green."

"Those same people say we're citizens of these United States," the boy says.

"I think I'm a citizen," the lady says.

"Citizens have certain rights," the boy says. "Name me one right that you have. One right, granted by the Constitution, that you can exercise in Bayonne."

The lady don't answer him. She just looks at him like she don't know what he's talking 'bout. I know I don't.

"Things changing," she says.

"Things are changing because some black men have begun to think with their brains and not their hearts," the boy says.

"You trying to say these people don't believe in God?"

"I'm sure some of them do. Maybe most of them do. But they don't believe that God is going to touch these white people's hearts and change things tomorrow. Things change through action. By no other way."

Everybody sit quiet and look at the boy. Nobody says a thing. Then the lady 'cross the room from me and Mama just shakes her head.

"Let's hope that not all your generation feel the same way you do," she says.

"Think what you please, it doesn't matter," the boy says. "But it will be men who listen to their heads and not their hearts who will see that your children have a better chance than you had."

"Let's hope they ain't all like you, though," the old lady says. "Done forgot the heart absolutely."

"Yes ma'am, I hope they aren't all like me," the boy says. "Unfortunately, I was born too late to believe in your God. Let's hope that the ones who come after will have your faith—if not in your God, then in something else, something definitely that they can lean on. I haven't anything. For me, the wind is pink, the grass is black."

9:     The nurse comes in the room where we all sitting and waiting and says the doctor won't take no more patients till one o'clock this evening. My mama jumps up off the bench and goes up to the white lady.

"Nurse, I have to go back in the field this evening," she says.

"The doctor is treating his last patient now," the nurse says. "One o'clock this evening."

"Can I at least speak to the doctor?" my mama asks.

"I'm his nurse," the lady says.

"My little boy's sick," my mama says. "Right now his tooth almost killing him."

The nurse looks at me. She's trying to make up her mind if to let me come in. I look at her real pitiful. The tooth ain't hurting me at all, but Mama say it is, so I make 'tend for her sake.

"This evening," the nurse says, and goes on back in the office.

"Don't feel 'jected, honey," the lady says to Mama. "I been round them a long time—they take you when they want to. If you was white, that's something else; but we the wrong color."

Mama don't say nothing to the lady, and me and her go outside and stand 'gainst the wall. It's cold out there. I can feel that wind going through my coat. Some of the other people come out of the room and go up the street. Me and Mama stand there a little while and we start walking. I don't know where we going. When we come to the other street we just stand there.

"You don't have to make water, do you?" Mama says.

"No, ma'am," I say.

We go on up the street. Walking real slow. I can tell Mama don't know where she's going. When we come to a store we stand there and look at the dummies. I look at a little boy wearing a brown overcoat. He's got on brown shoes, too. I look at my old shoes and look at his'n again. You wait till summer, I say.

Me and Mama walk away. We come up to another store and we stop and look at them dummies, too. Then we go on again. We pass a cafe´ where the white people in there eating. Mama tells me keep my eyes in front where they belong, but I can't help from seeing them people eat. My stomach starts to growling 'cause I'm hungry. When I see people eating, I get hungry; when I see a coat, I get cold.

A man whistles at my mama when we go by a filling station. She makes 'tend she don't even see him. I look back and I feel like hitting him in the mouth. If I was bigger, I say; if I was bigger, you'd see.

We keep on going. I'm getting colder and colder, but I don't say nothing. I feel that stuff running down my nose and I sniff.

"That rag," Mama says.

I get it out and wipe my nose. I'm getting cold all over now—my face, my hands, my feet, everything. We pass another little café, but this'n for white people, too, and we can't go in there, either. So we just walk. I'm so cold now I'm 'bout ready to say it. If I knowed where we was going I wouldn't be so cold, but I don't know where we going. We go, we go, we go. We walk clean out of Bayonne. Then we cross the street and we come back. Same thing I seen when I got off the bus this morning. Same old trees, same old walk, same old weeds, same old cracked pave—same old everything.

I sniff again.

"That rag," Mama says.

I wipe my nose real fast and jugg that handkerchief back in my pocket 'fore my hand gets too cold. I raise my head and I can see David's hardware store. When we come up to it, we go in. I don't know why, but I'm glad.

It's warm in there. It's so warm in there you don't ever want to leave. I look for the heater, and I see it over by them barrels. Three white men standing round the heater talking in Creole. One of them comes over to see what my mama want.

"Got any axe handles?" she says.

Me, Mama and the white man start to the back, but Mama stops me when we come up to the heater. She and the white man go on. I hold my hands over the heater and look at them. They go all the way to the back, and I see the white man pointing to the axe handles 'gainst the wall. Mama takes one of them and shakes it like she's trying to figure how much it weighs. Then she rubs her hand over it from one end to the other end. She turns it over and looks at the other side, then she shakes it again, and shakes her head and puts it back. She gets another one and she does it just like she did the first one, then she shakes her head. Then she gets a brown one and do it that, too. But she don't like this one, either. Then she gets another one, but 'fore she shakes it or anything, she looks at me. Look like she's trying to say something to me, but I don't know what it is. All I know is I done got warm now and I'm feeling right smart better. Mama shakes this axe handle just like she did the others, and shakes her head and says something to the white man. The white man just looks at his pile of axe handles, and when Mama pass him to come to the front, the white man just scratch his head and follows her. She tells me come on and we go on out and start walking again.

We walk and walk, and no time at all I'm cold again. Look like I'm colder now 'cause I can still remember how good it was back there. My stomach growls and I suck it in to keep Mama from hearing it. She's walking right 'side me, and it growls so loud you can hear it a mile. But Mama don't say a word.

10:     When we come up to the courthouse, I look at the clock. It's got quarter to twelve. Mean we got another hour and a quarter to be out here in the cold. We go and stand 'side a building. Something hits my cap and I look up at the sky. Sleet's falling.

I look at Mama standing there. I want stand close 'side her, but she don't like that. She say that's crybaby stuff. She say you got to stand for yourself, by yourself.

"Let's go back to that office," she says.

We cross the street. When we get to the dentist office I try to open the door, but I can't. I twist and twist, but I can't. Mama pushes me to the side and she twist the knob, but she can't open the door, either. She turns 'way from the door. I look at her, but I don't move and I don't say nothing. I done seen her like this before and I'm scared of her.

"You hungry?" she says. She says it like she's mad at me, like I'm the cause of everything.

"No, ma'am," I say.

"You want eat and walk back, or you rather don't eat and ride?"

"I ain't hungry," I say.

I ain't just hungry, but I'm cold, too. I'm so hungry and cold I want to cry. And look like I'm getting colder and colder. My feet done got numb. I try to work my toes, but I don't even feel them. Look like I'm go'n die. Look like I'm go'n stand right here and freeze to death. I think 'bout home. I think 'bout Val and Auntie and Ty and Louis and Walker. It's 'bout twelve o'clock and I know they eating dinner now. I can hear Ty making jokes. He done forgot 'bout getting up early this morning and right now he's probably making jokes. Always trying to make somebody laugh. I wish I was right there listening to him. Give anything in the world if I was home round the fire.

"Come on," Mama says.

We start walking again. My feet so numb I can't hardly feel them. We turn the corner and go on back up the street. The clock on the courthouse starts hitting for twelve.

The sleet's coming down plenty now. They hit the pave and bounce like rice. Oh, Lord; oh, Lord, I pray. Don't let me die, don't let me die, don't let me die, Lord.

11:     Now I know where we going. We going back of town where the colored people eat. I don't care if I don't eat. I been hungry before. I can stand it. But I can't stand the cold. I can see we go'n have a long walk. It's 'bout

17

a mile down there. But I don't mind. I know when I get there I'm go'n warm myself. I think I can hold out. My hands numb in my pockets and my feet numb, too, but if I keep moving I can hold out. Just don't stop no more, that's all.

The sky's gray. The sleet keeps on falling. Falling like rain now—plenty, plenty. You can hear it hitting the pave. You can see it bouncing. Somethimes it bounces two times 'fore it settles.

We keep on going. We don't say nothing. We just keep on going, keep on going.

I wonder what Mama's thinking. I hope she ain't mad at me. When summer come I'm go'n pick plenty cotton and get her a coat. I'm go'n get her a red one.

I hope they'd make it summer all the time. I'd be glad if it was summer all the time—but it ain't. We got to have winter, too. Lord, I hate the winter. I guess everybody hate the winter.

I don't sniff this time. I get out my handkerchief and wipe my nose. My hands's so cold I can hardly hold the handkerchief.

I think we getting close, but we ain't there yet. I wonder where everybody is. Can't see a soul but us. Look like we the only two people moving round today. Must be too cold for the rest of the people to move round in.

I can hear my teeth. I hope they don't knock together too hard and make that bad one hurt. Lord, that's all I need, for that bad one to start off.

I hear a church bell somewhere. But today ain't Sunday. They must be ringing for a funeral or something.

I wonder what they doing at home. They must be eating. Monsieur Bayonne might be there with his guitar. One day Ty played with Monsieur Bayonne's guitar and broke one of the strings. Monsieur Bayonne was some mad with Ty. He say Ty wasn't go'n ever 'mount to nothing. Ty can go just like Monsieur Bayonne when he ain't there. Ty can make everybody laugh when he starts to mocking Monsieur Bayonne.

I used to like to be with Mama and Daddy. We used to be happy. But they took him in the Army. Now, nobody happy no more. . . . I be glad when Daddy comes home.

Monsieur Bayonne say it wasn't fair for them to take Daddy and give Mama nothing and give us nothing. Auntie say, "Shhh, Etienne. Don't let them hear you talk like that." Monsieur Bayonne say, "It's God truth. What they giving his children? They have to walk three and a half miles to school hot or cold. That's anything to give for a paw? She's got to work in the field rain or shine just to make ends meet. That's anything to give for a husband?" Auntie say, "Shhh, Etienne, shhh." "Yes, you right," Monsieur Bayonne say. "Best don't say it in front of them now. But one day they go'n find out. One day." "Yes, I suppose so," Auntie say. "Then what, Rose Mary?" Monsieur Bayonne say. "I don't know, Etienne," Auntie say. "All we can do is us job, and leave everything else in His hand . . . ."

We getting closer, now. We getting closer. I can even see the railroad tracks.

We cross the tracks, and now I see the cafè. Just to get in there, I say. Just to get in there. Already I'm starting to feel little better.

12:     We go in. Ahh, it's good. I look for the heater; there 'gainst the wall. One of them little brown ones. I just stand there and hold my hands over it. I can't open my hands too wide 'cause they almost froze.

Mama's standing right 'side me. She done unbuttoned her coat. Smoke rises out of the coat, and the coat smells like a wet dog.

I move to the side so Mama can have more room. She opens out her hands and rubs them together. I rub mine together, too, 'cause this keep them from hurting. If you let them warm too fast, they hurt you sure. But if you let them warm just little bit at a time, and you keep rubbing them, they be all right every time.

They got just two more people in the cafè. A lady back of the counter, and a man on this side the counter. They been watching us ever since we come in.

Mama gets out the handkerchief and count up the money. Both of us know how much money she's got there. Three dollars. No, she ain't got three dollars, 'cause she had to pay us way up here. She ain't got but two dollars and a half left. Dollar and a half to get my tooth pulled, and fifty cents for us to go back on, and fifty cents worth of salt meat.

She stirs the money round with her finger. Most of the money is change 'cause I can hear it rubbing together. She stirs it and stirs it. Then she looks at the door. It's still sleeting. I can hear it hitting 'gainst the wall like rice.

"I ain't hungry. Mama," I say.

"Got to pay them something for they heat," she says.

She takes a quarter out the handkerchief and ties the handkerchief up again. She looks over her shoulder at the people, but she still don't move. I hope she don't spend the money. I don't want her spending it on me. I'm hungry, I'm almost starving I'm so hungry, but I don't want her spending the money on me.

She flips the quarter over like she's thinking. She's must be thinking 'bout us walking back home. Lord, I sure don't want walk home. If I thought it'd do any good to say something, I'd say it. But Mama makes up her own mind 'bout things.

She turns 'way from the heater right fast, like she better hurry up and spend the quarter 'fore she change her mind. I watch her go toward the counter.

19

The man and the lady look at her, too. She tells the lady something and the lady walks away. The man keeps on looking at her. Her back's turned to the man, and she don't even know he's standing there.

The lady puts some cakes and a glass of milk on the counter. Then she pours up a cup of coffee and sets it 'side the other stuff. Mama pays her for the things and comes on back where I'm standing. She tells me sit down at the table 'gainst the wall.

The milk and the cakes's for me; the coffee's for Mama. I eat slow and I look at her. She's looking outside at the sleet. She's looking real sad. I say to myself, I'm go'n make all this up one day. You see, one day, I'm go'n make all this up. I want say it now; I want tell her how I feel right now; but Mama don't like for us to talk like that.

"I can't eat all this," I say.

They ain't got but just three little old cakes there. I'm so hungry right now, the Lord knows I can eat a hundred times three, but I want my mama to have one.

Mama don't even look my way. She knows I'm hungry, she knows I want it. I let it stay there a little while, then I get it and eat it. I eat just on my front teeth, though, 'cause if cake touch that back tooth I know what'll happen. Thank God it ain't hurt me at all today.

After I finish eating I see the man go to the juke box. He drops a nickel in it, then he just stand there a little while looking at the record. Mama tells me keep my eyes in front where they belong. I turn my head like she say, but then I hear the man coming toward us.

"Dance, pretty?" he says.

Mama gets up to dance with him. But 'fore you know it, she done grabbed the little man in the collar and done heaved him 'side the wall. He hit the wall so hard he stop the juke box from playing.

"Some pimp," the lady back of the counter says. "Some pimp."

The little man jumps up off the floor and starts toward my mama. 'Fore you know it, Mama done sprung open her knife and she's waiting for him.

"Come on," she says. "Come on. I'll gut you from your neighbor to your throat. Come on."

I go up to the little man to hit him, but Mama makes me come and stand 'side her. The little man looks at me and Mama and goes on back to the counter.

"Some pimp," the lady back of the counter says. "Some pimp." She starts laughing and pointing at the little man. "Yes sir, you a pimp, all right. Yes sir-ree."

13:     "Fasten that coat, let's go," Mama says.
        "You don't have to leave," the lady says.

Mama don't answer the lady, and we right out in the cold again. I'm warm right now—my hands, my ears, my feet—but I know this ain't go'n last too long. It done sleet so much now you got ice everywhere you look.

We cross the railroad tracks, and soon 's we do, I get cold. That wind goes through this little old coat like it ain't even there. I got on a shirt and a sweater under the coat, but that wind don't pay them no mind. I look up and I can see we got a long way to go. I wonder if we go'n make it 'fore I get too cold.

We cross over to walk on the sidewalk. They got just one sidewalk back here, and it's over there.

After we go just a little piece, I smell bread cooking. I look, then I see a baker shop. When we get closer, I can smell it more better. I shut my eyes and make 'tend I'm eating. But I keep them shut too long and I butt up 'gainst a telephone post. Mama grabs me and see if I'm hurt. I ain't bleeding or nothing and she turns me loose.

I can feel I'm getting colder and colder, and I look up to see how far we still got to go. Uptown is 'way up yonder. A half mile more, I reckon. I try to think of something. They say think and you won't get cold. I think of that poem, "Annabel Lee." I ain't been to school in so long—this bad weather—I reckon they done passed "Annabel Lee" by now. But passed it or not, I'm sure Miss Walker go'n make me recite it when I get there. That woman don't never forget nothing. I ain't never seen nobody like that in my life.

I'm still getting cold. "Annabel Lee" or no "Annabel Lee," I'm still getting cold. But I can see we getting closer. We getting there gradually.

Soon 's we turn the corner, I see a little old white lady up in front of us. She's the only lady on the street. She's all in black and she's got a long black rag over her head.

"Stop," she says.

Me and Mama stop and look at her. She must be crazy to be out in all this bad weather. Ain't got but a few other people out there, and all of them's men.

"Y'all done ate?" she says.

"Just finish," Mama says.

"Y'all must be cold then?" she says.

"We headed for the dentist," Mama says. "We'll warm up when we get there."

"What dentist?" the old lady says. "Mr. Bassett?"

"Yes, ma'am," Mama says.

"Come on in," the old lady says. "I'll telephone him and tell him y'all coming."

Me and Mama follow the old lady in the store. It's a little bitty store, and it don't have much in there. The old lady takes off her head rag and folds it up.

"Helena?" somebody calls from the back.

"Yes, Alnest?" the old lady says.

"Did you see them?"

"They're here. Standing beside me."

"Good. Now you can stay inside."

The old lady looks at Mama. Mama's waiting to hear what she brought us in here for. I'm waiting for that, too.

"I saw y'all each time you went by," she says. "I came out to catch you, but you were gone."

"We went back of town," Mama says.

"Did you eat?"

"Yes, ma'am."

The old lady looks at Mama a long time, like she's thinking Mama might be just saying that. Mama looks right back at her. The old lady looks at me to see what I have to say. I don't say nothing. I sure ain't going 'gainst my mama.

"There's food in the kitchen," she says to Mama. "I've been keeping it warm."

Mama turns right around and starts for the door.

"Just a minute," the old lady says. Mama stops. "The boy'll have to work for it. It isn't free."

"We don't take no handout," Mama says.

"I'm not handing out anything," the old lady says. "I need my garbage moved to the front. Ernest has a bad cold and can't go out there."

"James'll move it for you," Mama says.

"Not unless you eat," the old lady says. I'm old, but I have my pride, too, you know."

Mama can see she ain't go'n beat this old lady down, so she just shakes her head.

"All right," the old lady says. "Come into the kitchen."

She leads the way with that rag in her hand. The kitchen is a little bitty little old thing, too. The table and the stove just 'bout fill it up. They got a little room to the side. Somebody in there laying 'cross the bed—'cause I can see one of his feet. Must be the person she was talking to: Ernest or Alnest—something like that.

"Sit down," the old lady says to Mama. "Not you," she says to me. "You have to move the cans."

"Helena?" the man says in the other room.

"Yes, Alnest?" the old lady says.

"Are you going out there again?"

"I must show the boy where the garbage is, Alnest," the old lady says.

"Keep that shawl over your head," the old man says.

"You don't have to remind me, Alnest. Come, boy," the old lady says.

We go out in the yard. Little old backyard ain't no bigger than the store or the kitchen. But it can sleet here just like it can sleet in any big backyard. And 'fore you know it, I'm trembling.

"There," the old lady says, pointing to the cans. I pick up one of the cans and set it right back down. The can's so light, I'm go'n see what's inside of it.

"Here," the old lady says. "Leave that can alone."

I look back at her standing there in the door. She's got that black rag wrapped round her shoulders, and she's pointing one of her little old fingers at me.

"Pick it up and carry it to the front," she says. I go by her with the can, and she's looking at me all the time. I'm sure the can's empty. I'm sure she could've carried it herself—maybe both of them at the same time. "Set it on the sidewalk by the door and come back for the other one," she says.

I go and come back, and Mama looks at me when I pass her. I get the other can and take it to the front. It don't feel a bit heavier than that first one. I tell myself I ain't go'n be nobody's fool, and I'm go'n look inside this can to see just what I been hauling. First, I look up the street, then down the street. Nobody coming. Then I look over my shoulder toward the door. That little old lady done slipped there quiet 's mouse, watching me again. Look like she knowed what I was go'n do.

"Ehh, Lord," she says. "Children, children. Come in here, boy, and go wash your hands."

I follow her in the kitchen. She points toward the bathroom, and I go in there and wash up. Little bitty old bathroom, but it's clean, clean. I don't use any of her towels; I wipe my hands on my pants legs.

When I come back in the kitchen, the old lady done dished up the food. Rice, gravy, meat—and she even got some lettuce and tomato in a saucer. She even got a glass of milk and a piece of cake there, too. It looks so good, I almost start eating 'fore I say my blessing.

"Helena?" the old man says.

"Yes, Alnest?"

"Are they eating?"

"Yes," she says.

"Good," he says. "Now you'll stay inside."

The old lady goes in there where he is and I can hear them talking. I look at Mama. She's eating slow like she's thinking. I wonder what's the matter now. I reckon she's thinking 'bout home.

The old lady comes back in the kitchen.

"I talked to Dr. Bassett's nurse," she says. "Dr. Bassett will take you as soon as you get there."

"Thank you, ma'am," Mama says.

"Perfectly all right," the old lady says. "Which one is it?"

Mama nods toward me. The old lady looks at me real sad. I look sad, too.

"You're not afraid, are you?" she says.

"No, ma'am," I say.

"That's a good boy," the old lady says. "Nothing to be afraid of. Dr. Bassett will not hurt you."

When me and Mama get through eating, we thank the old lady again.

"Helena, are they leaving?" the old man says.

"Yes, Alnest."

"Tell them I say good-bye."

"They can hear you, Alnest."

"Good-bye both mother and son," the old man says. "And may God be with you."

Me and Mama tell the old man good-bye, and we follow the old lady in the front room. Mama opens the door to go out, but she stops and comes back in the store.

"You sell salt meat?" she says.

"Yes."

"Give me two bits worth."

"That isn't very much salt meat," the old lady says.

"That's all I have," Mama says.

The old lady goes back of the counter and cuts a big piece off the chunk. Then she wraps it up and puts it in a paper bag.

"Two bits," she says.

"That looks like awful lot of meat for a quarter," Mama says.

"Two bits," the old lady says. "I've been selling salt meat behind this counter twenty-five years. I think I know what I'm doing."

"You got a scale there," Mama says.

"What?" the old lady says.

"Weigh it," Mama says.

"What?" the old lady says. "Are you telling me how to run my busines?"

"Thanks very much for the food," Mama says.

"Just a minute," the old lady says.

"James," Mama says to me. I move toward the door.

"Just one minute, I said," the old lady says.

Me and Mama stop again and look at her. The old lady takes the meat out of the bag and unwraps it and cuts 'bout half of it off. Then she wraps it up again and juggs it back in the bag and gives the bag to Mama. Mama lays the quarter on the counter.

"Your kindness will never be forgotten," she says. "James," she says to me.

We go out, and the old lady comes to the door to look at us. After we go a little piece I look back, and she's still there watching us.

The sleet's coming down heavy, heavy now, and I turn up my coat collar to keep my neck warm. My mama tells me turn it right back down.

"You not a bum," she says. "You a man."

THE SKY IS GRAY

Facts

1. Why did James and his Mother make a trip into Bayonne? How much money did they have? What type of transportation did they use?

2. How old was James? Who's his buddy?

3. Where was James' father?

4. Were James and his mother dressed for the weather?

5. How did James' mother make a living?

Strategies

1. Who is the narrator? What is the point-of-view?

2. What techniques did the author use to achieve the voice of a child?

3. What do you hear in James' voice? Which emotions?

4. The author uses more than one rhetorical strategy. Explain.

5. The author uses repetition in his dialogue. Why?

Issues

1. Why was James afraid of his mother? Was his mother too harsh?

2. Why was it necessary for James to kill the redbird?

3. Gaines profiles different types of manhood. Describe them and include the mother's version.

4. Why didn't the mother accept a free meal from Ernest (Alnest) and Helena? Why didn't she accept the extra salt meat?

5.   Does James learn the lesson(s) his mother is trying to teach? When and how do you know?

6.   Is James' father alive or dead?

Writing Assignments

1.   Write a narrative from the child's perspective and child's voice about a lesson you learned when you were 8 to 10 years old.

2.   Read *Momma* by Maya Angelou and analyze the different strategies used to capture the child's voice.

Connie Thomas (student)

THE DAY I LIED MY WAY OUT OF SUMMER SCHOOL

CONNIE THOMAS is a student at Compton Community College majoring in English with the goal of becoming a lawyer.

I awake to the sound of my mother flicking on the light and banging on the broken light switch cover. It's on the wall of our bedroom where she stands in the doorway. I hate the sound of that broken light switch cover hitting against the wall. "Wake up you guys; it's time to get ready for school," she would say every school day morning. Usually I would moan and groan about having to wake up so early, but this day was different. It was the last two days before summer vacation. Since my teacher hadn't given the class our summer school enrollment forms, I just knew there wouldn't be any summer school this year. I was home free.

It's a beautiful summer morning. I can hear the birds chirping outside my bedroom window. As I look out I see bees buzzing around and butterflies fluttering about trying to land on every flower they see. The sun seems to be shinning brighter today than usual as if it was smiling on me like it knew this would be the summer I would be spending more time playing in its warm rays.

All of us kids, my three sisters and I, are hurrying around, grabbing, and pulling clothes out of our tiny bedroom closet. "I'm first in the bathroom," says Alice. "You know we're told to go two at a time so we won't be late," I say to her. She's thirteen months younger than I am. We feel we're too old for the both of us to share the bathroom together. So I tell her to take Lisa with her; she's two years younger than Alice. Since I'm the oldest I get to choose, and I always choose Jackie because she's six years younger than I am, and the youngest of us all.

While we're washing up she doesn't ask questions about private things if she just so happens to see them. This we did every morning while getting ready for school. Fighting for the mirror to see if our clothes are just right. Tugging over the bathroom sink so we can brush our teeth, and spit out the toothpaste. This morning I missed and spit in my sister's hair. She came down just as I did, but she's a lot shorter. "I'll clean it out," I say pleading with her not to tell our mother. "I won't tell if you clean it all out," she says. Lucky for me it all came out.

Dressed and ready for school we head out the door saying, "bye Mommy," as if we are a singing group. Before walking straight to school we stop at the team post. This is a place where the neighborhood kids go after school and play games, dance, and put on plays, so we don't have to hang out in the streets. Every morning before school the team post gives away free breakfast to any kid who wants to eat. I have sausage, eggs, and grits.

Now, I head to school on a full stomach happy as I can be because I don't have to go to summer school. I can spend my first summer of no school playing all day.

I finally arrive at my fifth grade class. As I sit there daydreaming out the window, I faintly hear the teacher's voice. She's talking about our class assignment for today. Why, when we only have two days left of school. Still daydreaming out the window, I watch the trees slowly rock back and forth in the warm summer breeze. All the while thinking as the clock ticks away, the day seems so long. It's too nice outside to be in class.

The bell rings; it's lunch time. Yes! Now the day will go faster. I walk home for lunch. Good, my mother made spaghetti. Oh no! *Pink quick*, a strawberry powdered milk drink, I hate *pink quick*. Whoever saw a pink rabbit anyway? "Eat every thing on your plate," she says. I hurry and eat all my spaghetti, and hold my nose while I drink my *pink quick*. Yuck!! Lunch time is over; I'm on my way back to school.

The teacher is asking the class what our plans are for the summer. This boy, Frank, raises his hand. He wears big thick black-rimmed glasses, and talks a lot, but he's a nice boy. I like him. The teacher says, "What will you be doing this summer, Frank?" "My family and I are going to drive to Mexico to see my Tia." (Aunt, that was the first Spanish word I learned.) Some of the other kids are talking over each other trying to tell the teacher what they're going to be doing for the summer. Me, I just sit back and think about what I will be doing. Like playing until my father comes to pick me and my sisters up for visitation time. My parents are divorced. I like spending time with my father during the summer because he takes us traveling in his RV to different places.

It's a few minutes now before school is out. Oh no! The teacher is handing out letters for us to take home. That's alright! I'll just cross my fingers real hard. Yes, that'll work, then for sure she won't give us a summer school application form. Here's the first one. Good, it's not the one. Let me keep my fingers crossed. Here's the second one. It's, it's a summer school application form. What do I do now? I guess I'll have to give it to my mother, I thought.

Just then the bell rings and it's time to go home. "I'm taking the long way home," I tell my sisters. "Well, we're going to take the short way, bye." As I try and clear my head of the thought of having to go to summer school, I hear all the neighborhood sounds, babies crying, dogs barking, kids playing in their yards. Bet they don't have to go to summer school. I go every year. Can't I get just one break?

Here's that lot with the tall yellow grass the city burns every summer. WAIT A MINUTE! No. I shouldn't be thinking this. That's bad, it will be lying. I continue to walk past the lot. Then I stop and look at the application. I run back to the lot as fast as I can because I am supposed to come straight home from school. I don't want to get caught walking the wrong way. I ball up the form and stick it through the chain link fence.

After I got into our front yard I thought, why did I put it so close to the edge of the fence? I don't know. I was thinking that the wind would blow it out before the lot could be burned. I worried that my mother would find it even though we lived a block and a half away.

Now, I'm in the house. My sisters are handing our mother their summer school application form. Why do they look so happy about going to summer school? All it is, is hot work, work, hot, work and homework. My mother even seems happy about summer school.

"Connie," she says, "where is your application form?"

I swallow and try to breathe. Why did I feel caught off guard. I should have known she would ask me next.

"Umm, umm," I say. Then my mouth opens like it belongs to somebody else, and says, "My teacher said that we don't have summer school this year."

I couldn't believe I said that. Did she know I was lying? All I could think about was playing with my dolls, watching T.V., and playing, playing, playing under, what was this morning, a warm smiling, happy sun, which seemed to have vanished at this point as if it was in some kind of trouble.

By this time, my mother seems to be pretty upset. "Well, since you are the only one who doesn't have to go to summer school (why did it feel as if she knows I am lying), then you're going to clean your room, clean the house, and stay in your room all day for the next few weeks until your father comes and picks you up."

Right then I wanted to tell her where the application form was, but I was afraid of making matters worse, like getting a beating or something. Summer school was looking pretty good to me right about then.

I spent the rest of the summer doing exactly what I was told.

Some people might think I learned a valuable lesson about lying. They're right. I learned not to be so creative next time. Then, maybe it would be easier to fix it.

THE DAY I LIED MY WAY
OUT OF SUMMER SCHOOL

Questions

1. Do you think the author fulfilled her goal to play all day everyday all summer? Explain.

2. Name the emotions you hear in the author's voice.

3. The author mixes internal thoughts with real-life events. Is this an effective strategy? Explain.

Maya Angelou

MOMMA

MAYA ANGELOU (b. 1928) was born Marguerite Johnson in California, but traveled to Stamps, Arkansas, to live with her grandmother at the age of four. Along with her many accomplishments, Maya Angelou was appointed Poet Laureate of the United States in 1993. Everyone was in awe and inspired as she recited her poem, *On the Pulse of Morning*, during President Clinton's inauguration. Angelou is also noted for her five-volume autobiography beginning with *I Know Why The Caged Bird Sings* (1970), *Gather Together in My Name* (1974), *Singin' and Swingin' and Gettin' Merry Like Christmas* (1976), *The Heart of a Woman* (1981), and *All God's Children Have Traveling Shoes* (1986). "Momma" is an excerpt from the popular *I Know Why The Caged Bird Sings*. Maya Angelou directed the film *Down in the Delta* (1999) and continues as an English Professor at Wake Forest University in Winston-Salem, North Carolina.

The author's grandmother endeavors to teach her important lessons, which will help her navigate through life as a Black woman.

"Thou shall not be dirty" and "Thou shall not be impudent" were the two commandments of Grandmother Henderson upon which hung our total salvation.

Each night in the bitterest winter we were forced to wash faces, arms, necks, legs and feet before going to bed. She used to add, with a smirk that unprofane people can't control when venturing into profanity, "and wash as far as possible, then wash possible."

We would go to the well and wash in the ice-cold, clear water, grease our legs with the equally cold stiff Vaseline, then tiptoe into the house. We wiped the dust from our toes and settled down for schoolwork, cornbread, clabbered milk, prayers and bed, always in that order. Momma was famous for pulling the quilts off after we had fallen asleep to examine our feet. If they weren't clean enough for her, she took the switch (she kept one behind the bedroom door for emergencies) and woke up the offender with a few aptly placed burning reminders.

The area around the well at night was dark and slick, and boys told about how snakes love water, so that anyone who had to draw water at night and then stand there alone and wash knew that moccasins and rattlers, puff adders and boa constrictors were winding their way to the well and would arrive just as the person washing got soap in her eyes. But Momma convinced us that not only was cleanliness next to Godliness, dirtiness was the inventor of misery.

The impudent child was detested by God and a shame to its parents and could bring destruction to its house and line. All adults had to be addressed as Mister, Missus, Miss, Auntie, Cousin, Unk, Uncle, Buhbah, Sister, Brother and a thousand other appellations indicating familial relationship and the lowliness of the addressor.

Everyone I knew respected these customary laws, except for the powhitetrash children.

Some families of powhitetrash lived on Momma's farm land behind the school. Sometimes a gaggle of them came to the Store, filling the whole room, chasing out the air and even changing the well-known scents. The children crawled over the shelves and into the potato and onion bins, twanging all the time in their sharp voices like cigar-box guitars. They took liberties in my Store that I would never dare. Since Momma told us that the less you say to whitefolks (or even powhitetrash) the better, Bailey and I would stand, solemn, quiet, in the displaced air. But if one of the playful apparitions got close to us, I pinched it. Partly out of angry frustration and partly because I didn't believe in its flesh reality.

They called my uncle by his first name and ordered him around the Store. He, to my crying shame, obeyed them in his limping dip-straight-dip fashion.

My grandmother, too, followed their orders, except that she didn't seem to be servile because she anticipated their needs.

"Here's sugar, Miz Potter, and here's baking powder. You didn't buy soda last month, you'll probably be needing some."

Momma always directed her statements to the adults, but sometimes, Oh painful sometimes, the grimy, snotty-nosed girls would answer her.

"Naw, Annie . . ."—to Momma? Who owned the land they lived on? Who forgot more than they would ever learn? If there was any justice in the world, God should strike them dumb at once!—"Just give us some extry sody crackers, and some more mackerel."

At least they never looked in her face, or I never caught them doing so. Nobody with a smidgen of training, not even the worst roustabout, would look right in a grown person's face. It meant the person was trying to take the words out before they were formed. The dirty little children didn't do that, but they threw their orders around the Store like lashes from a cat-o'-nine-tails.

When I was around ten years old, those scruffy children caused me the most painful and confusing experience I had ever had with my grandmother.

One summer morning, after I had swept the dirt yard of leaves, spearmint-gum wrappers and Vienna-sausage labels, I raked the yellow-red dirt, and made half-moons carefully, so that the design stood out clearly and mask-like. I put the rake behind the Store and came through the back of the house to find Grandmother on the front porch in her big, wide white apron. The apron was so stiff by virtue of the starch that it could have stood alone. Momma was admiring the yard, so I joined her. It truly looked like a flat redhead that had been raked with a big-toothed comb. Momma didn't say anything but I knew she liked it. She looked over toward the school principal's house and to the right at Mr. McElroy's. She was hoping one of those community pillars would see the design before the day's business wiped it out. Then she looked upward to the school. My head had swung with hers, so at just about the same time we saw a troop of the powhitetrash kids marching over the hill and down by the side of the school.

I looked to Momma for direction. She did an excellent job of sagging from her waist down, but from the waist up she seemed to be pulling for the top of the oak tree across the road. Then she began to moan a hymn. Maybe not to moan, but the tune was so slow and the meter so strange that she could have been moaning. She didn't look at me again. When the children reached halfway down the hill, halfway to the Store, she said without turning, "Sister, go on inside."

I wanted to beg her, "Momma, don't wait for them. Come on inside with me. If they come in the Store, you go to the bedroom and let me wait on them. They only frighten me if you're around. Alone I know how to handle them." But of course I couldn't say anything, so I went in and stood behind the screen door.

Before the girls got to the porch I heard their laughter crackling and popping like pine logs in a cooking stove. I suppose my lifelong paranoia was born in those cold, molasses-slow minutes. They came finally to stand on the ground in front of Momma. At first they pretended seriousness. Then one of them wrapped her right arm in the crook of her left, pushed out her mouth and started to hum. I realized that she was aping my grandmother. Another said, "Naw, Helen, you ain't standing like her. This here's it." Then she lifted her chest, folded her arms and mocked that strange carriage that was Annie Henderson. Another laughed. "Naw, you can't do it. Your mouth ain't pooched out enough. It's like this."

I thought about the rifle behind the door, but I knew I'd never be able to hold it straight, and the .410, our sawed-off shot gun, which stayed loaded and was fired every New Year's night, was locked in the trunk and Uncle Willie had the key on his chain. Through the fly-specked screen door, I could see that the arms of Momma's apron jiggled from the vibrations of her humming. But her knees seemed to have locked as if they would never bend again.

She sang on. No louder than before, but no softer either. No slower or faster.

The dirt of the girls' cotton dresses continued on their legs, feet, arms and faces to make them all of a piece. Their greasy uncolored hair hung down, uncombed, with a grim finality. I knelt to see them better, to remember them for all time. The tears that had slipped down my dress left unsurprising dark spots, and made the front yard blurry and even more unreal. The world had taken a deep breath and was having doubts about continuing to revolve.

The girls had tired of mocking Momma and turned to other means of agitation. One crossed her eyes, stuck her thumbs in both sides of her mouth and said, "Look here, Annie." Grandmother hummed on and the apron strings trembled. I wanted to throw a handful of black pepper in their faces, to throw lye on them, to scream that they were dirty, scummy peckerwoods, but I knew I was as clearly imprisoned behind the scene as the actors outside were confined to their roles.

One of the smaller girls did a kind of puppet dance while her fellow clowns laughed at her. But the tall one, who was almost a woman, said something very quietly, which I couldn't hear. They all moved backward from the porch, still watching Momma. For an awful second I thought they were going to throw a rock at Momma, who seemed (except for the apron strings) to have turned into stone herself. But the big girl turned her back, bent down and put her hands flat on the ground—she didn't pick up anything. She simply shifted her weight and did a hand stand.

Her dirty bare feet and long legs went straight for the sky. Her dress fell down around her shoulders and she had on no drawers. The slick pubic hair made a brown triangle where her legs came together. She hung in the vacuum of that lifeless morning for only a few seconds, then wavered and tumbled. The other girls clapped her on the back and slapped their hands.

Momma changed her song to "Bread of Heaven, bread of heaven, feed me till I want no more."

I found that I was praying too. How long could Momma hold out? What new indignity would they think of to subject her to? Would I be able to stay out of it? What would Momma really like me to do?

Then they were moving out of the yard, on their way to town. They bobbed their heads and shook their slack behinds and turned, one at a time:

" 'Bye, Annie."

" 'Bye, Annie."

" 'Bye, Annie."

Momma never turned her head or unfolded her arms, but she stopped singing and said, " 'Bye, Miz Helen, 'bye, Miz Ruth, 'bye, Miz Eloise."

I burst. A firecracker July-the-Fourth burst. How could Momma call them Miz? The mean nasty things. Why couldn't she have come inside the sweet, cool store when we saw them breasting the hill? What did she prove? And then if they were dirty, mean and impudent, why did Momma have to call them Miz?

She stood another whole song through and then opened the screen door to look down on me crying in rage. She looked until I looked up. Her face was a brown moon that shone on me. She was beautiful. Something had happened out there, which I couldn't completely understand, but I could see that she was happy. Then she bent down and touched me as mothers of the church "lay hands on the sick and afflicted" and I quieted.

"Go wash your face, Sister." And she went behind the candy counter and hummed, "Glory, glory, hallelujah, when I lay my burden down."

I threw the well water on my face and used the weekday handkerchief to blow my nose. Whatever the contest had been out front, I knew Momma had won.

I took the rake back to the front yard. The smudged footprints were easy to erase. I worked for a long time on my new design and laid the rake behind the wash pot. When I came back in the Store, I took Momma's hand and we both walked outside to look at the pattern.

It was a large heart with lots of hearts growing smaller inside, and piercing from the outside rim to the smallest heart was an arrow. Momma said, "Sister, that's right pretty." Then she turned back to the Store and resumed, "Glory, glory, hallelujah, when I lay my burden down."

MOMMA

Facts

1.   Where did Grandma Henderson and her family live? Where did they work?

2.   Who owned the land?

3.   How old was the author?

4.   Name the other relatives mentioned in the story.

Strategies

1.   Maya Angelou uses the first person point of view. Why?

2.   The author reinforces the child's voice and perspective with an adult understanding and clarification. Find the paragraphs where this is apparent.

3.   The author uses physical techniques to indicate the child's perspective. Find the paragraphs and explain.

4.   Why does the author use both perspectives and voices—adult and child? What does she gain by using both?

Issues

1.   Why are the first five paragraphs important to the story?

2.   Why was the author crying?

3.   What lesson was Grandmother Henderson trying to convey? Did the author learn the lesson?

4.   What would the Grandmother have done if black children had approached her in that manner?

5. Why did the author create a new pattern in the yard? What did the pattern symbolize?

6. Why are both groups of people—black and white—locked in a prison? What prison?

Writing Assignments

1. Using the child's voice and adult perspective, write a narrative about an important event that happened while you were on an outing with one of your parents.

2. Write an essay analyzing race relations in your hometown from the child's perspective.

Audra Bronson (student)

THE GOOD LIFE

AUDRA BRONSON was a student at Compton Community College when she wrote this essay. Currently, she is studying English at California State University-Dominguez Hills.

Why did we have to move? Why did I have to go to this new school? Why? I love where we used to live. I loved my old raggedy neighborhood, the church at the end of the corner, the liquor store at the other end of the corner, my great grandma's house two doors down, and the fact that we were all the same, at least in my eyes because we were all black. Also, there was my school, it was great because I had lots of fun and a lot of friends, who were also, just like me. They understood the things I did; how I wore my hair, and how during the summer when it was extremely hot outside, we all wore corn rows in our hair, or when we would get our hair pressed with so much grease that even a tornado couldn't make our stiff hairdos move. And we all knew that if my hair got wet it would get nappy and believe me, they all knew what nappy meant. Furthermore, we all knew what chitterlings were and greens, sweet potato pies and hot water cornbread. This was the bond we shared and these were my friends.

"So, why? Please, tell me why we had to leave?" These questions hung so heavily in my mind that I was sure someone could hear my thoughts, and I did have an idea why we were moving. Momma thought she was gonna improve me and my sister's lives, and she thought that we were moving up in the world because we had moved to an all white neighborhood. The houses were all new with perfect little yards, perfect little streets, perfect little sidewalks and perfect little people—white people, that is.

My mother had bought into the idea that whiter was better and as I look back it was understandable. It was the early '70s, and I was about seven years old, the civil rights movement had opened doors to places most blacks could never have imagined entering. We stepped right through the doors into the white man's world—"The Good Life."

Our family was the only black family in the entire neighborhood besides the Downings. Needless to say, there weren't many black kids at the school I was now attending; it was lily white. I was the only black kid in my class, but since I was naive to all of this prejudice stuff, I wasn't really too concerned that all of them were white. I assumed I'd make the best of a new situation, play and learn with these kids just like I did at my other school. After all, we were all kids, we were all the same age, and all in the same classroom, so everything would be fine.

However, they soon let me know that I wasn't like them, at least not by my outside appearance. First, it was my lips, they said I had big lips. "Oh, really," I said. No one wanted to sit by the black girl during lunch time. Then there were all the questions: Why do you wear your hair like that? And why do you put grease in your hair? Why? Why? Why? To make matters worse, we began to study about slavery. My teacher said that blacks were the slaves and that they were chained like animals, branded like cattle, and considered less than human, and the white people were their masters. Since I was the only black in my classroom, I could feel everyone looking at me as if I was dirty. "I never knew that being black was such a bad thing." By now, I was starting to feel worse and worse about being in this classroom and being the only black among all these white kids. Then came the final blow, one day in class this blonde-haired, blue-eyed boy did the ultimate insult. He called me a *Nigger*! I really didn't know what the word meant; I just knew it was the worst thing in the whole world to be called, especially by a white person. I knew it was a bad word.

All I could do was run and hide, so I ran to the bathroom which was in our classroom, and I cried, and cried, and cried. I felt like the ugliest, worst, dirtiest, stupidest person in the world. When I emerged from the bathroom with swollen, teary eyes, I slowly headed to the front of the class where the teacher's desk was; she made him apologize. As I stood there facing all of them and all those white faces stared back at my little black face, I felt numb. I didn't even hear his apology all I knew was that there was an aching pain in my heart and my soul. I knew that things could never be like they used to be at my old school. I knew that I would never be happy here with all of them, that I would never fit in, and that I would never want to. And they knew it too.

My mom thought she was giving us all the privileges she never had. The white privileges. She thought that at this all white school we would receive an education far superior to hers. My mom thought she was giving us "The Good Life."

THE GOOD LIFE

Questions

1.   In the author's story good and better equals white and bad and negative equals black. Discuss this attitude that seems to permeate our society.

2.   Discuss the author's voice. How does it add to the story?

Gish Jen

"WHAT MEANS SWITCH?"

GISH JEN (b. 1955) was born in New York City. She graduated from Harvard University and earned her M.F.A. at the Iowa University Writers' Workshop in 1991. *Typical American*, her first novel, was published in 1991 and was nominated for the National Book Critics Circle Award. Ms. Jen has also published her work in many magazines including *The New Yorker*, *The Atlantic*, *The Yale Review*, *The Southern Review*, and *Growing up Asian*. She lives in Cambridge, Massachusetts.

Mona Chang, a twelve-year-old Chinese American, is a newcomer to a junior high school in Scarsdale, New York. This humorous story explores the sometimes tense relationship between the Japanese and Chinese because of World War II.

There we are, nice Chinese family—father, mother, two born-here girls. Where should we live next? My parents slide the question back and forth like a cup of ginseng neither one wants to drink. Until finally it comes to them, what they really want is a milkshake (chocolate) and to go with it a house in Scarsdale. What else? The broker tries to hint: the neighborhood, she says. Moneyed. Many delis. Meaning rich and Jewish. But someone has sent my parents a list of the top ten schools nation-wide (based on the opinion of selected educators and others) and so *many-deli* or not we nestle into a Dutch colonial on the Bronx River Parkway. The road's windy where we are, very charming; drivers miss their turns, plow up our flower beds, then want to use our telephone. "Of course," my mom tells them, like it's no big deal, we can replant. We're the type to adjust. You know—the lady drivers weep, my mom gets out the Kleenex for them. We're a bit down the hill from the private plane set, in other words. Only in our dreams do our jacket zippers jam, what with all the lift tickets we have stapled to them, Killington on top of Sugarbush on top of Stowe, and we don't even know where the Virgin Islands are—although certain of us do know that virgins are like priests and nuns, which there were a lot more of in Yonkers, where we just moved from, than there are here.

This is my first understanding of class. In our old neighborhood everybody knew everything about virgins and non-virgins, not to say the technicalities of staying in between. Or almost everybody, I should say; in Yonkers I was the laugh-along type. Here I'm an expert.

"You mean the man . . . ?" Pig-tailed Barbara Gugelstein spits a mouthful of Coke back into her can. "That is *so* gross!"

Pretty soon I'm getting popular for a new girl. The only problem is Danielle Meyers, who wears blue mascara and has gone steady with two boys. "How do *you* know," she starts to ask, proceeding to edify us all with how she French-kissed one boyfriend and just regular kissed another. ("Because, you know, he had braces.") We hear about his rubber bands, how once one popped right into her mouth. I begin to realize I need to find somebody to kiss too. But how?

Luckily, I just about then happen to tell Barbara Gugelstein I know karate. I don't know why I tell her this. My sister Callie's the liar in the family; ask anybody. I'm the one who doesn't see why we should have to hold our heads up. But for some reason I tell Barbara Gugelstein I can make my hands like steel by thinking hard. "I'm not supposed to tell anyone," I say.

The way she backs away, blinking, I could be the burning bush.

"I can't do bricks," I say—a bit of expectation management. "But I can do your arm if you want." I set my hand in chop position.

"Uhh, it's okay," she says. "I know you can. I saw it on TV last night."

That's when I recall that I too saw it on TV last night—in fact, at her house. I rush on to tell her I know how to get pregnant with tea.

"With *tea*?"

"That's how they do it in China."

She agrees that China is an ancient and great civilization that ought to be known for more than spaghetti and gunpowder. I tell her I know Chinese. "*Be-yeh fa-foon*," I say. "*Shee-veh. Ji nu.*" Meaning "Stop acting crazy. Rice gruel. Soy sauce." She's impressed. At lunch the next day, Danielle Meyers and Amy Weinstein and Barbara's crush, Andy Kaplan, are all impressed too. Scarsdale is a liberal town, not like Yonkers, where the Whitman Road Gang used to throw crabapple mash at my sister Callie and me and tell us it would make our eyes stick shut. Here we're like permanent exchange students. In another ten years, there'll be so many Orientals we'll turn into Asians; a Japanese grocery will buy out that one deli too many. But for now, the mid-sixties, what with civil rights on TV, we're not so much accepted as embraced. Especially by the Jewish part of town—which, it turns out, is not all of town at all. That's just an idea people have, Callie says, and lots of them could take us or leave us same as the Christians, who are nice too; I shouldn't generalize. So let me not generalize except to say that pretty soon I've been to so many bar and bas mitzvahs, I can almost say myself whether the kid chants like an angel or like a train conductor, maybe they could use him on the commuter line. At seder I know to forget the

44

bricks, get a good pile of that mortar. Also I know what is schmaltz. I know that I am a goy. This is not why people like me, though. People like me because I do not need to use deodorant, as I demonstrate in the locker room before and after gym. Also, I can explain to them, for example, what is tofu (*der-voo*, we say at home). Their mothers invite me to taste-test their Chinese cooking.

"Very authentic." I try to be reassuring. After all, they're nice people, I like them. "De-lish." I have seconds. On the question of what we eat, though, I have to admit, "Well, no, it's different than that." I have thirds. "What my mom makes is home style, it's not in the cookbooks."

Not in the cookbooks! Everyone's jealous. Meanwhile, the big deal at home is when we have turkey pot pie. My sister Callie's the one introduced them—Mrs. Wilder's, they come in this green-and brown-box—and when we have them, we both get suddenly interested in helping out in the kitchen. You know, we stand in front of the oven and help them bake. Twenty-five minutes. She and I have a deal, though, to keep it secret from school, as everybody else thinks they're gross. We think they're a big improvement over authentic Chinese home cooking. Oxtail soup—now that's gross. Stir-fried beef with tomatoes. One day I say, "You know Ma, I have never seen a stir-fried tomato in any Chinese restaurant we have ever been in, ever."

"In China," she says, real lofty, "we consider tomatoes are a delicacy."

"Ma," I say. "Tomatoes are *Italian*."

"No respect for elders." She wags her finger at me, but I can tell it's just to try and shame me into believing her. "I'm tell you, tomatoes *invented* in China."

"*Ma.*"

"Is true. Like noodles. Invented in China."

"That's not what they said in *school*."

"In *China*," my mother counters, "we also eat tomatoes uncooked, like apple. And in summertime we slice them, and put some sugar on top."

"Are you sure?"

My mom says of course she's sure, and in the end I give in, even though she once told me that China was such a long time ago, a lot of things she can hardly remember. She said sometimes she has trouble remembering her characters, that sometimes she'll be writing a letter, just writing along, and all of a sudden she won't be sure if she should put four dots or three.

"So what do you do then?"

"Oh, I just make a little sloppy."

"You mean you *fudge*?"

She laughed then, but another time, when she was showing me how to write my name, and I said, just kidding, "Are you sure that's the right number of dots now?" she was hurt.

45

"I mean, of course you know," I said. "I mean, *oy*."

Meanwhile, what *I* know is that in the eighth grade, what people want to hear does not include how Chinese people eat sliced tomatoes with sugar on top. For a gross fact, it just isn't gross enough. On the other hand, the fact that somewhere in China somebody eats or has eaten or once ate living monkey brains—now that's conversation.

"They have these special tables," I say, "kind of like a giant collar. With a hole in the middle, for the monkey's neck. They put the monkey in the collar, and then they cut off the top of its head."

"Whadda they use for cutting?"

I think. "Scalpels."

"*Scalpels*?" says Andy Kaplan

"Kaplan, don't be dense," Barbara Gugelstein says. "The Chinese *invented* scalpels."

Once a friend said to me, You know, everybody is valued for something. She explained how some people resented being valued for their looks; other resented being valued for their money. Wasn't it still better to be beautiful and rich than ugly and poor, though? You should be just glad, she said, that you have something people value. It's like having a special talent, like being good at ice-skating, or opera-singing. She said, You could probably make a career out of it.

Here's the irony: I am.

Anyway. I am ad-libbing my way through eighth grade, as I've described. Until one bloomy spring day, I come in late to homeroom, and to my chagrin discover there's a new kid in class.

Chinese.

So what should I do, pretend to have to go to the girls' room, like Barbara Gugelstein the day Andy Kaplan took his ID back? I sit down; I am so cool I remind myself of Paul Newman. First thing I realize, though, is that no one looking at me is thinking of Paul Newman. The notes fly:

"*I* think he's cute."

"Who?" I write back. (I am still at an age, understand, when I believe a person can be saved by aplomb.)

"I don't think he talks English too good. Writes it either."

"Who?"

"They might have to put him behind a grade, so don't worry."

"He has a crush on you already, you could tell as soon as you walked in, he turned kind of orangeish."

I hope I'm not turning orangeish as I deal with my mail; I could use a secretary. The second round starts:

"What do you mean who? Don't be weird. Didn't you *see* him???
Straight back over your right shoulder!!!!"

I have to look; what else can I do? I think of certain tips I learned in Girl
Scouts about poise. I cross my ankles. I hold a pen in my hand. I sit up as
though I have a crown on my head. I swivel my head slowly, repeating to
myself, *I could be Miss America.*

"Miss Mona Chang."

Horror raises its hoary head.

"Notes, please."

Mrs. Mandeville's policy is to read all notes aloud.

I try to consider what Miss America would do, and see myself, back
straight, knees together, crying. Some inspiration. Cool Hand Luke, on the other
hand, would, quick, eat the evidence. And why not? I should yawn as I stand
up, and boom, the notes are gone. All that's left is to explain that it's an old
Chinese reflex.

I shuffle up to the front of the room.

"One minute please," Mrs. Mandeville says.

I wait, noticing how large and plastic her mouth is.

She unfolds a piece of paper.

And I, Miss Mona Chang, who got almost straight A's her whole life
except in math and conduct, am about to start crying in front of everyone.

. . .

I am delivered out of hot Egypt by the bell. General pandemonium. Mrs.
Mandeville still has her hand clamped on my shoulder, though. And the next
thing I know, I'm holding the new boy's schedule. He's standing next to me like
a big blank piece of paper. "This is Sherman," Mrs. Mandeville says.

"Hello," I say.

"*Non how a,*" I say.

"I'm glad Barbara Gugelstein isn't there to see my Chinese in action.

"*Ji nu,*" I say. "*Shee veh.*"

Later I find out that his mother asked if there were any other Orientals in
our grade. She had him put in my class on purpose. For now, though, he looks
at me as though I'm much stranger than anything else he's seen so far. Is this
because he understands I'm saying "soy sauce rice gruel" to him or because he
doesn't?

"Sher-man," he says finally.

I look at his schedule card. Sherman Matsumoto. What kind of name is
that for a nice Chinese boy?

(Later on, people ask me how I can tell Chinese from Japanese. I shrug. You just kind of know, I say. *Oy!*)

Sherman's got the sort of looks I think of as pretty-boy. Monsignor-black hair (not monk brown like mine), bouncy. Crayola eyebrows, one with a round bald spot in the middle of it, like a golf hole. I don't know how anybody can think of him as orangeish; his skin looks white to me, with pink triangles hanging down the front of his cheeks like flags. Kind of delicate-looking, but the only truly uncool thing about him is that his spiral notebook has a picture of a kitty cat on it. A big white fluffy one, with a blue ribbon above each perky little ear. I get much opportunity to view this, as all the poor kid understands about life in junior high school is that he should follow me everywhere. It's embarrassing. On the other hand, he's obviously even more miserable than I am, so I try not to say anything. Give him a chance to adjust. We communicate by sign language, and by drawing pictures, which he's better at than I am; he puts in every last detail, even if it takes forever. I try to be patient.

A week of this. Finally I enlighten him. "You should get a new notebook."

His cheeks turn a shade of pink you mostly only see in hyacinths.

"Notebook." I point to his. I show him mine, which is psychedelic, with big purple and yellow stick-on flowers. I try to explain he should have one like this, only without the flowers. He nods enigmatically, and the next day brings me a notebook just like his, except that this cat sports pink bows instead of blue.

"Pret-ty," he says. "You."

He speaks English! I'm dumbfounded. Has he spoken it all this time? I consider: Pretty. You. What does that mean? Plus actually, he's said *plit-ty,* much as my parents would; I'm assuming he means pretty, but maybe he means pity. Pity. You.

"Jeez," I say finally.

"You are wel-come," he says.

I decorate the back of the notebook with stick-on flowers, and hold it so that these show when I walk through the halls. In class I mostly keep by book open. After all, the kid's so new; I think I really ought to have a heart. And for a livelong day nobody notices.

Then Barbara Gugelstein sidles up. "Matching notebooks, huh?"

I'm speechless.

"First comes love, then comes marriage, and then come chappies in a baby carriage."

"Barbara!"

"Get it?" she says. "Chinese Japs."

"Bar-*bra*," I say to get even.

"Just make sure he doesn't give you any *tea*," she says.

Are Sherman and I in love? Three days later, I hazard that we are. My thinking proceeds this way: I think he's cute, and I think he thinks I'm cute. On the other hand, we don't kiss and we don't exactly have fantastic conversations. Our talks *are* getting better, though. We started out, "This is a book." "Book." "This is a chair." "Chair." Advancing to, "What is this?" "This is a book." Now, for fun, he tests me.

"What is this?" he says.

"This is a book," I say, as if I'm the one who has to learn how to talk.

He claps. "Good!"

Meanwhile, people ask me all about him. I could be his press agent.

"No, he doesn't eat raw fish."

"No, his father wasn't a kamikaze pilot."

"No, he can't do karate."

"Are you sure?" somebody asks.

Indeed he doesn't know karate, but judo he does. I am hurt I'm not the one to find this out; the guys know from gym class. They line up to be flipped, he flips them all onto the floor, and after that he doesn't eat lunch at the girls' table with me anymore. I'm more or less glad. Meaning, when he was there, I never knew what to say. Now that he's gone, though, I seem to be stuck at the "This is a chair" level of conversation. Ancient Chinese eating habits have lost their cachet; all I get are more and more questions about me and Sherman. "I dunno," I'm saying all the time. *Are* we going out? We do stuff, it's true. For example, I take him to the department stores, explain to him who shops in Alexander's, who shops in Saks. I tell him my family's the type that shops in Alexander's. He says he's sorry. In Saks he gets lost; either that, or else I'm the lost one. (It's true I find him calmly waiting at the front door, hands behind his back, like a guard.) I take him to the candy store. I take him to the bagel store. Sherman is crazy about bagels. I explain to him that Lender's is gross, he should get his bagels from the bagel store. He says thank you.

"Are you going steady?" people want to know.

How can we go steady when he doesn't have an ID bracelet? On the other hand, he brings me more presents than I think any girl's ever gotten before. Oranges. Flowers. A little bag of bagels. But what do they mean? Do they mean thank you, I enjoyed our trip; do they mean I like you; do they mean I decided I liked the Lender's better even if they are gross, you can have these? Sometimes I think he's acting on his mother's instructions. Also I know at least a couple of the presents were supposed to go to our teachers. He told me that once and turned red. I figured it still might mean something that he didn't throw them out.

More and more now, we joke. Like, instead of "I'm thinking," he always says, "I'm sinking," which we both think is so funny, that all either one of us has to do is pretend to be drowning and the other one cracks up. And he tells me things—for example, that there are electric lights everywhere in Tokyo now.

"You mean you didn't have them before?"

"Everywhere now!" He's amazed too. "Since Olympics!"

"Olympics?"

"1960," he says proudly, and as proof, hums for me the Olympic theme song. "You know?"

"Sure," I say, and hum with him happily. We could be a picture on a UNICEF poster. The only problem is that I don't really understand what the Olympics have to do with the modernization of Japan, any more than I get this other story he tells me, about that hole in his left eyebrow, which is from some time his father accidentally hit him with a lit cigarette. When Sherman was a baby. His father was drunk, having been out carousing; his mother was very mad but didn't say anything, just cleaned the whole house. Then his father was so ashamed he bowed to ask her forgiveness.

"Your mother cleaned the house?"

Sherman nods solemnly.

"And your father *bowed*?" I find this more astounding than anything I ever thought to make up. "That is so weird," I tell him.

"Weird," he agrees. "This I no forget, forever. *Father* bow to *mother*!"

We shake our heads.

As for the things he asks me, they're not topics I ever discussed before. Do I like it here? Of course I like it here, I was born here, I say. Am I Jewish? Jewish! I laugh. *Oy!* Am I American? "Sure I'm American," I say. "Everybody who's born here is American, and also some people who convert from what they were before. You could become American." But he says no, he could never. "Sure you could," I say. "You only have to learn some rules and speeches."

"But I Japanese," he says.

"You could become American anyway," I say. "Like I *could* become Jewish, if I wanted to. I'd just have to switch, that's all."

"But you Catholic," he says.

I think maybe he doesn't get what means switch.

I introduce him to Mrs. Wilder's turkey pot pies. "Gross?" he asks. I say they are, but we like them anyway. "Don't tell anybody." He promises. We bake them, eat them. While we're eating, he's drawing me pictures.

"This American," he says, and he draws something that looks like John Wayne. "This Jewish," he says, and draws something that looks like the Wicked Witch of the West, only male.

"I don't think so," I say.

He's undeterred. "This Japanese," he says, and draws a fair rendition of himself. "This Chinese," he says, and draws what looks to be another fair rendition of himself.

"How can you tell them apart?"

"This way," he says, and he puts the picture of the Chinese so that it is looking at the pictures of the American and the Jew. The Japanese faces the wall. Then he draws another picture, of a Japanese flag, so that the Japanese has that to contemplate. "Chinese lost in department store," he says. "Japanese know how go." For fun, he then takes the Japanese flag and fastens it to the refrigerator door with magnets." "In school, in ceremony, we this way," he explains, and bows to the picture.

When my mother comes in, her face is so red that with the white wall behind her she looks a bit like the Japanese flag herself. Yet I get the feeling I better not say so. First she doesn't move. Then she snatches the flag off the refrigerator, so fast the magnets go flying. Two of them land on the stove. She crumples up the paper. She hisses at Sherman, *"This is the U.S. of A., do you hear me!"*

Sherman hears her.

"You call your mother right now, tell her come pick you up."

He understands perfectly. *I*, on the other hand, am stymied. How can two people who don't really speak English understand each other better than I can understand them? "But Ma," I say.

"Don't *Ma* me," she says.

Later on she explains that World War II was in China, too. "Hitler," I say. "Nazis. Volkswagens." I know the Japanese were on the wrong side, because they bombed Pearl Harbor. My mother explains about before that. The Napkin Massacre.

"*Nan*-king," she corrects me.

"Are you sure?" I say. "In school, they said the war was about putting the Jews in ovens."

"Also about ovens."

"About both?"

"Both."

"That's not what they said in school."

"Just forget about school."

Forget about school? "I thought we moved here for the schools."

"We moved here," she says, "for your education."

Sometimes I have no idea what she's talking about.

"I like Sherman," I say after a while.

"He's nice boy," she agrees.

Meaning what? I would ask, except that my dad's just come home, which means it's time to start talking about whether we should build a brick wall across the front of the lawn. Recently a car made it almost into our living room, which was so scary, the driver fainted and an ambulance had to come. "We should have discussion," my dad said after that. And so for about a week, every night we do.

"Are you just friends, or more than just friends?" Barbara Gugelstein is giving me the cross-ex.

"Maybe," I say.

"Come on," she says, "I told you *everything* about me and Andy."

I actually *am* trying to tell Barbara everything about Sherman, but everything turns out to be nothing. Meaning, I can't locate the conversation in what I have to say. Sherman and I go places, we talk, one time my mother threw him out of the house because of World War II.

"I think we're just friends," I say.

"You think or you're sure?"

Now that I do less of the talking at lunch, I notice more what other people talk about—cheerleading, who likes who, this place in White Plains to get earrings. On none of these topics am I an expert. Of course, I'm still friends with Barbara Gugelstein, but I notice Danielle Meyers has spun away to other groups.

Barbara's analysis goes this way: To be popular, you have to have big boobs, a note from your mother that lets you use her Lord & Taylor credit card, and a boyfriend. On the other hand, what's so wrong with being unpopular? "We'll get them in the end," she says. It's what her dad tells her. "Like they'll turn out too dumb to do their own investing, and then they'll get killed in fees and then they'll have to move to towns where the schools stink. And my dad should know," she winds up. "He's a broker."

"I guess," I say.

But the next thing I know, I have a true crush on Sherman Matsumoto. *Mis*ter Judo, the guys call him now, with real respect; and the more they call him that, the more I don't care that he carries a notebook with a cat on it.

I sigh. "Sherman."

"I thought you were just friends," says Barbara Gugelstein.

"We were," I say mysteriously. This, I've noticed, is how Danielle Meyers talks; everything's secret, she only lets out so much, it's like she didn't grow up with everybody telling her she had to share.

And here's the funny thing: The more I intimate that Sherman and I are more than just friends, the more it seems we actually are. It's the old imagination giving reality a nudge. When I start to blush; he starts to blush; we reach a point where we can hardly talk at all.

"Well, there's first base with tongue, and first base without," I tell Barbara Gugelstein.

In fact, Sherman and I have brushed shoulders, which was equivalent to first base I was sure, maybe even second. I felt as though I'd turned into one huge shoulder; that's all I was, one huge shoulder. We not only didn't talk, we didn't breathe. But how can I tell Barbara Gugelstein that? So instead I say, "Well there's second base and second base."

Danielle Meyers is my friend again. She says, "I know exactly what you mean," just to make Barbara Gugelstein feel bad.

"Like *what* do I mean?" I say.

Danielle Meyers can't answer.

"You know what I think?" I tell Barbara the next day. "I think Danielle's giving us a line."

Barbara pulls thoughtfully on one of her pigtails.

Sherman is leaving in a month. Already! I think, well, I suppose he will leave and we'll never even kiss. I guess that's all right. Just when I've resigned myself to it, though, we hold hands all five fingers. Once when we are at the bagel shop, then again in my parents' kitchen. Then, when we are at the playground, he kisses the back of my hand.

He does it again not too long after that, in White Plains.

I invest in a bottle of mouthwash.

Instead of moving on, though, he kisses the back of my hand again. And again. I try raising my hand, hoping he'll make the jump from my hand to my cheek. It's like trying to wheedle an inchworm out the window. You know. *This way, this way.*

All over the world, people have their own cultures. That's what we learned in social studies.

If we never kiss, I'm not going to take it personally.

It is the end of the school year. We've had parties. We've turned in our textbooks. Hooray! Outside the asphalt already steams if you spit on it. Sherman isn't leaving for another couple of days, though, and he comes to visit every morning, staying until the afternoon, when Callie comes home from her big-deal job as a bank teller. We drink Kool-Aid in the backyard and hold hands until they are sweaty and make smacking noises coming apart. He tells me how busy his parents are, getting ready for the move. His mother, particularly, is very tired. Mostly we are mournful.

The very last day we hold hands and do not let go. Our palms fill up with water like a blister. We do not care. We talk more than usual. How much airmail is to Japan, that kind of thing. Then suddenly he asks, will I marry him?

I'm only thirteen.

But when old? Sixteen?

If you come back to get me.

I come. Or you can come to Japan, be Japanese.

How can I be Japanese?

Like you become American. Switch.

He kisses me on the cheek, again and again and again.

His mother calls to say she's coming to get him. I cry. I tell him how I've saved every present he's ever given me—the ruler, the pencils, the bags from the bagels, all the flower petals. I even have the orange peels from the oranges.

All?

I put them in a jar.

I'd show him, except that we're not allowed to go upstairs to my room. Anyway, something about the orange peels seems to choke him up too. *Mister Judo,* but I've gotten him in a soft spot. We are going together to the bathroom to get some toilet paper to wipe our eyes when poor tired Mrs. Matsumoto, driving a shiny new station wagon, skids up onto our lawn.

"Very sorry!"

We race outside.

"Very sorry!"

Mrs. Matsumoto is so short that about all we can see of her is a green cotton sun hat, with a big brim. It's tied on. The brim is trembling.

I hope my mom's not going to start yelling about World War II.

"Is all right, no trouble," she says, materializing on the steps behind me and Sherman. She's propped the screen door wide open; when I turn I see she's waving. "No trouble, no trouble!"

"No trouble, no trouble!" I echo, twirling a few times with relief.

Mrs. Matsumoto keeps apologizing; my mom keeps insisting she shouldn't feel bad, it was only some grass and a small tree. Crossing the lawn, she insists Mrs. Matsumoto get out of the car, even though it means trampling some lilies-of-the-valley. She insists that Mrs. Matsumoto come in for a cup of tea. Then she will not talk about anything unless Mrs. Matsumoto sits down, and unless she lets my mom prepare her a small snack. The coming in and the tea and the sitting down are settled pretty quickly, but they negotiate ferociously over the small snack, which Mrs. Matsumoto will not eat unless she can call Mr.

Matsumoto. She makes the mistake of linking Mr. Matsumoto with a reparation of some sort, which my mom will not hear of.

"Please!"

"No no no no."

Back and forth it goes: "No no no no." "No no no no." "No no no no." What kind of conversation is that? I look at Sherman, who shrugs. Finally Mr. Matsumoto calls on his own, wondering where his wife is. He comes over in a taxi. He's a heavy-browed businessman, friendly but brisk—not at all a type you could imagine bowing to a lady with a taste for tie-on sun hats. My mom invites him in as if it's an idea she just this moment thought of. And would he maybe have some tea and a small snack?

Sherman and I sneak back outside for another farewell, by the side of the house, behind the forsythia bushes. We hold hands. He kisses me on the cheek again, and then—just when I think he's finally going to kiss me on the lips—he kisses me on the neck.

Is this first base?

He does it more. Up and down, up and down. First it tickles, and then it doesn't. He has his eyes closed. I close my eyes too. He's hugging me. Up and down. Then down.

He's at my collarbone.

Still at my collarbone. Now his hand's on my ribs. So much for first base. More ribs. The idea of second base would probably make me nervous if he weren't on his way back to Japan and if I really thought we were going to get there. As it is, though, I'm not in much danger of wrecking my life on the shoals of passion; his unmoving hand feels more like a growth than a boyfriend. He has his whole face pressed to my neck skin so I can't tell his mouth from his nose. I think he may be licking me.

From indoors, a burst of adult laughter. My eyelids flutter. I start to try and wiggle such that his hand will maybe budge upward.

Do I mean for my top blouse button to come accidentally undone?

He clenches his jaw, and when he opens his eyes, they're fixed on that button like it's a gnat that's been bothering him for far too long. He mutters in Japanese. If later in life he were to describe this as a pivotal moment in his youth, I would not be surprised. Holding the material as far from my body as possible, he buttons the button. Somehow we've landed up too close to the bushes.

What to tell Barbara Gugelstein? She says, "Tell me what were his last words. He must have said something last."

"I don't want to talk about it."

"Maybe he said, Good-bye?" she suggests. "Sayonara?" She means well.

"I don't want to talk about it."

"Aw, come on, I told you everything about—"

I say, "Because it's private, excuse me."

She stops, squints at me as though at a far-off face she's trying to make out. Then she nods and very lightly places her hand on my forearm.

The forsythia seemed to be stabbing us in the eyes. Sherman said, more or less, *You will need to study how to switch.*

And I said, *I think you should switch. The way you do everything is weird.*

And he said, *You just want to tell everything to your friends. You just want to have boyfriend to become popular.*

Then he flipped me. Two swift moves, and I went sprawling through the air, a flailing confusion of soft human parts such as had no idea where the ground was.

It is the fall, and I am in high school, and still he hasn't written, so finally I write him.

I still have all your gifts, I write. *I don't talk so much as I used to. Although I am not exactly a mouse either. I don't care about being popular anymore. I swear. Are you happy to be back in Japan? I know I ruined everything. I was just trying to be entertaining. I miss you with all my heart, and hope I didn't ruin everything.*

He writes back, *You will never be Japanese.*

I throw all the orange peels out that day. Some of them, it turns out, were moldy anyway. I tell my mother I want to move to Chinatown.

"Chinatown!" she says.

I don't know why I suggested it.

"What's the matter?" she says. "Still boy-crazy? That Sherman?"

"No."

"Too much homework?"

I don't answer.

"Forget about school."

Later she tells me if I don't like school, I don't have to go every day. Some days I can stay home.

"Stay home?" In Yonkers, Callie and I used to stay home all the time, but that was because the schools there were *waste of time.*

"No good for a girl be too smart anyway."

. . .

For a long time I think about Sherman. But after a while I don't think about him so much as I just keep seeing myself flipped onto the ground, lying there shocked as the Matsumotos get ready to leave. My head has hit a rock; my brain aches as though it's been shoved to some new place in my skull. Otherwise I am okay. I see the forsythia, all those whippy branches, and can't believe how many leaves there are on a bush—every one green and perky and durably itself. And past them, real sky. I try to remember about why the sky's blue, even though this one's gone the kind of indescribable gray you associate with the insides of old shoes. I smell grass. Probably I have grass stains all over my back. I hear my mother calling through the back door, "Mon-a! Everyone leaving now," and "Not coming to say good-bye?" I hear Mr. and Mrs. Matsumoto bowing as they leave—or at least I hear the embarrassment in my mother's voice as they bow. I hear their car start. I hear Mrs. Matsumoto directing Mr. Matsumoto how to back off the lawn so as not to rip any more of it up. I feel the back of my head for blood—just a little. I hear their chug-chug grow fainter and fainter, until it has faded into the whuzz-whuzz of all the other cars. I hear my mom singing, *"Mon-a! Mon-a!"* until my dad comes home. Doors open and shut. I see myself standing up, brushing myself off so I'll have less explaining to do if she comes out to look for me. Grass stains—just like I thought. I see myself walking around the house, going over to have a look at our churned-up yard. It looks pretty sad, two big brown tracks, right through the irises and the lilies of the valley, and that was a new dogwood we'd just planted. Lying there like that. I hear myself thinking about my father, having to go dig it up all over again. Adjusting. I think how we probably ought to put up that brick wall. And sure enough, when I go inside, no one's thinking about me, or that little bit of blood at the back of my head, or the grass stains. That's what they're talking about—that wall. Again. My mom doesn't think it'll do any good, but my dad thinks we should give it a try. Should we or shouldn't we? How high? How thick? What will the neighbors say? I plop myself down on a hard chair. And all I think is, we are the complete only family that has to worry about this. If I could, I'd switch everything to be different. But since I can't, I might as well sit here at the table for a while, discussing what I know how to discuss. I nod and listen to the rest.

"WHAT MEANS SWITCH?"

Facts

1.   The narrator's parents moved from where to where? What were the differences between the two places?

2.   What constitutes the narrator's expertise?

3.   According to the narrator's mother, where were tomatoes and noodles invented?

4.   What nationality does the narrator think the new boy is? What nationality is he?

5.   Why does the narrator's mother become angry when she sees the Japanese flag on the refrigerator door?

6.   From the exchange about history with her mother, the narrator learns something more than history. What does she learn?

Strategies

1.   Why does the narrator mention the Civil Rights Movement?

2.   The child's voice of the narrator is quite humorous. Select some humorous excerpts.

3.   The child's voice also changes readily. Select the parts where it changes from one emotion to another and describe that change with one word.

4.   When is switch first mentioned in this narrative and why?

5.   Toward the end of the narrative, the author uses a familiar fiction technique. Define the technique and explain how the author accomplishes her objective.

Issues

1. Discuss the importance of fitting into a new neighborhood and/or a new school. Discuss some of the things you've done to fit in.

2. Why did the narrator make a "career" out of telling stories about China?

3. Is the new kid, Sherman, a threat? Why or why not?

4. Discuss whether non-Asians can tell the different Asian nationalities apart. Can Asians tell the difference? Does it make a difference?

5. The narrator says, "I'd just like to switch, that's all." Who does she want to become and why?

6. When people from another culture become American citizens, do they switch? Discuss the meaning of "switch."

Writing Assignments

1. After reading "What Means Switch?" write a narrative essay, using the voice of a child and your own experiences, about living and surviving in two cultures.

2. Research other stories where young adults and/or adolescents have had to define themselves and their culture. Is there a common thread, a common effect? Write a cause/effect essay about your findings.

Sui Sin Far (Edith Eaton)

PAT AND PAN

SUI SIN FAR (b. 1867-d. 1915) grew up in the United States and Canada during an era of prejudice against most foreigners. "Pat and Pan" is an essay from her collection of short stories entitled *Mrs. Spring Fragrance*, which was published in 1912.

Pat, a little white boy, is adopted by Pan's Chinese parents. Pat loves Pan but abandons her when he realizes it is not prudent to befriend someone Chinese.

I

They lay there, in the entrance to the joss house, sound asleep in each others' arms. Her tiny face was hidden upon his bosom and his white, upturned chin rested upon her black, rosetted head.

It was that white chin which caused the passing Mission woman to pause and look again at the little pair. Yes, it was a white boy and a little Chinese girl; he, about five, she, not more than three years old.

"Whose is that boy?" asked the Mission woman of the peripatetic vender of Chinese fruits and sweetmeats.

"That boy! Oh, him is boy of Lum Yook that make the China gold ring and bracelet."

"But he is white."

"Yes, him white; but all same, China boy. His mother, she not have any white flend, and the wife of Lum Yook give her lice and tea, so when she go to the land of spilit, she give her boy to the wife of Lum Yook. Lady, you want buy lichi?"

While Anna Harrison was extracting a dime from her purse the black, rosetted head slowly turned and a tiny fist began rubbing itself into a tiny face.

"Well, chickabiddy, have you had a nice nap?"

"Tjo ho! tjo ho!"

The black eyes gazed solemnly and disdainfully at the stranger.

"She tell you to be good," chuckled the old man.

"Oh, you quaint little thing!"

The quaint little thing hearing herself thus apostrophized, turned herself around upon the bosom of the still sleeping boy and, reaching her arms up to his neck, buried her face again under his chin. This, of course, awakened him. He sat up and stared bewilderedly at the Mission woman.

"What is the boy's name?" she asked, noting his gray eyes and rosy skin.

His reply, though audible, was wholly unintelligible to the American woman.

"He talk only Chinese talk," said the old man.

Anna Harrison was amazed. A white boy in America talking only Chinese talk! She placed her bag of lichis beside him and was amused to see the little girl instantly lean over her companion and possess herself of it. The boy made no attempt to take it from her, and the little thing opened the bag and cautiously peeped in. What she saw evoked a chirrup of delight. Quickly she brought forth one of the browny-red fruit nuts, crushed and pulled off its soft shell. But to the surprise of the Mission woman, instead of putting it into her own mouth, she thrust the sweetish, dried pulp into that of her companion. She repeated this operation several times, then cocking her little head on one side, asked:

"Ho 'm ho? Is it good or bad?"

"Ho! ho!" answered the boy, removing several pits from his mouth and shaking his head to signify that he had had enough. Whereupon the little girl tasted herself of the fruit.

"Pat! Pan! Pat! Pan!" called a woman's voice, and a sleek-headed, kindly-faced matron in dark blue pantalettes and tunic, wearing double hooped gold earrings, appeared around the corner. Hearing her voice, the boy jumped up with a merry laugh and ran out into the street. The little girl more seriously and slowly followed him.

"Him mother!" informed the lichi man.

II

When Anna Harrison, some months later, opend her school for white and Chinese children in Chinatown, she determined that Pat, the adopted son of Lum Yook, the Chinese jeweller, should learn to speak his mother tongue. For a white boy to grow up as a Chinese was unthinkable. The second time she saw him, it was some kind of a Chinese holiday, and he was in great glee over a row of red Chinese candles and punk which he was burning on the curb of the street, in company with a number of Chinese urchins. Pat's candle was giving a brighter and bigger flame than any of the others, and he was jumping up and down with his legs doubled under him from the knees like an india-rubber ball, while Pan, from the doorstep of her father's store, applauded him in vociferous, infantile Chinese.

Miss Harrison laid her hand upon the boy's shoulder and spoke to him. It had not been very difficult for her to pick up a few Chinese phrases. Would he not like to come to her school and see some pretty pictures? Pat shook his ruddy curls and looked at Pan. Would Pan come too? Yes, Pan would. Pan's memory was good, and so were lichis and shredded coconut candy.

Of course Pan was too young to go to school—a mere baby; but if Pat could not be got without Pan, why then Pan must come too. Lum Yook and his wife, upon being interviewed, were quite willing to have Pat learn English. The foster father could speak a little of the language himself, but as he used it only when in business or when speaking to Americans, Pat had not benefited thereby. However, he was more eager than otherwise to have Pat learn "the speech of his ancestors," and promised that he would encourage the little ones to practise "American" together when at home.

So Pat and Pan went to the Mission school, and for the first time in their lives suffered themselves to be divided, for Pat had to sit with the boys and tiny Pan had a little red chair near Miss Harrison, beside which were placed a number of baby toys. Pan was not supposed to learn, only to play.

But Pan did learn. In a year's time, although her talk was more broken and babyish, she had a better English vocabulary than Pat. Moreover, she could sing hymns and recite verses in a high, shrill voice; whereas, Pat, though he tried hard enough, poor little fellow, was unable to memorize even a sentence. Naturally, Pat did not like school as well as did Pan, and it was only Miss Harrison's persistent ambition for him that kept him there.

One day, when Pan was five and Pat was seven, the little girl, for the first time, came to school alone.

"Where is Pat?" asked the teacher.

"Pat, he is sick today," replied Pan.

"Sick!" echoed Miss Harrison. "Well, that is too bad. Poor Pat! What is the matter with him?"

"A big dog bite him."

That afternoon, the teacher, on her way to see the bitten Pat, beheld him up an alley busily engaged in keeping five tops spinning at one time, while several American boys stood around, loudly admiring the Chinese feat.

The next morning Pat received five strokes from a cane which Miss Harrison kept within her desk and used only on special occasions. These strokes made Pat's right hand tingle smartly, but he received them with smiling grace.

Miss Harrison then turned to five-year-old Pan, who had watched the caning with tearful interest.

"Pan!" said the teacher, "you have been just as naughty as Pat, and you must be punished too."

"I not stay away from school!" protested Pan.

"No,"—severely—"you did not stay away from school, but you told me a dog had bitten Pat, and that was not true. Little girls must not say what is not true. Teacher does not like to slap Pan's hands, but she must do it, so that Pan will remember that she must not say what is not true. Come here!"

Pan, hiding her face in her sleeve, sobbingly arose.

The teacher leaned forward and pulling down the uplifted arm, took the small hand in her own and slapped it. She was about to do this a second time when Pat bounded from his seat, pushed Pan aside, and shaking his little fist in the teacher's face, dared her in a voice hoarse with passion:

"You hurt my Pan again! You hurt my Pan again!"

They were not always lovers—those two. It was aggravating to Pat, when the teacher finding he did not know his verse, would turn to Pan and say:

"Well, Pan, let us hear you."

And Pan, who was the youngest child in school and unusually small for her years, would pharisaically clasp her tiny fingers and repeat word for word the verse desired to be heard.

"I hate you, Pan!" muttered Pat on one such occasion.

Happily Pan did not hear him. She was serenely singing:

"Yesu love me, t'is I know,
For the Bible tell me so."

But though a little seraph in the matter of singing hymns and repeating verses, Pan, for a small Chinese girl, was very mischievous. Indeed, she was the originator of most of the mischief which Pat carried out with such spirit. Nevertheless, when Pat got into trouble, Pan, though sympathetic, always had a lecture for him. "Too bad, too bad! Why not you be good like me?" admonished she one day when he was suffering "consequences."

Pat looked down upon her with wrathful eyes.

"Why," he asked, "is bad people always so good?"

III

The child of the white woman, who had been given a babe into the arms of the wife of Lum Yook, was regarded as their own by the Chinese jeweller and his wife, and they bestowed upon him equal love and care with the little daughter who came two years after him. If Mrs. Lum Yook showed any favoritism whatever, it was to Pat. He was the first she had cradled to her bosom; the first to gladden her heart with baby smiles and wiles; the first to call her Ah Ma; the first to love her. On his eighth birthday, she said to her husband: "The son of the white woman is the son of the white woman, and there are many tongues wagging because he lives under our roof. My heart is as heavy as the blackest heavens."

"Peace, my woman," answered the easygoing man. "Why should we trouble before trouble comes?"

When trouble did come it was met calmly and bravely. To the comfortably off American and wife who were to have the boy and "raise him as an American boy should be raised," they yielded him without protest. But deep in their hearts was the sense of injustice and outraged love. If it had not been for their pity for the unfortunate white girl, their care and affection for her helpless offspring, there would have been no white boy for others to "raise."

And Pat and Pan? "I will not leave my Pan! I will not leave my Pan!" shouted Pat.

"But you must!" sadly urged Lum Yook. "You are a white boy and Pan is Chinese."

"I am Chinese too! I am Chinese too!" cried Pat.

"He Chinese! He Chinese!" pleaded Pan. Her little nose was swollen with crying; her little eyes red-rimmed.

But Pat was driven away.

. . .

Pat, his schoolbooks under his arm, was walking down the hill, whistling cheerily. His roving glance down a side street was suddenly arrested.

"Gee!" he exclaimed. "If that isn't Pan! Pan, oh, Pan!" he shouted.

Pan turned. There was a shrill cry of delight, and Pan was clinging to Pat, crying: "Nice Pat! Good Pat!"

Then she pushed him away from her and scanned him from head to foot.

"Nice coat! Nice boot! How many dollars?" she queried.

Pat laughed good-humoredly. "I don't know," he answered. "Mother bought them."

"Mother!" echoed Pan. She puckered her brows for a moment.

"You are grown big, Pat," was her next remark.

"And you have grown little, Pan," retorted Pat. It was a year since they had seen one another and Pan was much smaller than any of his girl schoolfellows.

"Do you like to go to the big school?" asked Pan, noticing the books.

"I don't like it very much. But, say, Pan, I learn lots of things that you don't know anything about."

Pan eyed him wistfully. Finally she said: "O Pat! A-Toy, she die."

"A-Toy! Who is A-Toy?"

"The meow, Pat; the big gray meow! Pat, you have forgot to remember."

Pat looked across Pan head and far away.

"Chinatown is very nice now," assured Pan. "Hum Lock has two trays of brass beetles in his store and Ah Ma has many flowers!"

"I would like to see the brass beetles," said Pat.

"And father's new glass case?"

"Yes."

"And Ah Ma's flowers?"

"Yes."

"Then come, Pat."

"I can't, Pan!"

"Oh!"

Again Pat was walking home from school, this time in company with some boys. Suddenly a glad little voice sounded in his ear. It was Pan's.

"Ah, Pat!" cried she joyfully. "I find you! I find you!"

"Hear the China kid!" laughed one of the boys.

Then Pat turned upon Pan. "Get away from me," he shouted. "Get away from me!"

And Pan did get away from him—just as fast as her little legs could carry her. But when she reached the foot of the hill, she looked up and shook her little head sorrowfully. "Poor Pat!" said she. "He Chinese no more; he Chinese no more!"

PAT AND PAN

Facts

1.   What nationality is Pat? What nationality is Pan?

2.   Where did they live? In what part of the city?

3.   Why did Pat leave Pan and the only parents he knew?

4.   Why did Pat snub Pan? How did Pan feel?

Strategies

1.   In this essay, the author creates a child's voice full of innocence. Discuss the strategy and technique the author used to capture the voice of innocence.

2.   When Pat was adopted by a white American couple, he spoke broken English like Pan. How did the author indicate his language had changed?

Issues

1.   When the mission woman, Anna Harrison, attempted to register Pat, she also had to register Pan. Explain her attitude about this situation.

2.   Discuss Pat's parents' attitude toward his education and his place in the Chinese community.

3.   Explain Pan's comment, "He Chinese no more; he Chinese no more."

Writing Assignments

1.   Write an essay using the child's voice of innocence.

2.   Analyze the essays "What Means Switch?" and "Pat and Pan," then write an essay on the meaning of "switch."

Jana MacCullen (student)

CHICKEN TETRAZZINI

JANA MACCULLEN is a student at Long Beach City College.

I'm not picky and my mom isn't a bad cook; she just makes the wrong things sometimes. Like when she makes macaroni and cheese, or corn dogs, or chicken pot pie, or fish, or chicken, or ham sandwiches, or turkey rice soup, or chicken rice casserole, or enchiladas, or green beans, or carrots, or melon, or taco salad, or strawberry shortcake, or burned cookies, or anything with mushrooms or melted cheese, or especially Chicken Tetrazzini; that's the stuff that's bad. It's not that I don't love my mom or anything, she is one of my most favorite people. I just really hate it when she makes Chicken Tetrazzini. Whenever we have it, I always get sent to my room after dinner for the rest of the night.

We had it the other night. I came home from my best friend Kim's house to see what we were going to have for dinner. My mom always gets upset when I ask her, though I can't seem to figure out why. When I got to the Loveday's house, that's our next door neighbor, I could tell what she was making. That Chicken Tetrazzini had such an awful smell. I didn't even need to ask my mom what was for dinner. I stood at the edge of my neighbor's yard. I didn't know what to do. Maybe I could tell my mom that I was feeling sick and wasn't very hungry. I really wasn't feeling very well at all; I was just curious to know what everyone else was going to eat. I wondered what my mom's reaction would be if I told her that. I decided not to tell her because she probably wouldn't believe me. I decided to go to Kim's house. Kim's mom is a good cook and she knows how to make the right stuff. She always asks me if I would like to eat with them. She's real nice like that. Besides, I needed to eat something; it would make me feel better as long as it's the right food.

So I walked down to Kim's house and knocked on the door. I have to knock real hard because they can never hear it. I think that they need to have a big bell or something so their guests don't get hurt knocking on their door.

"Hi Jana!"

"Hi Kim! Can you still play?"

"Well, we're about to eat dinner right now, but I probably can after."

"It smells good! What are you having?"

"Oh, just spaghetti."

"Spaghetti! That's my favorite!"

"Really? What are you having for dinner?"

"Yucky Chicken Tetrazzini! I hate it!"

"Hey, want me to ask my mom and see if you can just eat with us?"

"Sure, then we can play after!"

"Okay, I'll be right back!"

Well, it turned out that they were having family night. They do that a lot. I sure wish I was a part of their family tonight.

I walked back home trying to think of what I could do next. Maybe I could just plug my nose so that my stomach wouldn't know what was coming in it. Or maybe I could sit there until everyone else was done and then give it to my dog, Missy. I just wondered if my mom would know what I was up to. She might have thought that I was doing it because I didn't like her. I just didn't want to hurt my stomach.

When I got to my house, my whole family was already at the dinner table waiting for me. "Have a seat little late bird," my mom said. I could feel the smell of Chicken Tetrazzini making my stomach turn. There was gooey cheese all over the noodles and chicken and olives. I dreaded the time when it would have to be in my mouth.

The blessing seemed awfully short that night and, right after, the bowl was passed directly to me. I stared. My arm wouldn't move. It just stayed right where it was. My mom picked up the spoon, and my stomach felt sick again. She plopped a bunch of that slop on my plate. I still felt sick. My poor mom, she worked so hard to make it, but it really was awful stuff. It should be against the law to make any good kid eat it. She just didn't know what she was doing. I had to eat it though. I had to do it for my mom. I picked up my fork and stared at the pasta. I thought that I could maybe make it taste like water if I thought hard enough. I could make it not taste as bad with my imagination. I could be like magic!

I sat there for a real long time. Everyone was done except me. I was the only one at the table, except for my mom who was cleaning it off. She wasn't very happy. If only she could understand that it's not her fault that Chicken Tetrazzini is so yucky. She's a good cook; she just needs to learn how to cook the right stuff. She came and sat next to me.

"Jana! Eat it!"

"I'm trying mommy!"

"Well, you're not trying hard enough! Now, eat it!"

She took my fork out of my hand and tried to feed it to me like I was a baby.

"You are not getting up from this table until you have cleaned your plate off!"

She tried to put it in my mouth, but for some reason my mouth wouldn't open. I think it was because my stomach didn't want it. My stomach was sure doing everything it could to keep that Chicken Tetrazzini out! My mommy wasn't very happy with me. I told her that it was my stomach's fault and that just made her even more upset. Then, she took her hands and opened up my mouth and put it in. There was Chicken Tetrazzini in my mouth. My eyes were all watery and hot and I felt sweaty. My stomach was all nervous and shaky feeling. There was Chicken Tetrazzini in my mouth and I didn't know what to do with it. My stomach didn't want it, but neither did my mom. I tried to push it down, but it just wouldn't go. My stomach threw it up. I wasn't my fault though! My stomach just didn't want it! I can't hardly tell my stomach what to do. It wouldn't know what I was saying.

My mom didn't know what I was saying either. She said that I could have eaten it if I wanted to. I still love her though! Just because I don't love Chicken Tetrazzini doesn't mean that I don't love her. It doesn't. I had to stay in my room for the whole night because of that stupid stuff. Now my mom thinks that I don't like anything she cooks. She might even think that I don't love her. I hate Chicken Tetrazzini.

CHICKEN TETRAZZINI

Questions

1. The author writes that she loves her mother even though she doesn't cook the "right stuff." Is the author equating food with love? Explain.

2. In the author's opinion, what is the "right stuff"?

3. Do you think the author ever gets away with "not" eating her dinner?

Gus Lee

TOUSSAINT

GUS LEE (b. 1946) was born in San Francisco and lived in a poor primarily African-American neighborhood called the "Panhandle." Mr. Lee attended West Point and eventually graduated from the University of California at Davis with a degree in law. He is the author of *Honor and Duty* (1994), and his most recent work, *No Physical Evidence*, was published in 1998. "Toussaint" is an excerpt from Mr. Lee's first novel, *China Boy*, published in 1991.

Toussaint, an African-American boy, befriends Kai Ting, known as "China Boy," in his struggle to survive the neighborhood bullies and the classic "mean" stepmother.

A rail-thin nine-year-old named Toussaint LaRue looked on during these beatings and only hit me once. I therefore assumed that he occupied some lower social niche than mine. Like a snail's.

He took no pleasure in the China Boy rituals. He instead talked to me. I suspected that he had devised a new method of pain infliction.

"Toussaint," he said, offering his hand. "Ya'lls supposed ta shake it." He grinned when I put my hand out with the same enthusiasm with which I would pet Mr. Carter's bulldog. Toussaint, like Evil, had a big gap between his front teeth.

Toussaint would become my guide to American boyhood.

My primary bond to him was for the things he did not do. He did not pound or trap me. He never cut me down. Or laughed with knives in his eyes. Then he opened his heart by explaining things to me, giving me his learning, and taking me into his home.

"China. Don be cryin no mo'. Don work on dis her block, no sir, Cap'n! Give 'er up. When ya'll cry, hol' it insida yo'self. Shif' yo' feet an air-out, go park-side. Preten ya'll gone fishin. Don run, now. Ain't cool."

"Fish in park?" I asked

"Cheez! Ya'll don colly nothin! Ferget da fish, China. Dry yo' tears."

He told me about the theory of fights. That kids did it because it was how you became a man later on.

"Momma tole me," he said, "in ole days, no Negro man kin hit or fight. We belongs to da whites, like hosses.

"Man fight 'notha man, be damagin white man goods. So he get whipped. An I mean *whipped*." He shook his head and rubbed the top of it, easing the pain of the thought.

"Now, ain't no mo' dat," he said, smiling. "We kin fights, like men." He was speaking very seriously. Fighting was a measure of citizenship. Of civilization. I didn't think so.

"China, stan up."

"Why?" I whined.

"Putchur fists up. Make a fist! Right. Bof han's."

"Dis one__," he said, holding my left. "It fo' guardin yo' face. Dis here one—dat's fo' poundin da fool who call ya out. Here come a punch, and ya'll block it. China—you listenin ta me?"

"No fight, no reason!" I said hotly.

"No reason!?" he yelled. "You can fight wif no *reason*? Boy! What-chu *talkin* about?"

Uh-oh, I thought. Toussaint's hands were on his hips.

"Evera kid on dis here block like ta knock you upside da head and make you *bleed* and ya'll got no *reason*? China. Ain't no dude in da Handle got mo' cause fo' fightin *evera* day den *you*!"

"Too many boy fight," I said, drawing back from his heat.

"Uh-*uh*! No sir, Cap'n! Big-time nossir! Lissen. Some kids, dey fight *hard*. But ain't *never* gonna be no gangin up on one kid. *Dat* ain't cool." He shook his head. "Kid stan on his feet. No one else feet. Ain't *nobody* gonna stan inaway a dat. An youse best colly dat."

"Hittin' long," I tried.

"Say what?" he said.

"Long. Not light!"

"Wrong? Ya'll sayin fightin's *wrong*?"

"Light," I said.

"Howzat?"

"Bad yuing chi," I explained.

"Say *what*?"

"Bad, uh, karma!" I said, finding the East Indian word often used by my sisters.

"Well, China, ya'll thinks awful funny. Don have nothin ta do wif no *caramels*. No matta Big Willie take yo' candies. Ain't *candies*. It not bein *chicken*. Not bein yella. Ya'll don havta like it. Sakes, China, no one like ta Fist City.

Well, maybe Big Willie, he like it. But like it or don like it, no matter none. Ya'll jus *do* it."

He invited me to play in his house. Many of the games involved capturing cockroaches. "Ya'll ready?" he would ask, and I would nod, nervously. Toos would kick the wall next to the sink, and roaches would slither out of the dust and the cracked plaster. Toos would use his plastic cup, smacking it quickly onto the floor, smiling as he watched the captured roach's antennae struggle to escape, its hard body clicking angrily against the plastic.

He made his closest buddies tolerate me. His mother took me to the church of Reverend Jones on Sundays until Edna changed my religion. The simple presence of his company, and that of his pals, saved me from innumerable thrashings and gave me time to breathe.

I had never had a friend before, and I cared for him as few lads have for another. My heart fills now when I think of him. That will never change.

Toussaint was, next to me, the skinniest kid on the block. He ran no faster than I since he lacked the sincerity of my efforts, but he was as tough as a slum rat and had the guts of Carmen Basilio. Basilio, the big-headed middle-weight who fought while his blood ran down his bruised face like cascading crimson rain in a summer monsoon. Basilio, whose busted face was on the front page of every pinned-up sports section in every barber shop in the city. Kids respected bravery above all else. It was what allowed you to put your pants on in the morning.

My courage was so low that putting on my big-boy underpants was a task. Toussaint was deemed crazy to buddy with me. But he was my friend because I needed one. He got nothing for himself, in the hard world of our peers' respect, for his generosity.

Outside of a table service, we had few possessions and less cash, but Toos's home made ours look like a gilded palace of Babylon. The LaRue family lived in a windowless converted storage room in a shambling tenement on Masonic, next door to Brook's Mortuary. The stone steps to the main door were chipped, crumbling, and dangerous for old people and toddlers. The entryway was a garbage dump for rotted food, and the stairways reeked of old and pungent uric acid.

A sad, small alcoholic named Sippy Suds lived next door to Toussaint. Suds's apartment produced the worst smell in the Panhandle, a rancid sour waft of vomit and urine so strong in the closed space of the hallway that it made you crazy with the badness of it. He used to mess on himself. Suds was one of several people in the 'hood whose speech evaded understanding. I thought it was related to my eyes. Whenever I concentrated and tried to fight through his thick, inebriated Mississippi babble, my eyes watered from the pungent toxins in the air. Suds had everything no one wanted, down to flies that liked his clothes and odors that would cause others to change jobs.

Many of the kids on the block despised Suds, taking his pitiful coins by incessant begging.

"C'mon, Suds, gimme nickel. Yeah! Gimme dollah!"

Toussaint respected him.

"Leave da man be," he said to a whole battalion of yammering kids. "Ain't cool, takin poor man's coins. C'mon! Back off!" he shouted, pushing them back. " 'Sides. Man yoosta be a fighta," he said.

Heck, I thought. *Everyone* around here is a fighter.

I had seen dead rats before in our house, looking pitiful and scary in the traps, their little feet tucked up in death, thick round tails looking like remnants of ancient lizards. But I had never seen families of them alive. They were on Toussaint's stairs, sluggish, bunched up, and squeaky, and the first time I saw them I stopped and cried. Toussaint looked at me, nodding his head. The rats were pushy and one ran over my foot, small, heavy, sharp-clawed, and warm.

"Won hurtcha none," he said, taking my arm as I began to faint.

An elderly and toothless woman lived in a shamble of newspapers and produce cartons on top of the stairs in the hall. Toussaint called her Missus Hall. She wore old shawls, discarded and unmatched men's shoes, and staggered on broken hips with wriggling loose shoelaces, aided by a short stick wrested from a fruit crate. She would sit on the neighborhood stoops, her crackled fingers pulling splinters from each other, her aged and wrinkled face scrunched with the effort of finding the torment in her hands. During these efforts, her fleshy nose could touch her lips. She was missing clumps of hair, eyelashes, eyebrows. Missus Hall did not look like someone who had been very pretty in her youth. But her durability, her will to survive, were attractive, and I liked her very much.

My mother had been beautiful. And she had died.

Missus Hall would relieve herself on old newspapers in the alleyways on Central Avenue. She never spoke to anyone but would nod at Toussaint, who brought her shares of their meager food. The LaRue and the Ting families did not look even a little bit alike, but we had the same caloric intake, while enjoying strong differences on the meaning of Christian charity.

Mrs. LaRue offered to feed me as well, and I was inclined to eat anything that wasn't going to run away from me. This easily included plain, unbuttered grits, which resembled *tze*, rice gruel. But Toussaint's friends never took food from his mother. Her son was too thin.

One Halloween night, after I had been friends with the LaRues for more than five years, Missus Hall smiled at me. I remember that when she showed her teeth I thought she was angry. It took a moment to realize that she was greeting me with a smile, and I beamed back at her, offering her witches' teeth candy, the world full of light.

I asked Mrs. LaRue why Missus Hall never spoke.

"I honestly don't know, Kai," she said. "I figure somethin almighty drastic happened in her life, and it probly happened twice. Once early, and once late. She's not gonna do nothin fancy with her life. She's jes getting ready for the next blow."

The LaRue home had no furniture, only milk cartons and fruit crates that his momma got from the Reliance Market.

Toussaint had no toys and never asked to play with those belonging to others. He had no father. His mother was wonderful and caring and had convinced Toos that toys and living fathers were not necessary in this mysterious physical world. She carried the whole load, all the way. Toussaint had the gift of love, and they shared everything they had. I was testament to that fact. His smile, shining from a high-cheekboned, high-foreheaded, almost skull-like face, was beatific and had the force of the Prophet. I thought he was the handsomest boy in the world.

As a streetfighter, Toussaint was unusual. He cared nothing for style, which was becoming an extremely big deal to the others.

"Toos," said Jerome Washington. "Ya'll fights like a ole' lady. Ya'll fights like Missus Hall." He giggled. "Ain't dat right, Toos?" Jerome was not looking for a fight. He just enjoyed stirring feces with his tongue.

"Dat probly be true, Jerome," said Toussaint, slowly. He was smiling, frustrating Jerome in some mysterious way. Jerome cursed and moved on.

"See, China? Jerome don mess wif me. He wanna hurt mah feelins, an I jes talk blahdee-blah trash back at 'em. 'China Bashers.' Dat's a lota *crap*. Misser Pueblo, in Cutty's Garage. He tole me: fight fo' da fight. Don pay no mind ta no lookers. Style, dat fo' *girls*.

"Fists. Be fo' da boy dookin Fist City wif ya."

Toos threw unending series of berserk punches, ignoring incoming rounds as if they were raindrops on a pleasant spring day. He would punch until the fight was over—until Toussaint collapsed or the other kid stopped. I didn't know how he could do that.

When he fought, the smile beat feet, and he became all business. He did not have to do this often. It usually occured when a Haight kid crossed the border of Fell Street and strutted north up Masonic, looking to break some bones.

Toos's home was on the cross-'hoods thoroughfare. It was Indian Country; trouble came calling with the rising sun.

Toos was skinny and occasionally got picked. He would stand up straight, like an older boy, and roll his shoulders back, like a grown man. He would measure the challenge, giving the Handle crosser a chance to move on. Sometimes his quiet, unfearing gaze was as articulate as my mother's face. When parley failed, he met aggression with his own fury. He was never called out twice by the same youth.

The Haight, six blocks south, was bogeymanland. Boys carried knives, men had zip guns, and women looked more dangerous than twenty San Juan streetfighters with switchblades. Some of the Haight boys wore old-skinned Big Ben coveralls and carried barber shaving razors in the cup of the hand, hiding the flash of steel inside their arm-swaying struts. They could punch a guy and move on. It took a moment to realize that the face had been opened, blood everywhere, the searing pain following long moments after the incision.

"Ya'll stay outa dere," said Toussaint, pointing with a long and skinny thumb at our rival 'hood. "Be boogeymen, big-time."

Until I learned English, I understood it as The Hate.

The Panhandle lay between our 'hoods like no-man's-land, a DMZ that operated without U.N. intervention. Panhandle boys entered the park with great care and only in daylight. It was a jungle of thick eucalyptus, corpses, tangled azalea, and memories of aimless nocturnal screams. Men gathered there at night to smoke and drink and discuss this new land of California. When they disagreed, people died.

The Haight was largely populated by trekkers from Alabama and Louisiana. Mrs. LaRue said their heartaches came from not having a minister. Reverend M. Stamina Jones had followed the LaRues, the Joneses, the Scotts, and the Williamses—the Panhandle families—from Georgia. Others in the neighborhood hailed from Mississippi, Maryland, and Tennessee. I thought they were names of streets.

"No ministers in the Haight, just knife fighters," she said. "They'se lost. Toussaint LaRue and Kai Ting, you listen to Momma! Don't be goin into the Haight, no how and no way. Now. *That* be gospel."

Toussaint taught me about music. He tried to translate the words of the chorus in the church of Reverend Jones, but I always suspected that he lacked certainty in his explanations. But he knew that the chorus moved me, and would rub the hair on my head whenever I found myself weeping in time with its singing. I did not have to be an Imperial Scholar to know that crying in this temple house was accepted; the congregation's choral majesty was salted with tears and accented by open weeping. Sobs often served as confirmation of the truth of Reverend Jones's ministry. A dry-eyed assembly meant that his delivery was off the mark.

Toos also introduced me to Mr. Carter, who owned Evil the bulldog. Mr. Carter was a shipyard worker at Hunters Point who lived across the street from us, with the LaRue home around the corner. He had a platoon of ex-wives, no prospects of any more, two radios and a record player, and everyone on the block liked him while hating his dog.

Evil was moody. Somedays he raised his black-and-white head to you on a loose leash, anxious for a pat, his eyes half-closed, his teeth looking sadly overused and brownishly old.

Other days he growled, the fangs angry and huge and brightly wet. He would run around like a broken top with his jaws open, all the kids screaming as they scattered. Evil never caught me; I was the flight expert. He would clamp his maws around a kid's leg and throw his neck back and forth and Mr. Carter would blow that whistle in Evil's ear until he let go. He would then use a fat clothes-hanger dowel to beat the starch out of the dog, and I was the only one who felt sorry for him.

"Oughta jes give dat dog *away*," said Toos.

I shook my head. "Give doggie mo' food," I said. "He too much hungry."

"China, you'se a very funny boy," he said. "Now. Don let no dog smell yo' fear. He smell dat, he get feared hisself and eat yo' pants in a *big* hurry."

The men who had been in the army would sit on the wide stairs of Mr. Carter's place and sing "What the Best-Dressed Man in Harlem Is Wearing Tonight," "The Blues in the Night," and I could close my eyes and sway to their unearthly beautiful voices. They also sang songs they called Jodies. I knew them; my father used to chant them while he chopped vegetables in the kitchen when our mother was still alive.

> *"Yo' momma was dere when ya lef"*
> *"YO' RIGHT!"*
> *"Jody was dere when ya lef"*
> *"YO' RIGHT!"*
> *"Sound off—"*
> *"ONE-TWO!"*
> *"Sound off—"*
> *"THREE-FO'!"*
> *"Bring it on down—"*
> *"ONE-TWO-THREE-FO'!"*
> *"ONE-TWO-THREE-FO'!"*
>
> *"Jody got somethin dat you ain't got"*
> *"I'S BIN SO LONG AH ALMOS' FO'GOT"*
> *"Yo' baby's as lonely as lonely can be"*

"WIF ONLY JODY FO' COM-PANY"
"Ain't it great ta have a pal"
"TA HELP KEEP UP HER MO-RALE"
"Sound off. . . ."
"Yo' not gonna get till da enda da war"
"IN NINET'IN HUNDRA' AN' SEVENTY-FOUR. . . ."

Adults and kids gathered on Mr. Carter's stoop to sing and clap hands, or to gently swing to "Harlem Nocturne" and the high throaty jazz of Billie Holiday's "Strange Fruit," "The Way You Look Tonight," and "God Bless the Child." Toos told me that the words to that song meant that if God did not love you, you were soon dead, because little came to short people without God's grace.

"Good news is, China," said Toos, "dat God love all chilun."

"Me, too?" I asked.

"Dat *gotta* be true," he said. " God get dibs on all da little chilun he kin find. And," he said, elbowing me, "you'se little."

We would keep time and tap with one foot while keeping the other ready to exit stage left if Evil felt the urge. The muse didn't come cheap in the Panhandle.

"Mista Carter," said Toussaint's mom. "That's not right, namin a dog Evil. You can come up with a better name'n that, I know you can. Callin something a name sometime make it so."

"Charlotte, you think it be a big favor to all de chilun on dis block be comin up ta dis here dog an callin 'em *Spot?* or *Fido?*

"See. His firs' name, it was Winston. The name offered no warnin. Folks like ta pet 'em. Den he start ta eat kids? He gots too much crust. I call 'em what he is: Evil." He whacked his pants leg with the dowel.

Kids learned to make their own music, without radios. I thought this was because of Evil, since the price of listening to radios could be a pint of dog-drawn blood. But I was wrong. Kids, even poor and unhappy ones, love to sing, warbling the purity of expression, the unsullied and miraculous poetry of a child's honesty. Happy kids sing better. Toos sat on his crumbling steps with Titus McGovern and Alvin Sharpes—boys who had pledged their lives to him—to sing the "Papa Ditty," and other rapadiddle tunes from the not-so-distant South.

"Well, I don know but I been tole,
Papa gonna buy me a pile a coal.
If dat coal don burn fo' me,
Papa gonna take me to da sea.

> *If dat sea don make me wet,*
> *Papa gonna sink us deeper in debt.*
> *If dat debt don eat our food,*
> *Papa gonna thank da good Saint Jude."*

And so on.

Each kid would sing a two-line stanza, making it up as he went. I always shook my head, lowering it as I blushed when it was my turn.

"Dang!" cried Alvin Sharpes. "Lookit China's face. It all red! How you do dat, China?" It was easy. I couldn't rhyme.

"Missa LaRue," I asked, struggling to align the *L*'s and the *R*'s. "Kin rearn me 'Papa Ditty'?"

"The 'Papa Ditty'? I don't think I know that, Kai. Can you sing a little of it for me?"

I tried. She laughed and hugged me.

"Oh, sweetnin, that's 'The Mockinbird's Song.' Listen to me," she said, bending over, her smoothly angular and pretty face bright with life, looking at me with a great smile, singing in a deep mystic voice that scratched the itches in my heart.

> *"Well, I'll tell you what I've learned:*
> *Papa's gonna buy me a mockinbird.*
> *If that mockinbird don't sing,*
> *Papa's gonna buy me a diamond ring.*
> *If that diamond ring don't shine,*
> *Papa's gonna buy me a bottle of wine.*
> *If that bottle of wine don't pour,*
> *Papa's gonna take us to the shore. . . ."*

"My momma rike shore, rike ocean," I said.
"Well, Kai, that big blue sea, it's somethin, all right."

Toussaint told me that Big Willie Mack, the glandular error in the guise of a twelve-year-old, had been the first to punch me on my inaugural day on the street. Big Willie was the toughest dude on the block, a bad combination of vicious clothes-taking bully and mean, gutsy fighter.

Toussaint had hit me on the arm that day with that second, harmless blow, to make sure that Willie didn't wind up and do it again.

"China, ya'lls gotta fight. Pretty soon, he be takin yo' clothes."

"No. Crows too small. Him long size," I said.

"China, he don't take 'em ta wear. He take 'em to *take 'em*. You'se gotta punch it out wif him, China."

"Ohnry make worse, mo' hit."

"Den *you* hit back mo'. Dat how it is. It hard be livin, be a stan-up-boy on dis here block, ya'll don fight. Don havta *win*, jes *fight*. Make it so's da other boy think fightin you's too much work! Make it easy on *bof* of us."

"Kin you whup Big Wirry?" I asked.

"Nah, don think so. But he know I fights 'em, won give in. He wan *my* shoes, he gonna havta give me some *blood*."

We both look at Toos's shoes. I didn't think Toos had to worry about anyone taking them unless Evil went crazy or a starving rat was driven to extreme means.

I tried to explain yuing chi, the responsibility of the future, God's ever-watchful scorecard, to Toussaint, but the concept exceeded my vocabulary. I had understood the idea so easily when it was conveyed by the dark, shimmering, expressive eyes of my mother. I was so anxious to explain that fighting was wrong, and would cause later pain, but winning this inarticulate debate was as difficult as prevailing in its subject matter.

I thought desperately about fighting but could not figure it out. I would be noticed, cut down, called horrific names, shoulder-bumped or shoved into the soft tar of the old streets of the Handle. A kid would challenge me and fear would rise inside my stomach like fog on the Bay and swamp me. My lights would get punched out and I would bawl like a newborn.

Flight always overcame Fight.

The very best I could do was control my tears, to a point. It was my only victory over the weakness of my body, the paucity of my combat power, the horror of fighting.

"China, I need yo' help someday too," said Toos.

I looked at him, confused.

"Say dude from da Haight strut here wif a razor, break mah bones and bleed me. Hustle to yo' door, ya'll lemme in. Right?

I thought of Edna. Edna wouldn't let *me* in.

"Hmm," I said.

Toussaint was a preacher of the handshake. He already knew at this tender age that people got by because they gave each other the biggest gift in the book: time. His momma provided it for him whenever he wanted it. They had a handshake on it, and it gave him the strength of angels.

"You'all lookin at me kinda strange, Kai. Whatcha thinkin?" said his momma, as Toos went out the door.

"Toos ask fo' wata. You *give* wata."

She studied me for a bit, passing me a sad little cup of water, as well. I
drank. "Say that again?" she said. So I did.

"Kai. I love my son. Now look here. *Everybody* love their kids. Yo'
daddy and his wife, they surely love you, too. Jus' everabody don't know *how*.

"If the Good Lord took my boy from me I would curl up and die; I truly
would," she said very solemnly. "He sent me Toussaint LaRue so's I could *love*
him, give him my life, my heart." She smiled. "I have the Lord Jesus and I have
Toussaint, and they'se my joys.

"Kai. You 'member this, chile. Someday you'all gonna have yo' own
little Kai, a little Janie Ting. When yo' child want yo' time, you *give* it. That's
our—our *callin*. I *love* my boy, but sometime he want ta play the cockroach game
and I'm jes sick of it? Oh, Lord, *really sick of it*." She looked down at the old
floor, clicking her tongue. "Or, he tell me the mos' *borin*, stop-your-mind stuff
ever? My little man, Toussaint, he tell the longest and mos' unfunniest jokes in
the world! But I *listen*, and I laugh fo' his joy, and I play him roaches, cuz I'm his
momma, he's my son. It's my God-given duty."

She dried her hands on a rag, and exhaled, looking away from me.
"Toussaint's daddy got killed in truck acciden' in Benning," she said softly. "He
was an officer. He went inta the army a private, and came back a cap'n, two
bright silver railroad tracks on his collar. Lord, what a man he was! Well, the
war, it was over, and he made it back from overseas, a pure hero, and he gave me
Toussaint, and then we lost him. . . ." Her voice faded.

"He was a good man, Little Kai, and I miss him *evera day*." Her voice was
choked. She stopped to blow her nose, shaking her head, hot tears coursing
down her cheeks. "God wanted him bad, and took him." She looked toward the
door. "Oh, Lord. What a price You exact. . . .

"John LaRue made a promise to me. I think his son done made one to
you. Promises be powerful things. I take care of my son's wants. Then he give
water to other men when they need it. And we'll have another John LaRue in the
world. You want some more water?"

That was yuing chi, karma! And she let Missus Hall and the rats live on
the stairs, and roaches in the wall. Mrs. LaRue was Chinese! She just didn't *look*
it.

Could you give water to children who asked for it *and* beat the stuffing
out of them if a fight was offered? I frowned with the difficulty of the riddle.
She was offering me more water.

I took the plastic cup from Mrs. LaRue again, looking at the liquid within
it as I drew it to my mouth. The plastic was old and scarred, with a history
probably longer than mine. Innumberable scratches and half-cracks made it look
tired, as if the serving of its masters and the catching of roaches had somehow

cost too much. The water inside the cup sloshed, like the surf in the ocean, and for a transcendent moment all the scale and sense of proportion in the world dissolved, and I could see my mother placing her feet in the roaring waters of the cup. She was communicating with Na-Gung, an ocean away, and with me, from another world. My eardrums tickled, making me shudder, with her reaching for me. The cup was against my lip, and I stared inside it, cross-eyed. I could not drink this water.

"Tank you, Momma," I said. "I keep wata?"

"You want ta take it on home?" she asked.

"No. Want keep here, on sink. Same wata," I said. "Special. Uh, big-time, special."

"You can take it, chile."

"No," I said, shaking my head. "Mo' betta here." I heard Toos come in. Mrs. LaRue took the cup and placed it on the sink.

"China. Ya'll wanna be mah fren'?" asked Toos. Mrs. LaRue smiled and moved away from my field of vision. Maybe three feet.

"Chure, yep," I said. I sensed something weighing in the balance, an unasked question, a favor awaiting fulfillment.

"Den shake on it," he said, extending his hand. Again? I wondered. He took my hand and molded it into his. His was so hard, so rough.

"Squeeze, squeeze hard, China," he said, "like milk'd come out if ya squoze hard. You'se gotta know how." I gripped, and he smiled.

"Now. We'se frens, fo' sure," he said.

"An you can ask him yo' question, honey," said Momma.

"China," said Toos.

"Toos?" I said.

"China. Tell me 'bout yo' daddy."

I frowned. "Tell what?" I asked.

"Anythin, China, Jes *talk* 'bout him."

I began breathing heavily, not knowing what to say.

"I think yo' daddy was in the war, right?" said Mrs. LaRue. I nodded. "He in China army, for war," I said. "He fry airprane wif guns, bomb. He—" I made motions with my hands—" fall in pallashoot. Shoot gun. Save my mama." I was licking my lips. "He very smart. Read books. Pray catch wif me. . . ."

There was a long silence.

"Thanks, chile," said Momma. "Listen. You share yo' daddy with Toussaint, here? Dat's what frens do."

Toussaint was all smiles, and I halfway grinned at him, trying to hide my teeth so the Teeth God would not want them.

It was now another day, and my friend, my friend of the handshake, my friend of the water, was staring at me. I jumped a little when I realized he had been staring at me.

"China, ya'll knows how ta laff?" asked Toos. We had been playing marbles. I was pretty good at marbles, for the short shots. I was also becoming something of a demon in penny-pitching, and card-tossing. Parlor games, not at the level of the Bigs of street-thumping and ball-playing, but something, after all. It was all in the wrist.

"Chure, yep," I said, worried by his question.

He opened his eyes wide and showed his teeth. He giggled. It was high, and silly, and warm.

"So les hear yo' laff!" he giggled.

I started to explain to him about the Teeth God, realizing that I could neither describe it nor prove its existence. I didn't even know if it was a boy or a girl. This was, like karma, a matter of faith. I suddenly wondered what all this god-fearing was worth. Mother had respected every god known, and they had taken her.

I opened my mouth and tried to make a laughing sound. It must've been ridiculous, because Toos bent over and guffawed, slapping his knees and putting his head between his knees while making a wonderful sound of a strange animal. My ears perked as I heard what I could later favorably compare to a spasm-ridden rum-crazed jackass. Now I was hearing something that reminded me of the distant laughter of my father. I giggled with him, still holding back.

Even through the laughter came the whistle of my stepmother. She never called when I needed her.

I could not discuss my street whippings at home. Stepmother Edna pretended that no problem existed, washing out the blood from my clothes with astounding tolerance. I began to believe that she took pleasure in my fear. I felt that my shame was mine, and somehow my father's and even my mother's, and did not see it as transferable.

Janie was involved in a struggle for survival with Edna. It was a war between two de facto mother figures. One by blood and death, one by marriage and expectation, neither by choice.

As the lastborn kid of four, I did not understand Janie's tenacious resistance to Edna's supreme power. Kids in the lower birth order, like me, seldom resisted parental authority as did the first born, the vanguards. Jennifer Sung-ah and Megan Wai-la were in Berkeley; Janie was now the functional older sibling.

Edna was a grown-up and could slap you silly and dance fandangos on your face. But she hadn't touched Jane for months. If Edna had left me alone like that I would have written poetry for her.

"Kai, I'm doing this for both of us. She is *not* our mom."

I know dat," I said. I just didn't know what it meant. Janie's eyes were bright in anger.

"Edna told me not to read this to you," she said, pulling a stained and torn book from her aging schoolbag. "It's called *Hansel and Gretel*. It's about a stepmother who gets the father to get rid of the kids. Edna threw it out, and I dug it out of the garbage." Janie looked very intense, very determined.

We sat on the front stairs of our house. I pretended to look at the book, but was watching for Big Willie and the Bashers.

"You China Boy sister? asked Reginald Tufts.

"His name is Kai," said Janie. "Can you say that? Kai."

"Kai," said Reginald. My mouth was, again, as open as the Red Sea was for Moses. Hearing a boy say my first name was astonishing, and I squinted with the pressure of it, waiting to see what else in the world might change next.

"I'm going to read a book. Want to listen?" she asked.

"A book? Yeah!" he cried, and I glared at him, not wanting to share Janie with a Basher, or a friend of a Basher. Even if he had said my name.

Janie opened the book, which was missing its cover.

"Once upon a time," she began, "there was a poor woodcutter who lived at the edge of a large forest with his wife and two children. The boy was named Hansel, and the girl was named Gretel. Many years before, his wife had died, and he had remarried. They had always been poor. . . ."

Toos and Alvin Sharpes arrived and sat on the stairs to listen to the story and stare at the storyteller. Janie smiled at them and received their smiles in return. I grinned.

The stepmother in this story gave the two children a last meal and left them in the woods to be taken by wolves. She had done this to allow the father and stepmother to live without the burden of the kids, whose voracious appetites were consuming too much of the limited food. It was a credible tale.

I later asked Toos what he would do if his momma left and another mother moved in.

"My momma, she no go nowhere wif out me. Dere ain't no other momma," he said.

"But she go bye-bye anyway," I said.

"Den I goes wif her."

"If she jus, *gone*?"

"I fin her," he said.

"Can fin her, den . . . ?"

"Keep lookin," he said.

"Where rook?" I asked.

"Dunno, China. Lord. *All* over." He looked at me. "Ya'll miss yo' momma, doncha. Yeah." Then he looked up, squinting. "I 'member her. She yoosta tote da um-brella when dere was no rain. Ya'll was a big saprise, comin outa dat 'partment. Didn know you'se in dere."

I looked down at the stairs.

"Ya'll don like yo' stepmomma?"

I shook my head, fearing that somehow, even around the corner of buildings and the rise of streets, she knew I was admitting it, and that this knowledge would hurt me.

"She be a white lady," he said, and I nodded. "Wif yella hair," he added. "Don think she like *us*," he concluded.

"What I do, Toos?" I asked.

"She yo momma, now. Dang, China. I get it; dat's hard." He studied it for a bit. "I'd as' da Lord."

"I did dat," I said.

To my father, the combat between the females was Women's War, the incomprehensible tensions between disenfranchised females. In Shanghai, there was an unquestionable hierarchy, an immutable order of rank. It did not call for the involvement of men, and he had no experience to make himself Ward Cleaver, who in any event was a fantasy designed to sell Mapo. He could not find an intellectual guide to the current problem and knew that he did not wish to reestablish the old order. I found guidance in comic books.

I loved Superman and Mighty Mouse. I had lost my funnies in the revolutionary storm. Alvin Sharpes had a deep and endless collection and I began to draw from his castaways. I read them, two inches from my face, again and again. I began to imagine myself as a fighter. Who did good for others and beat the crap out of bad guys. Good karma. I projected myself into the cartoon sequences. I was unconquerable. Here I come, to save the day. . . . It means that Mighty Mouse is on his way. . . .

After my stunning victories over evil incarnate, I received the appreciative accolades of my family, laurels from a grateful nation, a citation from the President of the United States, free milk at our doorstep, and a new copy of *The Tales of Lu Hsun*.

After a pounding on the street, I would take out my comics and pore over them with shaking hands and a teary face, trying desperately to incorporate their messages into my body. But the correspondence-school method of street fighting proved unsuccessful.

Then I tried reason. Be pal? I would offer. Pow! I don wan twubble wit you. Wham! Here, candy? Snatch!

Forget reason. I returned to comics and running.

Then Edna rediscovered the comic books, and they were gone.

I wondered if I was going crazy. I would awaken at night, crying from a dream in which I was fleeing my stepmother. Edna would enter my room and slap me in an effort to stop the weeping, which had awakened her. By the time I figured out that the dream had merged with reality, she was gone and I would squint at the closed door, trying to separate images of light and dark.

Despite the fact that I now had Toussaint and his mother in the periphery of my life, I tried to run away again.

Knowing that silence was imperative to successful flight, I took my time. It was not difficult to sneak down the staircase, my footfalls absorbed by the carpet that had through long wear become part of the risers. The front door made a sound like a cherry bomb when opened by the remote handle. I had seen Father lubricate it. I put oil in the hinges and gave the task five minutes, and the door opened with all the sound that a mouse makes when it sniffs cheese.

Golden Gate Avenue was utterly dark and surprisingly cold, the lone streetlamp at the corner of Central Avenue offering few clues and no warmth. But the street was mine, surrendered only for blinding moments as cars with overbright headlights passed.

The first time a car approached I ran from it, thinking it was an agent of Edna in hot pursuit. I could run very fast on a cold night on an empty sidewalk, my lungs bellowing as I humped arms high and hard to let my legs pump, my head vibrating synchronously with the effort as I fled my fears.

I roamed McAllister, leaning against the cold steel doors of Cutty's Garage, peering into the barred windows of the Reliance Market, missing the winos who kept guard at the Double Olive Bar, trying to recapture the now departed aromas of sizzling french fries in the General Lew Wallace Eatery. I wondered if Rupert and Dozer, the fratricidal siblings, argued after they closed the Eatery and went home to the large apartment building on Grove. Without the aromas of food, McAllister smelled sour and old. I played imaginary checkers on the linoleum grid of the barber shop floor. I projected the more complex figures of Chinese chess, *shiang chi*, onto the black-and-white squares, but could not remember all the moves for both players.

I strolled to Broderick Street, over the pavement where I had once raced when I had a home in which to hide. I looked through the iron-grate fence of Fremont Elementary, retracing beatings by Big Willie and the Bashers. I surveyed the kickball-field benches, the lunch tables, where food had been taken and little bodies stomped. I looked at that spot of the yard, knowing a truth lay in it. I looked away.

Cats chased shadowy rats on the street where Big Willie had stood on my chest. Dogs rousted garbage cans. One growled at me and I froze, waiting ten or fifteen minutes like a man who has stepped on a pressure-release-trigger landmine, until the dog had taken his pleasure with the waste. With light feet, his mangy tail down, he padded away from me and I breathed again.

This was my street, McAllister. Now, in the solace of the night, with its bullies and angry words and fists absent, I liked it. I wanted to sleep by day and to walk McAllister to the east at night. It felt safe, the biting cold welcome and fitting. For an instant, I did not want to go any farther, my feet immobilized by the vast, dark unknowns that surrounded the 'hood. I wondered if *wupo*, witches, awaited me inside alleys, or if *dufei*, bandits, were hoping to snatch the only son of the Ting clan tonight.

Ah, I thought. The *wupo* is *inside* the house, not here.

Feeling mildly suicidal, I crossed McAllister to Fulton, which was bold for any kid north of the park. I headed south, keeping to the shadows, crossing Grove, Hayes, and Fell, the final boundary between sanity and simple stupidity. I watched the night traffic on Fell, a big, wide thoroughfare. Where were these people going? Could I go too?

Now I was in the tall eucalyptus trees of the Panhandle itself, the glare of the streetlights swallowed in the darkness of gnarled, interwoven trees. I was in the demilitarized zone, the place of mysterious human sounds, secret passions, and dark bleeding. This was not a child's place.

I crept through the brush as only a boy with bad night vision can. Slowly, patiently, silently, over a detritus of cans, wrappers, boxes, papers. If I made a noise, I stopped. I crawled past a man and a woman, whispering to each other with an intensity beyond comprehension. I shimmied up to a group of talkers sitting around a burning trash can. The fire crackled and cloaked my advance.

I listened to the men in the park. "Boogeymen" from the Haight, with deep, gravelly, bitter voices, raspy with old rumbling hungers. The humor was strained. Some of the speakers were drunk and flared at each other like the trash fire finding fuel to combust a gunfire-like consumption.

What would they do if they found me? I wondered. Nothing, I decided. They didn't care about little boys. There was little talk about sports and fighting. Someone mentioned Joe Louis, and I heard DiMaggio's name.

They were mostly concerned with women, and their meanness and beauty. The mystery of women. These men blamed women for all their woes. Always taking things, wanting more, refusing love, yelling, complaining, comparing. I nodded my head, watching the shadowed figures gesturing, belching in hunger, nodding heads, tippling bottles.

One man held their attention as he spoke of the great Southern Pacific trains that ran from the China Basin docks to Mexico with empty freight cars, no railroad police, and a free meal at the train stops for veterans. I was the son of a veteran. Did that count? I didn't have a mother. Did that matter?

China Basin. It was somewhere in San Francisco, and it sounded like China Boy, like me. It was *my* train. I could go to Mexico. No Edna. No Willie and no Bashers. I would be leaving Janie. Could I do that?

In my mind I heard the wail of the engine calling, its thunderous power promising fast, determined movement, high-pumping wheels chugging tirelessly, taking me away even while I slept in its cars.

I watched the firefly sparks of the trash fire flicker into the night sky, looking like the stack flames of a southbound freight, disappearing into the swallowing blackness. For years I would deride myself, assailing my manhood, for not taking the China Basin train. The decision had been in my hands, but I lacked the ability to seize an early opportunity to die a boy's lonesome death on a distant track.

When I reached Masonic and Golden Gate, I was drawn to Toussaint's apartment building. I climbed the outside stairs with great stealth, thinking of Mrs. LaRue, wanting a glass of water, happy with the mere thought that she was on the other side of the door, resting. Truly there, actually alive, to be seen and heard again. I touched a leg. A big leg. I knew that I was dead from fright and would be beaten afterward for clumsiness.

It was Sippy Suds, his horrendous odors mysteriously absent in the cool of the night. He stirred slightly and began to snore softly. He looked huge lying down, folded inside his faded, moth-eaten, navy pea jacket. In his bent, inebriated, staggering postures on the street, I had thought him as short as Missus Hall. He was actually a tall man. His hands were pinned between his drawn-up knees. They were huge, the fingers bent and black with the dirt of past labor. His wrists were bony but very thick. Hands that gave precious coins to greedy children.

His face looked as if it had been hit often by hard objects or by an angry stepmother. It was square and hard, different colors shading it. Bruising colors. His nose was very flat at the bridge, the bottom of the nose turned to the side, as if an anvil had been dropped on it from an angle. The closed, trusting eyes were surrounded by scars and small mounds of built-up skin. The rough pebbles of scar tissue interrupted the deep lines that laughter had once carved into his temples.

He was a fighta, Toussaint had said.

I sat next to him, looking at him, edging closer, absorbing his kindly silent companionship, feeling safety, defeating loneliness with every moment in his company. I held my breath.

Then we breathed together, and I matched his cycle, my small puff of air emerging with his thicker cloud, both of us slowly exhaling our fatigues with bright, streetlit, vaporous breath into the foggy night. My lungs filled with soulful strength.

I wanted him to awaken and to tell me about his fights. I wanted to hear that he had won, somehow, somewhere, in his past. Together, I thought, the two of us could do anything. I sat until my bottom ached from the hardness of the stairs, and I began shivering, my thin body capsized in cold.

Bye-bye Suds, I whispered, smiling as he stirred again. I returned with small steps to the house of my stepmother, ready for neither the beginning of sleep nor the start of day.

TOUSSAINT

Facts

1. What are the ethnicities of Kai Ting and Toussaint LaRue?

2. What is the neighborhood called?

3. What advice does Toussaint give Kai about fighting?

4. What does Kai think about Tousaint's mother?

5. What does Toussaint think about Kai's father?

6. What was Toussaint's favorite game?

7. Who is Evil and why is he mentioned?

Strategies

1. The narrator speaks about his lack of courage, but he believes his friend, Toussaint, is courageous. How does the narrator communicate Toussaint's courage to the reader?

2. What does the narrator mean when he says, "happy kids sing better"?

3. Why is the dialogue so important in this story? What purpose does the prose serve?

4. What is the main idea of this narrative?

5. Why did Janie think it important to read *Hansel and Gretel* to Kai? Why didn't Edna want the story read to him?

Issues

1. What constitutes friendship? Can two people from different ethnic backgrounds truly be friends?

2.   Where did Toussaint get his self-confidence and his wisdom?

3.   Why was it important for Kai to share his father with Toussaint and for Toussaint to share his mother with Kai?

4.   Why did Kai run away from home? Why did he return?

5.   "... a deep mystic voice that scratched the itches of my heart." What is the narrator revealing with this statement?

Writing Assignments

1.   Write a narrative essay using dialogue to communicate the ethnicity and voice of the child.

2.   Write a compare/contrast essay analyzing the little boy's character in Gaines's "The Sky Is Gray," and the character of Toussaint in Lee's "Toussaint."

Danny Santiago

COUNTY HOSPITAL

DANNY SANTIAGO (b. 1911-d. 1988) was the pseudonym of Daniel James. Born in Kansas City, Missouri, James served as a volunteer social worker in the East Los Angeles neighborhood portrayed in *Famous All Over Town*. "County Hospital" is an excerpt from *Famous All Over Town*, which was published in 1983.

In "County Hospital," the third chapter in Famous All Over Town, the narrator, Chato Medina, starts his journey of self-discovery and purpose during his stay at the Los Angeles County Hospital.

Curtains came rolling on squeaky wheels, then swung out to make a fence around my bed, I wondered why. It was dark and there were snorers outside the curtains. Inside was a big white bear that stood beside my head and a black bear that moved around and talked.

"Has he been confirmed?" the black one said. "It makes a difference."

If he meant me, the answer was yes but I didn't bother to tell him so.

"Poor little lad," he said, "did you call the family?"

That black bear talked very funny. I could barely understand him.

"Pity not to wait for them," he said, "but I've another one on Seven."

Another what?

He snapped open a little box that smelled of church. He lit a cigarette or maybe it was a candle. I heard dishes clank, then Latin. He touched me here and there, on my foot and on my head, and mumbled. If I still hurt I couldn't feel it. Possibly they had given me something because I was flying. All of us were flying, me, the bed, the rolling curtains, the black bear and the white one. Where to, who knows?

The next I remember, those rolling curtains were gone and I was in a tall bright room with eight beds of strangers, which was no doubt a hospital ward, and how are you supposed to act? I wondered. Do you wave and say Hi to everybody or only speak when spoken to? To be on the safe side, I shut my eyes because who can criticize you when you're asleep? I was hurting but like very far away. Mostly what I felt was uneasy. Something was very very wrong down underneath the covers. I slided my hand down under very slow and sneaky so nobody would get any wrong ideas, and found a big fat bandage on my belly. That I had expected because no doubt they operated me, but lower down felt very unfamiliar. I went exploring You Know Where. My fingers touched something and I jerked my hand away like bitten. What was it?

A snake?

Like that milk-sucker in Mexico? No. Too skinny.

A worm then?

Which had crawled into my thing to feed on my insides? Except it didn't squirm. Possibly it died in there.

A wire?

Some mad scientist could have me hooked up to a big machine like on the television, to change me to a monster, with lights blinking and needles whipping around on various dials.

Or was it a lesson to me?

For certain little sins I might have committed down there. Like that bad day with Pelon. "Puto," my father yelled at me, "do you let him use you for a woman?" And wouldn't listen when I told him No, no, no.

Or wait!

It could be a mistake, something they forgot to take out after the operation. Everybody knows how they treat Mexicans at County Hospital. Like that little lady on Milflores Street, she went there to get cough medicine and came out a corpse, I forget her name.

Should I ask a nurse? They were trotting in and out, but they were white ladies and if I called attention to myself Down There, they would be sure to scream and slap my face. No, whatever that thing might be, I had to get rid of it by myself. Slowly, slowly I started pulling. It came out inch by inch, slick and slimy, I could barely stand to touch it. It came out forever, till finally I felt it loose and squirmy on my legs. I quickly kicked it out of bed and it flip-flopped on the floor.

You might think I had burned down their hospital.

Nurses came scolding from near and far.

"Look what you've done, bad boy!"

"I told you we should of tied his hands."

"Call the Resident!"

He turned out to be that same tiny doctor which came to our house last night or whenever. The one that possibly saved my life, and for a wonder he took my side against the nurses.

"It's time for The Thing to come out anyway," he said.

"But it's ordered," the boss nurse said. She had a cap with horns like a bull, and brass hair. "Dr. *Wenty* ordered it," she said.

"I'm changing the orders," Dr. Penrose said which seemed to be his name.

"And what if he wets the bed, doctor?"

"Then you will change the sheets, nurse."

They didn't love each other. She stomped away broadcasting her twenty years nursing experience. Dr. Penrose sat down on my bed like an old friend and explained me everything. "That snaky thing was to piss through while asleep," he said, "and Catheter was its name." Next he drew a picture of my operation. It seemed my appendix busted which poisoned my insides and they call it Peritonitis. Later he would show it to me in a bottle. I was three hours on the table, Dr. Penrose said, while surgeons swabbed me out. They barely pulled me through. Another hour and I would be dead, it seemed, but now with ten days' bed rest I would be as good as new. Dr. Penrose, who had been quite cranky in our house, today was very cheery and even combed me with his personal comb.

That afternoon my father was admitted with the news. My mother got well half an hour after they took me to the hospital, he reported.

"How's Rigoberto?" I asked.

"Dolores," he said disgusted.

After that he couldn't find too much to say. Mexican-style he kept his hat on but he didn't seem real happy about it and kept taking it off and putting it on while he searched the ceiling for conversation. I wished I could see my mother but of course she couldn't leave the house till her forty days were up.

"Where's Lena?" I asked.

"Down in the Buick praying for you."

Then I remembered. When Li'l Angel got knifed she went to the hospital to see him, he was like a boyfriend almost, and she found him quite lively and cracking jokes, but next morning he was dead and after that Lena never dared to visit the sick, especially not in County Hospital.

My father handed me her Get Well card. "Thanks be to God I never get sick," he said. "No sir, never been in one of these places except to visit friends to see you get well quick and come home soon."

He kissed me loudly and left, still fiddling with his hat. My poor father, he might be King of the Aztecs' club but here in County Hospital he looked uneasy and out of place for all his coat and tie. Every day he came to see me after work, and I appreciated him, but the high point of my hospital days was when Dr. Penrose visited the ward.

Where other residents interns looked as if they wore their clothes to bed, Dr. Penrose was always spotless in his white doctor-suit with earphones dangling casual from the pocket. He had that real sharp Ivy League look which I only wished I had myself and his trousers were recut by personal tailor. They fitted him so tight he had to unscrew his feet to take them off, he said. The whole ward cheered up when Dr. Penrose marched in. He always winked at me first, then passed on to his graver cases, never too impatient to listen to all their troubles, even those poor old winos they had in there. With needle, nobody else could find your vein like him, the others poked you like a pincushion. Everybody was crazy about Dr. Penrose except the nurses.

"Why hasn't this bed been changed?" he'd ask. "Who wrote this idiot chart? Fill that man's water jug. Where's the ice packs I ordered?"

He really kept those nurses hopping, and then after he'd checked the ward he would perch on my bed which he seldom if never did on any others.

"What's new?" he'd say like any other guy, "how's the aches and pains today?" He never once discriminated me. In fact, Mexicans seemed to be his most favorite class of people, and last year he flew down there to Acapulco with his friend Colin for vacation. He showed me their pictures on the beach, all very tanned and more muscley than you might guess. They had more or less adopted a shoeshine boy around my age, it seemed. Personally I didn't care too much for the guy's looks. He smiled too much. In every snapshot there was old Pepe with all his teeth on display. Dr. Penrose said they really had a ball in Acapulco except somebody stole his gold wristwatch worth $400. I could guess who but naturally I didn't say anything. You can't trust those Mexicans down there. They aren't like us. I would never steal from a friend, never, even if I could get away with it.

Dr. Penrose found a lot to talk about. He told me about the rare and interesting cases they had there in the hospital, and about those hotshot staff doctors who look so saintly when they come cruising through your ward with a dozen interns following along like mice. You might not believe it, but a lot of those doctors are drunks, and others cheat on their wives and they all blame each other for butchering up the patients, just like anybody else. Then too, Dr. Penrose explained me all those hospital words like OB, RN, EKG and ETKM meaning Every Test Known to Man, which doctors call for when they run into puzzling patients. Dr. Penrose was very pleased how fast I learned that language. We could talk together like a couple of pros.

The priest dropped by to see me too, the one that ministered me my Last Rites. He talked football mostly, the way they do, but later turned quite solemn.

"You're a very lucky boy," he told me. "Do you go every Sunday to mass?"

"Sometimes," I confessed.

"You should, laddie. You owe God a big debt. The doctors gave you up for lost. They left you in God's hands and in His mercy he chose to spare your life. Perhaps he has in mind some great work you'll do in this world."

What type of work? I wondered.

The father mentioned Altar Boy and left me with a Rosary. The beads felt friendly to my fingers and I tried out a prayer or two. My life was a real mess. I was sinning more than my share both by thought and act, and getting very poor grades in school besides. Why would God bother to save me with my record? I thought quite a lot about what that priest said, and asked Dr. Penrose if it was true God brought me back to life? He told me possibly but blamed penicillin more.

I thought about it. Could it be He spared me to cure the sick? "How do you get to be a doctor?" I asked.

That same day Dr. Penrose brought me a Book of Bones to study. It had a spooky fold-out skeleton which you could dance the arms and legs around. Your ear was on another page with tiny bones inside almost too small to notice. A lot of bones have names as long as freight trains but Dr. Penrose taught me how to say them and it sounded quite a lot like Spanish. I promised to learn two bones per day. After I got them all by heart I could start memorizing my muscles and my inside organs, and after that a Book of Germs, and then I would be in business.

But I would have to graduate too and Audubon Junior High School stood in my way. In Social Studies, Life Science, and Spanish Language my grades were pure C's and D's, and I had a gang of U's for Unsatisfactory in Cooperation, Personal Hygiene and Habits of Thrift.

What happened to me?

Back there in 6th grade everything came so easy. Mrs. Cully was my teacher then. She was a chubby red-haired lady, very motherly but with bad breath, and she really made you learn. I even got 100's in arithmetic, and how that lady used to love my handwriting! She made me the official writer for Open House when parents were invited to see our work, except mine always failed to show up.

I was quite sickly with the asthma in those days so while others played baseball, she got me into marble-shooting and introduced me to the Boys' Club where Ernie Zapata coached me every day. That was the year I came in runner-up in the All-City Playgrounds Marbles Championship, twelve and under. Mr. Zapata helped me a lot but not like Mrs. Cully. I'll never forget the day I graduated. "Rudy, Rudy," she told me. "You're so darned gifted but what's going to happen to you in Junior High? Will you get lost like all the rest?"

How right that lady was! She hugged and kissed me too, in front of everybody, but when I dropped by last spring to say hello, it seemed they had moved her to another district.

So anyway, I worked very hard on my Book of Bones, and when they let me walk I started practicing a little medicine on my own. I used to crank beds up and down when the nurses were busy gabbing at their station. I brought fresh ice water and helped the patients to drink, those little old winos especially which their hands were all the time playing the guitar. I emptied forgotten bedpans and sometimes even, I translated Spanish-speakers to the doctors which my own father never trusted me to do. Lena was always interpreter with us.

Another time they brought in a colored kid around my age and he had caught his hand in a meat-grinder so they had to chop it off. He was quite upset and hollered around Why not die better?

"Cheer up and make the best of it," I told the guy. "They'll put a hook on you, man, with a real sharp point on it so nobody would ever dare to mess with you."

It failed to cheer him up and when I loaned him my Classic Comic about Dr. Jekyll and Mr. Hyde which Dr. Penrose gave me, the guy didn't even return it, which shows you how those people are. Then too I read charts when nobody was looking so I could inform my friends if their temperature was up or down. I got quite popular up there in ward 1017 and several said they didn't know what they would do without me, grown men too. But forget about those nurses. They were not one tiny bit like on TV. Fat and ugly was their style and they seemed to come in two colors only, Alabama black or silver blondie with never a Mexican in the crowd. And were they ever bossy? You should have heard them when they caught me reading charts.

"You're the limit!" they yelled. "Back to your bed, you little snotnose. You know the rules."

"So throw me out of the hospital," I suggested. "Report me to the District Attorney."

I stood there two weeks. Most people might get homesick, but me never. Except maybe once or twice in the middle of the night, like the time I got restless and climbed out on the fire escape for fresh air, ten dizzy stories up. There was old familiar Eastside spread out under me. I felt like God or an angel at the very least. Shamrock I couldn't see. It was in a puddle of black between the brewery and the S.P. tracks, but there was the river, and beyond the Civic Center with lights climbing City Hall to the sky. There was Sunset Boulevard curving off toward the ocean, and Wilshire like a chain of Xmas lights. The whole city stretched out under me and there was no end to it, my L.A. which I was once almost marbles champion of. It made me proud and I pitied guys from poor little Oxnard and El Centro and all those towns they have to keep apologizing for.

A low humming and a buzzing came up from all those snoring people, and from dishwashers coming home by bus, night shifts changing, trucks bringing in tomorrow's groceries and the latest styles. So many millions of people and only one of me. How easy to get lost down there, one tiny ant chasing around with all those other ants. Was that all that God had spared me for? He had given me a second chance but what could I possibly do with it.

"Why don't you jump?" came to me suddenly. "Jump and all your worries will be over." My knees shook so hard I had to hang onto the railing. And then the iron door swung open and there was Dr. Penrose.

"Looked for you everywhere," he said. "Thought you flew the coop."

His voice was quite muddy. Possibly he'd been drinking, or did he take some kind of pill? Anyway he took my hand.

"Trust me?" he asked.

"Como no?" I said. How not?

"Then let's fly," he said and flapped both arms.

"Hey!" I grabbed the railing.

"Coward," he told me. "Time for bed."

He bolted the door after us, then led me along the hall. Nobody else in sight.

"Wrong way," I informed him.

"I'm promoting you to a private room," he said.

The bed was made up in there so I laid down on it, wondering what next?

"Now," he told me, "I'm going to give you a back rub to raise the dead."

"Since when do doctors give back rubs?" I asked.

"Since tonight."

He untied my neck strings and peeled the gown off my shoulders. His hands were just right, not too hot and not too cold. He held the alcohol in his palm to warm it, and not like the nurses. And let me tell you something. In all my nights in the hospital I never had a back rub like that one. Dr. Penrose seemed to know each tiny bone and muscle from my neck all the way down. Mine wasn't the first back he ever rubbed, you could tell. Right away my eyes got heavy and I started floating into sleep, till he folded back my covers and I was naked to my heels.

"Hey," I said embarrassed.

"Never be ashamed of your body," he told me. "Your body is a beautiful thing."

"My legs are too skinny."

"So are a deer's," he said.

"Don't you feel anything?" he said.

What should I feel? He stood looking down. Then he gave my butt a friendly slap, pulled up my covers and left before I could even tell him thanks.

As it turned out, that was the last night I spent at County Hospital. Dr. Wenty checked me over in the morning and gave me my release. I could finish getting well at home, he said but no school for the next few days which didn't break my heart. I was hoping Dr. Penrose would drop in and say goodbye but he didn't, and when I packed up, along with various other things I took his Book of Bones, only hoping it was a gift and not just a loaner.

COUNTY HOSPTIAL

Facts

1. Why is the narrator, Medina, in the hospital?

2. What does he mean by ". . . little sins I might have committed down there"?

3. Why was he afraid to call the white nurses to ask for help "down there"?

4. Explain the attitude of the people who had to use County Hospital for their primary health care needs.

Strategies

1. Who was Dr. Penrose? Why is he important?

2. Why does the catheter removal sequence begin the narrative?

3. List the adjectives that describe the child's voice in "County Hospital."

4. What is the main focus of this excerpt from *Famous All Over Town*?

5. Why did Dr. Penrose give Medina a back rub?

6. What does this question mean, "Don't you feel anything?" Which section(s) of the narrative reinforces your interpretation?

Issues

1. The priest tells the author he was spared because God has a special purpose for him. Does everyone have a special purpose in life?

2. Is the sexual awakening for a boy different than that of a girl?

3. Why is the doctor/patient relationship important? Or is it important?

4.   Are county hospital professionals less qualified than the professionals in private facilities? Do they treat the poor differently?

Writing Assignments

1.   From a child's perspective, write a narrative about your neighborhood.

2.   Write an issue analyzing some of your neighborhood's prejudices.

Ed Malave (student)

MY SHARKSKIN SUIT

ED MALAVE was a student a Los Angeles City College when he wrote this essay. He is currently studying English at California State University-Los Angeles.

Two years ago when I was eight, I got the scare of my life. It was in the Spring because the mornings was always sunny 'n' the air was cool. It was the beginning of Spring 'cause I remember we had the last snow storm on Easter. I remember that day very well 'cause on Easter Sunday, I wore my sharkskin suit. My father had to dig deep into his pocket to buy me that suit. My four brothers got the usual clothes for Easter and my little sister too, but I got the sharkskin suit 'cause I begged my dad to get it for me. My mother wanted us to stay home that Easter Sunday 'cause of all the snow, but I was goin' ta church, regardless. Not that I liked goin' ta church. In fact, I hated it with all their strict rules about how to live my life and I couldn't do nuthin' without gettin' a sin for it. But I was gonna wear my suit and show all the kids that I had a sharkskin suit. I was gonna become popular 'cause I was prob'bly the only kid in the whole projects who could afford a suit like that. Well, not really, but anyway, they were very hip in nineteen-sixty-three, two years ago in Queens, New York.

I gotta tell about this suit. It was light gray with a sort of lavender under-color to it. It had a velvet collar with velvet flaps on the pockets, and a velvet belt on the back of the jacket with a button holdin' it up on both sides. When the sun hit it, the rays made it shine almost to the point of blinding ya, 'n' it fit so perfect like it was tailor-made jus' for me.

Anyway, the snow was up to my chest, about three-to-four feet high. But I didn't care, I was gonna go to church regardless, which was the same distance as to my school, in my new suit "come hell or high water" 'n' nuthin' was gonna stop me. The church was right next to my school, so it was always the same walk whether it was walkin' ta school or walkin' ta church. By the time I got to church, sloshing through the snow like I was "Rudolph the Red Nosed-Rain Deer," I was soakin' wet, 'n' frezin', 'n' waitin' for the priest to finish mass so I could go home 'n' get warm. None of my friends were at church 'cause of all the snow, so I felt cheated of my efforts. I went through all that trouble for nuthin', so I got really disappointed.

When I got to the altar to receive my "Holy Communion," my body was shiverin' 'n' I couldn't keep my mouth open 'cause all my teeth was rattlin' somepin awful. But I forced myself to open my mouth although my teeth kep' rattlin', that I thought I would bite the priest's finger. Think of the sin I would be committin', bitin' the priest. The nuns would prob'bly have a field day taking turns pulling at my ears which I prob'bly wouldn't have felt anyway on a count na my ears were frozen numb.

The mass seemed like it would never end 'cause all I could think about was how cold I was. Then another thought crossed my mind which turned out even more of a problem. I began to think that I was gonna be in some big trouble when I got home. My mother would see the suit all soakin' wet and she would really blow her top 'cause she didn't want me goin' ta church in the firs' place, especially in the suit. So as much as I wanted to go home, I was scared of what my mother would do to me once I got there. I also dreaded walkin' through all that snow again and gettin' even more wetter. The mass was finally over so I jus' started walkin'.

The walk to my house seemed to take forever, like it would never end. Truckin' through all that snow like I was Santa Claus 'cept this was no joyous occasion, no sirree! But I kep' walkin', 'n' walkin', 'n' the faster I walked the colder 'n' wetter I became. The suit was doubly wetter by the time I got halfway home, and I thought by now it was ruined. I was tryin' ta walk as fast as possible thinkin' I can get home in time to save my suit. But instead, the suit had shrunken at least three sizes. The tips of my sleeves were practically up to my forearms between my elbows and wrists, the jacket had gotten too tight for me to button, 'n' the hem of my pants had shrunken halfway between my knees and ankles. I couldn't go home now, my mother would kill me.

I finally got to the building where I lived, 'n' I ran up the stairs as fast as I could, passing my front door where I could hear my mother screamin' at my little brother, Peter. Up the stairs I kep' runnin', two 'n' three at-a-time, to a landing just above the sixth floor, below the door that led to the roof and I stayed there, shiverin' and scared, 'n' lookin' out the window at the snow fallin', 'n' thinkin' 'bout what I was gonna do next. I thought if I sneaked into the house I could hang the suit up to dry, hiding it behind the shower curtain, no questions asked. It would dry and I could hang it way inside my closet in the back so nobody could see it, 'n' if my mother asked me about the suit I could tell her that I'm savin' it for a special occasion with the hope that eventually she would forget about it. But everybody was home 'cause of the snow storm. I could still hear their voices from down at the second floor. The thought of the worse beatin' of my life was the main thought in my head with no room for nuthin' else 'cept how hungry I was 'n' that thought jus' kep' comin' 'n' goin'. I was up there for about four hours 'n' I knew what was goin' on in my house 'cause I could hear the commotion down there, my mother all upset 'n' worried 'bout me, 'n' wondrin' where I could be.

My big brother, Ralph, had an idea 'cause I could hear him talkin'. He knew that I always went up to the top landing whenever I got upset 'bout somepin, 'cause I could be alone to think up there, then I could hear his footsteps running up the stairs 'n' before I knew it, I was looking up at my brother 'n' he was lookin' down at me with this funny grin on his face that said "I got you, 'n' now you're in big trouble," kinda look. I started cryin' 'cause I was so scared, sittin' on the floor with my knees to my chest and my arms wrapped around my legs like they were poles for me to hold on to, to keep me from being dragged down the stairs. But my brother picked me up like I was a heavy box, polls 'n' all, 'n' carried me down the stairs to where I lived, my body shivering not from being cold but from being scared. I could feel my heart poundin' somepin terrible like it was gonna explode inside my chest, 'cause I dreaded lookin' into my mother's eyes 'cause I was sure to find a lot of rage in there, a familiar look in her eyes whenever she got mad 'bout somepin, that was somepin really scary to see. But instead, I found love in her eyes which shocked me 'n' at the same time made me feel suspicious 'cause my mother had a way of trickin' us with her looks.

As it turned out, she was happy to see that I was fine, and even though I ruined my sharkskin suit that cost my father a lot of money, she was glad I was home. Like she knew how scared I was, made her feel sorry for me. She got me out of my sharkskin suit, all wet from the snow, makin' it harder to take it off of me 'cause it got smaller even, 'n' she put me in a warm blanket and gave me a bowl of homemade chicken soup. It felt great to be home 'n' get some warmth from the blanket and my mother's arms that held me. But I'll never forget how scared I was on that Easter Sunday, two years ago.

My Sharkskin Suit

Questions

1.   Why did the author want a sharkskin suit? What did the suit symbolize?

2.   The author said he hid because he damaged his suit. What were the other reasons he hid?

3.   The voice of the author captures his emotions. Explain.

Zitkala-Sa (Gertrude Bonnin)

IMPRESSIONS OF AN INDIAN CHILDHOOD

ZITKALA-SA (b. 1876-d. 1938) was born Gertrude Simmons on the Yankton Reservation in South Dakota. In 1901, Ms. Simmons changed her name to Zitkala-Sa (Red Bird). She married Raymond Bonnin in 1902. Her first eight years were spent on the reservation with her mother at which time, against her mother's wishes, she went to study at White's Manual Institute in Indiana. In January 1900, the first of a series of autobiographical essays, "The Impressions of An Indian Childhood," was published in the *Atlantic Monthly*. "The School Days of an Indian Girl" and "An Indian Teacher Among Indians," were published in the *Atlantic Monthly* in February and March of 1900, respectively.

The author's idyllic life on the reservation is captured and described through the eyes and voice of an eight-year-old child.

I.

MY MOTHER.

A wigwam of weather-stained canvas stood at the base of some irregularly ascending hills. A footpath wound its way gently down the sloping land till it reached the broad river bottom; creeping through the long swamp grasses that bent over it on either side, it came out on the edge of the Missouri.

Here, morning, noon, and evening, my mother came to draw water from the muddy stream for our household use. Always, when my mother started for the river, I stopped my play to run along with her. She was only of medium height. Often she was sad and silent, at which times her full arched lips were compressed into hard and bitter lines, and shadows fell under her black eyes. Then I clung to her hand and begged to know what made the tears fall.

"Hush, my little daughter must never talk about my tears;" and smiling through them, she patted my head and said, "Now let me see how fast you can run to-day." Whereupon I tore away at my highest possible speed, with my long black hair blowing in the breeze.

I was a wild little girl of seven. Loosely clad in a slip of brown buckskin, and light-footed with a pair of soft moccasins on my feet, I was as free as the wind that blew my hair, and no less spirited than a bounding deer. These were my mother's pride,—my wild freedom and overflowing spirits. She taught me no fear save that of intruding myself upon others.

Having gone many paces ahead I stopped, panting for breath, and laughing with glee as my mother watched my every movement. I was not wholly conscious of myself, but was more keenly alive to the fire within. It was as if I were the activity, and my hands and feet were only experiments for my spirit to work upon.

Returning from the river, I tugged beside my mother, with my hand upon the bucket I believed I was carrying. One time, on such a return, I remember a bit of conversation we had. My grown-up cousin, Warca-Ziwin (Sunflower), who was then seventeen, always went to the river alone for water for her mother. Their wigwam was not far from ours; and I saw her daily going to and from the river. I admired my cousin greatly. So I said: "Mother, when I am tall as my cousin Warca-Ziwin, you shall not have to come for water. I will do it for you."

With a strange tremor in her voice which I could not understand, she answered, "If the paleface does not take away from us the river we drink."

"Mother, who is this bad paleface?" I asked.

"My little daughter, he is a sham,—a sickly sham! The bronzed Dakota is the only real man."

I looked up into my mother's face while she spoke; and seeing her bite her lips, I knew she was unhappy. This aroused revenge in my small soul. Stamping my foot on the earth, I cried aloud, "I hate the paleface that makes my mother cry!"

Setting the pail of water on the ground, my mother stooped, and stretching her left hand out on the level with my eyes, she placed her other arm about me; she pointed to the hill where my uncle and my other sister lay buried.

"There is what the paleface has done! Since then your father too has been buried in a hill nearer the rising sun. We were once very happy. But the paleface has stolen our lands and driven us hither. Having defrauded us of our land, the paleface forced us away.

"Well, it happened on the day we moved camp that your sister and uncle were both very sick. Many others were ailing, but there seemed to be no help. We traveled many days and nights; not in the grand happy way that we moved camp when I was a little girl, but we were driven, my child, driven like a herd of buffalo. With every step, your sister, who was not as large as you are now, shrieked with the painful jar until she was hoarse with crying. She grew more and more feverish. Her little hands and cheeks were burning hot. Her little lips were parched and dry, but she would not drink the water I gave her. Then I discovered that her throat was swollen and red. My poor child, how I cried with her because the Great Spirit had forgotten us!

"At last, when we reached this western country, on the first weary night your sister died. And soon your uncle died also, leaving a widow and an orphan daughter, your cousin Warca-Ziwin. Both your sister and uncle might have been happy with us to-day, had it not been for the heartless paleface."

My mother was silent the rest of the way to our wigwam. Though I saw no tears in her eyes, I knew that was because I was with her. She seldom wept before me.

II.

THE LEGENDS.

During the summer days, my mother built her fire in the shadow of our wigwam.

In the early morning our simple breakfast was spread upon the grass west of our tepee. At the farthest point of the shade my mother sat beside her fire, toasting a savory piece of dried meat. Near her, I sat upon my feet, eating my dried meat with unleavened bread, and drinking strong black coffee.

The morning meal was our quiet hour, when we two were entirely alone. At noon, several who chanced to be passing by stopped to rest, and to share our luncheon with us, for they were sure of our hospitality.

My uncle, whose death my mother ever lamented, was one of our nation's bravest warriors. His name was on the lips of old men when talking of the proud feats of valor; and it was mentioned by younger men, too, in connection with deeds of gallantry. Old women praised him for his kindness toward them; young women held him up as an ideal to their sweethearts. Every one loved him, and my mother worshiped his memory. Thus it happened that even strangers were sure of welcome in our lodge, if they but asked a favor in my uncle's name.

Though I heard many strange experiences related by these wayfarers, I loved best the evening meal, for that was the time old legends were told. I was always glad when the sun hung low in the west, for then my mother sent me to invite the neighboring old men and women to eat supper with us. Running all the way to the wigwams, I halted shyly at the entrances. Sometimes I stood long moments without saying a word. It was not any fear that made me so dumb when out upon such a happy errand; nor was it that I wished to withhold the invitation, for it was all I could do to observe this very proper silence. But it was a sensing of the atmosphere, to assure myself that I should not hinder other plans. My mother used to say to me, as I was almost bounding away for the old people: "Wait a moment before you invite any one. If other plans are being discussed, do not interfere, but go elsewhere."

The old folks knew the meaning of my pauses; and often they coaxed my confidence by asking, "What do you seek, little granddaughter?"

"My mother says you are to come to our tepee this evening," I instantly exploded, and breathed the freer afterwards.

"Yes, yes, gladly, gladly I shall come!" each replied. Rising at once and carrying their blankets across one shoulder, they flocked leisurely from their various wigwams toward our dwelling.

My mission done, I ran back, skipping and jumping with delight. All out of breath, I told my mother almost the exact words of the answers to my invitation. Frequently she asked, "What were they doing when you entered their tepee?" This taught me to remember all I saw at a single glance. Often I told my mother my impressions without being questioned.

While in the neighboring wigwams sometimes an old Indian woman asked me, "What is your mother doing?" Unless my mother had cautioned me not to tell, I generally answered her questions without reserve.

At the arrival of our guests I sat close to my mother, and did not leave her side without first asking her consent. I ate my supper in quiet, listening patiently to the talk of the old people, wishing all the time that they would begin the stories I loved best. At last, when I could not wait any longer, I whispered in my mother's ear, "Ask them to tell an Iktomi story, mother."

Soothing my impatience, my mother said aloud, "My little daughter is anxious to hear your legends." By this time all were through eating, and the evening was fast deepening into twilight.

As each in turn began to tell a legend, I pillowed my head in my mother's lap; and lying flat upon my back, I watched the stars as they peeped down upon me, one by one. The increasing interest of the tale aroused me, and I sat up eagerly listening for every word. The old women made funny remarks, and laughed so heartily that I could not help joining them.

The distant howling of a pack of wolves or the hooting of an owl in the river bottom frightened me, and I nestled into my mother's lap. She added some dry sticks to the open fire, and the bright flames leaped up into the faces of the old folks as they sat around in a great circle.

On such an evening, I remember the glare of the fire shone on a tattooed star upon the brow of the old warrior who was telling a story. I watched him curiously as he made his unconscious gestures. The blue star upon his bronzed forehead was a puzzle to me. Looking about, I saw two parallel lines on the chin of one of the old women. The rest had none. I examined my mother's face, but found no sign there.

After the warrior's story was finished, I asked the old woman the meaning of the blue lines on her chin, looking all the while out of the corners of my eyes at the warrior with the star on his forehead. I was a little afraid that he would rebuke me for my boldness.

Here the old woman began: "Why, my grandchild, they are signs,—secret signs I dare not tell you. I shall, however, tell you a wonderful story about a woman who had a cross tattooed upon each of her cheeks."

It was a long story of a woman whose magic power lay hidden behind the marks upon her face. I fell asleep before the story was completed.

Ever after that night I felt suspicious of tattooed people. Wherever I saw one I glanced furtively at the mark and round about it, wondering what terrible magic power was covered there.

It was rarely that such a fearful story as this one was told by the camp fire. Its impression was so acute that the picture still remains vividly clear and pronounced.

III.

THE BEADWORK.

Soon after breakfast, mother sometimes began her beadwork. On a bright clear day, she pulled out the wooden pegs that pinned the skirt of our wigwam to the ground, and rolled the canvas part way up on its frame of slender poles. Then the cool morning breezes swept freely through our dwelling, now and then wafting the perfume of sweet grasses from newly burnt prairie.

Untying the long tasseled strings that bound a small brown buckskin bag, my mother spread upon a mat beside her bunches of colored beads, just as an artist arranges the paints upon his palette. On a lapboard she smoothed out a double sheet of soft white buckskin; and drawing from a beaded case that hung on the left of her wide belt a long, narrow blade, she trimmed the buckskin into shape. Often she worked upon small moccasins for her small daughter. Then I became intensely interested in her designing. With a proud, beaming face, I watched her work. In imagination, I saw myself walking in a new pair of snugly fitting moccasins. I felt the envious eyes of my playmates upon the pretty red beads decorating my feet.

Close beside my mother I sat on a rug, with a scrap of buckskin in one hand and an awl in the other. This was the beginning of my practical observation lessons in the art of beadwork. From a skein of finely twisted threads of silvery sinews my mother pulled out a single one. With an awl she pierced the buckskin, and skillfully threaded it with the white sinew. Picking up the tiny beads one by one, she strung them with the point of her thread, always twisting it carefully after every stitch.

It took many trials before I learned how to knot my sinew thread on the point of my finger, as I saw her do. Then the next difficulty was in keeping my thread stiffly twisted, so that I could easily string my beads upon it. My mother required of me original designs for my lessons in beading. At first I frequently ensnared many a sunny hour into working a long design. Soon I learned from self-inflicted punishment to refrain from drawing complex patterns, for I had to finish whatever I began.

After some experience I usually drew easy and simple crosses and squares. These were some of the set forms. My original designs were not always symmetrical nor sufficiently characteristic, two faults with which my mother had little patience. The quietness of her oversight made me feel strongly responsible and dependent upon my own judgment. She treated me as a dignified little individual as long as I was on my good behavior; and how humiliated I was when some boldness of mine drew forth a rebuke from her!

In the choice of colors she left me to my own taste. I was pleased with an outline of yellow upon a background of dark blue, or a combination of red and myrtle-green. There was another of red with a bluish gray that was more conventionally used. When I became a little familiar with designing and the various pleasing combinations of color, a harder lesson was given me. It was the sewing on, instead of beads, some tinted porcupine quills, moistened and flattened between the nails of the thumb and forefinger. My mother cut off the prickly ends and burned them at once in the centre fire. These sharp points were poisonous, and worked into the flesh wherever they lodged. For this reason, my mother said, I should not do much alone in quills until I was as tall as my cousin Warca-Ziwin.

Always after these confining lessons I was wild with surplus spirits, and found joyous relief in running loose in the open again. Many a summer afternoon, a party of four or five of my playmates roamed over the hills with me. We each carried a light sharpened rod about four feet long, with which we pried up certain sweet roots. When we had eaten all the choice roots we chanced upon, we shouldered our rods and strayed off into patches of a stalky plant under whose yellow blossoms we found little crystal drops of gum. Drop by drop we gathered this nature's rock-candy, until each of us could boast of a lump the size of a small bird's egg. Soon satiated with its woody flavor, we tossed away our gum, to return again to the sweet roots.

I remember well how we used to exchange our necklaces, beaded belts, and sometimes even our moccasins. We pretended to offer them as gifts to one another. We delighted in impersonating our own mothers. We talked of things we had heard them say in their conversations. We imitated their various manners, even to the inflection of their voices. In the lap of the prairie we seated ourselves upon our feet; and leaning our painted cheeks in the palms of our hands, we rested our elbows on our knees, and bent forward as old women were most accustomed to do.

While one was telling of some heroic deed recently done by a near relative, the rest of us listened attentively, and exclaimed in undertones, "Han! han!" (yes! yes!) whenever the speaker paused for breath, or sometimes for our sympathy. As the discourse became more thrilling, according to our ideas, we raised our voices in these interjections. In these impersonations our parents were led to say only those things that were in common favor.

No matter how exciting a tale we might be rehearsing, the mere shifting of a cloud shadow in the landscape near by was sufficient to change our impulses; and soon we were all chasing the great shadows that played among the hills. We shouted and whopped in the chase; laughing and calling to one another, we were like little sportive nymphs on that Dakota sea of rolling green.

On one occasion, I forgot the cloud shadow in a strange notion to catch up with my own shadow. Standing straight and still, I began to glide after it, putting out one foot cautiously. When, with the greatest care, I set my foot in advance of myself, my shadow crept onward too. Then again I tried it; this time with the other foot. Still again my shadow escaped me. I began to run; and away flew my shadow, always just a step beyond me. Faster and faster I ran, setting my teeth and clenching my fists, determined to overtake my own fleet shadow. But ever swifter it glided before me, while I was growing breathless and hot. Slackening my speed, I was greatly vexed that my shadow should check its pace also. Daring it to the utmost, as I thought, I sat down upon a rock imbedded in the hillside.

So! My shadow had the impudence to sit down beside me!

Now my comrades caught up with me, and began to ask why I was running away so fast.

"Oh, I was chasing my shadow! Didn't you ever do that?" I inquired, surprised that they should not understand.

They planted their moccasined feet firmly upon my shadow to stay it, and I arose. Again my shadow slipped away, and moved as often as I did. Then we gave up trying to catch my shadow.

Before this peculiar experience I have no distinct memory of having recognized any vital bond between myself and my own shadow. I never gave it an afterthought.

Returning our borrowed belts and trinkets, we rambled homeward. That evening, as on other evenings, I went to sleep over my legends.

IV.

THE COFFEE-MAKING.

One summer afternoon, my mother left me alone in our wigwam, while she went across the way to my aunt's dwelling.

I did not much like to stay alone in our tepee, for I feared a tall, broad-shouldered crazy man, some forty years old, who walked loose among the hills. Wiyaka-Napbina (Wearer of a Feather Necklace) was harmless, and whenever he came into a wigwam he was driven there by extreme hunger. He went nude except for the half of a red blanket he girdled around his waist. In one tawny arm he used to carry a heavy bunch of wild sunflowers that he gathered in his aimless ramblings. His black hair was matted by the winds, and scorched into a dry red by the constant summer sun. As he took great strides, placing one brown bare foot directly in front of the other, he swung his long lean arm to and fro.

Frequently he paused in his walk and gazed far backward, shading his eyes with his hand. He was under the belief that an evil spirit was haunting his steps. This was what my mother told me once, when I sneered at such a silly big man. I was brave when my mother was near by, and Wiyaka-Napbina walking farther and farther away.

"Pity the man, my child. I knew him when he was a brave and handsome youth. He was overtaken by a malicious spirit among the hills, one day, when he went hither and thither after his ponies. Since then he cannot stay away from the hills," she said.

I felt so sorry for the man in his misfortune that I prayed to the Great Spirit to restore him. But though I pitied him at a distance, I was still afraid of him when he appeared near our wigwam.

Thus, when my mother left me by myself that afternoon, I sat in a fearful mood within our tepee. I recalled all I had ever heard about Wiyaka-Napbina; and I tried to assure myself that though he might pass near by, he would not come to our wigwam because there was no little girl around our grounds.

Just then, from without a hand lifted the canvas covering of the entrance; the shadow of a man fell within the wigwam, and a large roughly moccasined foot was planted inside.

For a moment I did not dare to breathe or stir, for I thought that could be no other than Wiyaka-Napbina. The next instant I sighed aloud in relief. It was an old grandfather who had often told me Iktomi legends.

"Where is your mother, my little grandchild?" were his first words.

113

"My mother is soon coming back from my aunt's tepee," I replied.

"Then I shall wait awhile for her return," he said, crossing his feet and seating himself upon a mat.

At once I began to play the part of a generous hostess. I turned to my mother's coffeepot.

Lifting the lid, I found nothing but coffee grounds in the bottom. I set the pot on a heap of cold ashes in the centre, and filled it half full of warm Missouri River water. During this performance I felt conscious of being watched. Then breaking off a small piece of our unleavened bread, I placed it in a bowl. Turning soon to the coffeepot, which would never have boiled on a dead fire had I waited forever, I poured out a cup of worse than muddy warm water. Carrying the bowl in one hand and cup in the other, I handed the light luncheon to the old warrior. I offered them to him with an air of bestowing generous hospitality.

"How! how!" he said, and placed the dishes on the ground in front of his crossed feet. He nibbled at the bread and sipped from the cup. I sat back against a pole watching him. I was proud to have succeeded so well in serving refreshments to a guest all by myself. Before the old warrior had finished eating, my mother entered. Immediately she wondered where I had found coffee, for she knew I had never made any, and that she had left the coffeepot empty. Answering the question in my mother's eyes, the warrior remarked, "My granddaughter made coffee on a heap of dead ashes, and served me the moment I came."

They both laughed, and mother said, "Wait a little longer, and I shall build a fire." She meant to make some real coffee. But neither she nor the warrior, whom the law of our custom had compelled to partake of my insipid hospitality, said anything to embarrass me. They treated my best judgment, poor as it was, with the utmost respect. It was not till long years afterward that I learned how ridiculous a thing I had done.

V.

THE DEAD MAN'S PLUM BUSH.

One autumn afternoon, many people came streaming toward the dwelling of our near neighbor. With painted faces, and wearing broad white bosoms of elk's teeth, they hurried down the narrow footpath to Haraka Wambdi's wigwam. Young mothers held their children by the hand, and half pulled them along in their haste. They overtook and passed by the bent old grandmothers who were trudging along with crooked canes toward the centre of excitement. Most of the young braves galloped hither on their ponies. Toothless warriors, like the old women, came more slowly, though mounted on lively ponies. They sat proudly erect on their horses. They wore their eagle plumes, and waved their various trophies of former wars.

In front of the wigwam a great fire was built, and several large black kettles of venison were suspended over it. The crowd were seated about it on the grass in a great circle. Behind them some of the braves stood leaning against the necks of their ponies, their tall figures draped in loose robes which were well drawn over their eyes.

Young girls, with their faces glowing like bright red autumn leaves, their glossy braids falling over each ear, sat coquettishly beside their chaperons. It was a custom for young Indian women to invite some older relative to escort them to the public feasts. Though it was not an iron law, it was generally observed.

Haraka Wambdi was a strong young brave, who had just returned from his first battle, a warrior. His near relatives, to celebrate his new rank, were spreading a feast to which the whole of the Indian village was invited.

Holding my pretty striped blanket in readiness to throw over my shoulders, I grew more and more restless as I watched the gay throng assembling. My mother was busily broiling a wild duck that my aunt had that morning brought over.

"Mother, mother, why do you stop to cook a small meal when we are invited to a feast?" I asked, with a snarl in my voice.

"My child, learn to wait. On our way to the celebration we are going to stop at Chanyu's wigwam. His aged mother-in-law is lying very ill, and I think she would like a taste of this small game."

Having once seen the suffering on the thin, pinched features of this dying woman, I felt a momentary shame that I had not remembered her before.

On our way, I ran ahead of my mother, and was reaching out my hand to pick some purple plums that grew on a small bush, when I was checked by a low "Sh!" from my mother.

"Why, mother, I want to taste the plums!" I exclaimed, as I dropped my hand to my side in disappointment.

"Never pluck a single plum from this bush, my child, for its roots are wrapped around an Indian's skeleton. A brave is buried here. While he lived, he was so fond of playing the game of striped plum seeds that, at his death, his set of plum seeds were buried in his hands. From them sprang up this little bush."

Eyeing the forbidden fruit, I trod lightly on the sacred ground, and dared to speak only in whispers, until we had gone many paces from it. After that time, I halted in my ramblings whenever I came in sight of the plum bush. I grew sober with awe, and was alert to hear a long-drawn-out whistle rise from the roots of it. Though I had never heard with my own ears this strange whistle of departed spirits, yet I had listened so frequently to hear the old folks describe it that I knew I should recognize it at once.

The lasting impression of that day, as I recall it now, is what my mother told me about the dead man's plum bush.

VI.

THE GROUND SQUIRREL.

In the busy autumn days, my cousin Warca-Ziwin's mother came to our wigwam to help my mother preserve foods for our winter use. I was very fond of my aunt, because she was not so quiet as my mother. Though she was older, she was more jovial and less reserved. She was slender and remarkably erect. While my mother's hair was heavy and black, my aunt had unusually thin locks.

Ever since I knew her, she wore a string of large blue beads around her neck,—beads that were precious because my uncle had given them to her when she was a younger woman. She had a peculiar swing in her gait, caused by a long stride rarely natural to so slight a figure. It was during my aunt's visit with us that my mother forgot her accustomed quietness, often laughing heartily at some of my aunt's witty remarks.

I loved my aunt threefold: for her hearty laughter, for the cheerfulness she caused my mother, and most of all for the times she dried my tears and held me in her lap, when my mother had reproved me.

Early in the cool mornings, just as the yellow rim of the sun rose above the hills, we were up and eating our breakfast. We awoke so early that we saw the sacred hour when a misty smoke hung over a pit surrounded by an impassable sinking mire. This strange smoke appeared every morning, both winter and summer; but most visibly in midwinter it rose immediately above the marshy spot. By the time the full face of the sun appeared above the eastern horizon, the smoke vanished. Even very old men, who had known this country the longest, said that the smoke from this pit had never failed a single day to rise heavenward.

As I frolicked about our dwelling, I used to stop suddenly, and with a fearful awe watch the smoking of the unknown fires. While the vapor was visible, I was afraid to go very far from our wigwam unless I went with my mother.

From a field in the fertile river bottom my mother and aunt gathered an abundant supply of corn. Near our tepee, they spread a large canvas upon the grass, and dried their sweet corn in it. I was left to watch the corn, that nothing should disturb it. I played around it with dolls made of ears of corn. I braided their soft fine silk for hair, and gave them blankets as various as the scraps I found in my mother's workbag.

There was a little stranger with a black-and-yellow-striped coat that used to come to the drying corn. It was a little ground squirrel, who was so fearless of me that he came to one corner of the canvas and carried away as much of the sweet corn as he could hold. I wanted very much to catch him, and rub his pretty fur back, but my mother said he would be so frightened if I caught him that he would bite my fingers. So I was as content as he to keep the corn between us. Every morning he came for more corn. Some evenings I have seen him creeping about our grounds; and when I gave a sudden whoop of recognition, he ran quickly out of sight.

When mother had dried all the corn she wished, then she sliced great pumpkins into thin rings; and these she doubled and linked together into long chains. She hung them on a pole that stretched between two forked posts. The wind and sun soon thoroughly dried the chains of pumpkin. Then she packed them away in a case of thick and stiff buckskin.

In the sun and wind she also dried many wild fruits,—cherries, berries, and plums. But chiefest among my early recollections of autumn is that one of the corn drying and the ground squirrel.

I have few memories of winter days, at this period of my life, though many of the summer. There is one only which I can recall.

Some missionaries gave me a little bag of marbles. They were all sizes and colors. Among them were some of colored glass. Walking with my mother to the river, on a late winter day, we found great chunks of ice piled all along the bank. The ice on the river was floating in huge pieces. As I stood beside one large block, I noticed for the first time the colors of the rainbow in the crystal ice. Immediately I thought of my glass marbles at home. With my bare fingers I tried to pick out some of the colors, for they seemed so near the surface. But my fingers began to sting with the intense cold, and I had to bite them hard to keep from crying.

From that day on, for many a moon, I believed that glass marbles had river ice inside of them.

VII.

THE BIG RED APPLES.

The first turning away from the easy, natural flow of my life occurred in an early spring. It was in my eighth year; in the month of March, I afterward learned. At this age I knew but one language, and that was my mother's native tongue.

117

From some of my playmates I heard that two paleface missionaries were in our village. They were from that class of white men who wore big hats and carried large hearts, they said. Running direct to my mother, I began to question her why these two strangers were among us. She told me, after I had teased much, that they had come to take away Indian boys and girls to the East. My mother did not seem to want me to talk about them. But in a day or two, I gleaned many wonderful stories from my playfellows concerning the strangers.

"Mother, my friend Judéwin is going home with the missionaries. She is going to a more beautiful country than ours; the palefaces told her so!" I said wistfully, wishing in my heart that I too might go.

Mother sat in a chair, and I was hanging on her knee. Within the last two seasons my big brother Dawée had returned from a three years' education in the East, and his coming back influenced my mother to take a farther step from her native way of living. First it was a change from the buffalo skin to the white man's canvas that covered our wigwam. Now she had given up her wigwam of slender poles, to live, a foreigner, in a home of clumsy logs.

"Yes, my child, several others besides Judéwin are going away with the palefaces. Your brother said the missionaries had inquired about his little sister," she said, watching my face very closely.

My heart thumped so hard against my breast, I wondered if she could hear it.

"Did he tell them to take me, mother?" I asked, fearing lest Dawée had forbidden the palefaces to see me, and that my hope of going to the Wonderland would be entirely blighted.

With a sad, slow smile, she answered: "There! I knew you were wishing to go, because Judéwin has filled your ears with the white man's lies. Don't believe a word they say! Their words are sweet, but, my child, their deeds are bitter. You will cry for me, but they will not even soothe you. Stay with me, my little one! Your brother Dawée says that going East, away from your mother, is too hard an experience for his baby sister."

Thus my mother discouraged my curiosity about the lands beyond our eastern horizon; for it was not yet an ambition for Letters that was stirring me. But on the following day the missionaries did come to our very house. I spied them coming up the footpath leading to our cottage. A third man was with them, but he was not my brother Dawée. It was another, a young interpreter, a paleface who had a smattering of the Indian language. I was ready to run out to meet them, but I did not dare to displease my mother. With great glee, I jumped up and down on our ground floor. I begged my mother to open the door, that they would be sure to come to us. Alas! They came, they saw, and they conquered!

Judéwin had told me of the great tree where grew red, red apples; and how we could reach out our hands and pick all the red apples we could eat. I had never seen apple trees. I had never tasted more than a dozen red apples in my life; and when I heard of the orchards of the East, I was eager to roam among them. The missionaries smiled into my eyes and patted by head. I wondered how mother could say such hard words against him.

"Mother, ask them if little girls may have all the red apples they want, when they go East," I whispered aloud, in my excitement.

The interpreter heard, and answered: "Yes, little girl, the nice red apples are for those who pick them; and you will have a ride on the iron horse if you go with these good people."

I had never seen a train, and he knew it.

"Mother, I am going East! I like big red apples, and I want to ride on the iron horse! Mother, say yes!" I pleaded.

My mother said nothing. The missionaries waited in silence; and my eyes began to blur with tears, though I struggled to choke them back. The corners of my mouth twitched, and my mother saw me.

"I am not ready to give you any word," she said to them. "Tomorrow I shall send you my answer by my son."

With this they left us. Alone with my mother, I yielded to my tears, and cried aloud, shaking my head so as not to hear what she was saying to me. This was the first time I had ever been so unwilling to give up my own desire that I refused to hearken to my mother's voice.

There was a solemn silence in our home that night. Before I went to bed I begged the Great Spirit to make my mother willing I should go with the missionaries.

The next morning came, and my mother called me to her side. "My daughter, do you still persist in wishing to leave your mother?" she asked.

"Oh, mother, it is not that I wish to leave you, but I want to see the wonderful Eastern land," I answered.

My dear old aunt came to our house that morning, and I heard her say, "Let her try it."

I hoped that, as usual, my aunt was pleading on my side. My brother Dawée came for mother's decision. I dropped my play, and crept close to my aunt.

"Yes, Dawée, my daughter, though she does not understand what it all means, is anxious to go. She will need an education when she is grown, for then there will be fewer real Dakotas, and many more palefaces. This tearing her away, so young, from her mother is necessary, if I would have her an educated woman. The palefaces, who owe us a large debt for stolen lands, have begun to pay a tardy justice in offering some education to our children. But I know my daughter must suffer keenly in this experiment. For her sake, I dread to tell you my reply to the missionaries. Go, tell them that they may take my little daughter, and that the Great Spirit shall not fail to reward them according to their hearts."

Wrapped in my heavy blanket, I walked with my mother to the carriage that was soon to take us to the iron horse. I was happy. I met my playmates, who were also wearing their best thick blankets. We showed one another our new beaded moccasins, and the width of the belts that girdled our new dresses. Soon we were being drawn rapidly away by the white man's horses. When I saw the lonely figure of my mother vanish in the distance, a sense of regret settled heavily upon me. I felt suddenly weak, as if I might fall limp to the ground. I was in the hands of strangers whom my mother did not fully trust. I no longer felt free to be myself, or to voice my own feelings. The tears trickled down my cheeks, and I buried my face in the folds of my blanket. Now the first step, parting me from my mother, was taken, and all my belated tears availed nothing.

Having driven thirty miles to the ferryboat, we crossed the Missouri in the evening. Then riding again a few miles eastward, we stopped before a massive brick building. I looked at it in amazement, and with a vague misgiving, for in our village I had never seen so large a house. Trembling with fear and distrust of the palefaces, my teeth chattering from the chilly ride, I crept noiselessly in my soft moccasins along the narrow hall, keeping very close to the bare wall. I was as frightened and bewildered as the captured young of a wild creature.

IMPRESSIONS OF AN INDIAN CHILDHOOD

Facts

1. What were the two things about the author that filled her mother with pride?

2. After a brief conversation with her mother, the author hated the paleface. Why?

3. Describe the lessons the author learned in each section of the essay.

4. What was the missing ingredient in the author's coffee-making?

5. In "The Ground Squirrel," the author relates three reasons why she loved her aunt. What were they?

6. After meeting the paleface, the author wanted to go with them. Why? Why did her mother let her go?

Strategies

1. Why did the author divide her essay into seven sections? How does this division impact the story?

2. What technique(s) does the author use to get the reader to hear the child's voice?

3. The reader doesn't encounter the brother, Dawée, until Section VII, "The Red Apples." Why isn't he introduced earlier? What is his role in the narrative? Is his late introduction a mistake?

4. The author prepared the reader for the grandfather's impromptu visit in Section IV, "The Coffee-Making." What is this technique called?

5. Discuss the actions in "The Coffee-Making" section that help the author communicate the child's voice.

Issues

1.   Parents teach their children lessons in many ways. For instance, there were lessons learned by the author before, during, and after the legends. Discuss other ways in which parents teach lessons.

2.   In "The Coffee-Making" section, the author treats the visitor with dignity and respect as does her mother. The adults treat the child in the same manner. In today's society, are children treated with dignity and respect?

3.   Discuss the missionaries and their relationship to other peoples they have attempted to convert to Christianity, such as Hawaiians, the Aztecs, Africans, etc.

4.   Discuss the meaning of this statement, ". . . the Great Spirit shall not fail to reward them according to their hearts."

5.   There are substantial changes in attitude made by the author's mother in Section VII when compared to Section I. What are they?

Writing Assignments

1.   Write an essay, using a childhood event and in the voice of a child, about a parental contradiction.

2.   Write an essay on an important decision you had to make as a child.

George King (student)

THE CRUELTY OF CHILDREN AND POLITICS

GEORGE KING was a student at Compton Community College when he wrote this essay. He is currently attending Santa Monica College.

I got suspended from school yesterday for fighting again. And yes, it was for the same reason; someone called me a name. I have been told constantly by my mother that I should know better than to pay attention to the kids who tease me at school. That lesson seems to be one I'm having a hard time learning. My days at Stephen C. Foster Elementary are so long and hard. There have been many days where I would fantasize about not going to school at all, but instead hitchhiking a ride somewhere else. I was never really sure of where I would go, I just knew that any place besides that jail would be a good place to start. It helps that some of the teachers are nice and some of the students seem to like me. Even then, I can't help but think that they like me because of my older sister. She and her wild friends ruled Foster last year and I think the memory of them is enough to make anybody think twice about messing with George King.

Anyway I'm at home now because of something that started about two weeks ago. My teacher, Mrs. Marsh, told my sixth-grade class that student-government elections were coming up soon. At first I didn't really care. Well actually, it's not that I didn't care, I wasn't really paying attention to her. I was talking to my friend Kellie who told me during recess that somebody said that I liked to play with Barbie dolls. I was trying to get her to tell me who said it so that I could show them what a boy who played with Barbie dolls really acted like. It wasn't until Mrs. Marsh screamed at me that I really started to listen. As I sat there embarrassed I began to think about what it would mean to be President. I thought about how fun it would be to rule Foster Elementary. Then everyone would like me and want me to be his friend. And if they didn't, I was gonna make rules so they'd have to. Ronald Reagan would have nothing on me. I even thought about my first duty as soon as I was elected: destroy Mrs. Marsh.

I started making plans of all the things I was gonna do to become President. I was so excited. I was scared too. What would I say? How would I say it? Then after a few moments my thoughts turned to, Who would care? Who would listen? I knew no one liked me or at least not enough did to make me win. Thinking about that hurt my feelings. At first I was feeling so happy and then I started to feel really really sad. All I could do was cry. I mean, I wanted to cry. I

123

really hate crying in front of people so I put my head down on my desk. Why did I do that? As soon as I did, Mrs. Marsh, the evil witch that she is, screamed, "George get your head up from that desk. We didn't come here to look at your head!" When she finished, she slammed down hard on the desk and this made me jump and the whole class began laughing like crazy. I began to think about the TV show I watched the night before. It was the Equalizer and in this episode there was this man named Dr. Woo who wanted to kill his wife for money or jewels or something. Up until that morning, I could not understand why a man would want to kill anyone, let alone a woman. By the end of the school day, I understood totally. Dr. Woo was my hero.

Before we left school, Mrs. Marsh gave us permission slips and applications for the kids who wanted to run for a spot on student government. The permission slips were handed out because the next day some guy was coming to our class to speak to us about something called AIDS. I didn't understand why we needed our parents' permission to talk about the teachers' helpers, but I took the slip anyway.

When I got home, I was still pretty sad. I had sort of stopped thinking about being president. To me being President was like being He-Man or Spiderman, like a fantasy. I put the two sheets of paper on the kitchen table and went outside to play GI Joe with Raymond, Shemar and Boozie. When I got back in the house, I saw that somebody had picked up the two sheets. Right when I noticed they were missing, my mama called me into her room. When I walked in I noticed that she had both sheets of paper on the bed to her side while she sat there rolling her hair. I sat down on the bed and waited for her to talk. When she did, she wanted to know what the papers were for. I told her one was for the kids who wanted to be in government and the other was because some guy was coming to talk to us about the teachers' aides. She started laughing when I know I wasn't trying to be funny. She asked me, So why don't you run for president? I told her that I thought about it, but that I changed my mind. I didn't feel like going into it, so I just left it like that. She then told me what she told my brother and sister before, "You'll never know what you can do until you try." And just like my mama twitched her nose like Samantha on Bewitched, I wanted to be president again.

The next day I couldn't wait to get to school. My mama signed both slips and I sprinted to school like I was Carl Lewis or something. When Mrs. Marsh came in, the first thing she screamed was for us to hand in our slips. She then said that those students who couldn't stay to hear that guy come talk to us, would be going to the cafeteria for an assembly. That really made me mad. Why did my mama have to be one of the ones to make her kids listen to this man? Anyway, the man came and put these weird words on the board. The one word

I remember was AIDS and another one began with an H. He wasn't gonna be talking about teachers' aides like I thought. Is that what my mama was laughing at? I felt so stupid. AIDS meant some other things kind of like G.L.O.W. means Gorgeous Ladies of Wrestling. I just can't remember exactly what it was. The same thing with that H word; it meant something else too. To be totally honest, the only letter I could think about was P and that stood for President. I knew that.

Finally, Mrs. Marsh got past all of the stuff that wasn't important and got to the student elections. She asked who all in class wanted to be secretary, treasurer, then class rep. None of these smaller offices meant anything to me. When she got to asking the class who wanted to run for President, I shot my hand up before she even finished the word. Right after I raised my hand two other students did the same. One of the students was Clifford McKee. I wasn't worried about him; he was new to the school and that meant he wouldn't get many votes. The other student was Nicole Perry. She scared me. Not only was she the smartest girl in school, but she had a lot of friends and a thousand cousins.

Two days after we got through all the requirements and other stuff, we were set to have a debate in the school cafeteria. The three main candidates for president were going to be asked questions by the teachers and students. I wasn't really worried or nervous about this. Well when I got on the stage and I looked and saw all those people looking at me; I started getting butterflies in my stomach. I just thanked God I was already seated or else I would have fallen straight to the floor. When I looked over at Nicole and Cliff, I saw that he was worse off than I was. He looked like he was about to cry or something. That made me feel better. When I looked at her, she was over there smiling and waving to a big part of the cafeteria that had nothing but her cousins in it. She didn't look nervous. She looked ready. None of this made me feel any better. The first question was What will you do to make Foster better? I was up first and I said something like I was gonna help clean up the school and try to help students get better grades. When Cliff was asked this question he looked like he froze. He just stood at the microphone staring out at the back door. He then said, I will do a lot of stuff for Foster. Most of the students, even a few teachers started laughing. He had this weird look on his face and he went to sit down. When Nicole was asked the question she stood up, walked to the microphone and began to talk. I can't remember exactly what she said; I just remember thinking, I wish I had said that to a lot of the things she said. When she finished the students went crazy. They clapped so hard they hurt my ears. I said for the next question that I was gonna say something really good. I was asked a different question, but because I couldn't think of anything, I gave the same answer I gave to the first question. I heard some people start to chuckle as I stood up there fumbling over words. I began to feel really bad when some of the teachers put their heads down or just looked away when I looked at them. I felt like a fool so I just sat down. Cliff didn't do much better. As a matter of fact, he did worse. When he was asked the question, he said nothing. I know he was just about to cry when the teacher said "Thank you" and sat him down. I was feeling better because then the attention was off me and my dumb answer. Once again, unfortunately, Nicole answered the question and got a lot of applause.

By the end I wasn't feeling too bad. The next day was the elections, but I still had a few tricks up my sleeves. On that morning before school, I stopped by the candy store and bought $2 worth of 1-cent bubble gum. At recess, I threw out the gum and big crowds of people were following me. That was fun. I asked some of them if they'd vote for me and they all said that they would. I didn't see Nicole doing any of this, so I felt really good.

I went home happy and excited about my chances for being president. That night before the election I sat in my bed fantasizing about all the good things I would be able to do. The biggest thing for me would be the fact that, as president, people would really like me and I'd have a lot more friends. The name-calling would stop and that would mean I wouldn't have to fight anymore. I wanted this so badly. I actually fell asleep praying to God that He make me president.

When I got to school I threw out more gum and more people told me they would vote for me. I was too happy. The whole school was going to vote after P.E. and that time couldn't come soon enough. I was so ready for this to be over so that I could begin my rule. I had never been happier. It didn't take long for me to finish my voting. When I finished I walked up to the teacher and gave her my sheet and smiled. She didn't smile back. I went back to my seat and sat and watched everyone as they were voting for me. When everyone finished she told us the results would be in the next day.

I thought that if I got to school the next day before everyone else, that Mrs. Marsh would tell me who won. She wouldn't. I had to wait until recess. The class time in between the start of school and recess meant nothing to me. I could think of nothing but the election. The bell rang for recess and, everyone ran out of the class to the cafeteria where the results were. I had already decided that I wanted to look cool as I got the news. So I walked. As I got closer, I saw Riley jumping up and down; he had gotten the position of Secretary. I saw Telley laughing; she won the position of Treasurer. Then I saw Nicole. She was just standing there staring at the poster. I remember thinking, poor thing, like my mama always says. I waited until most of the crowd disappeared to walk up and see my name up there as the new President. I couldn't believe what my eyes showed me. Nicole had 178 votes; I had 18 votes. I didn't win. Nicole won. I didn't win. I didn't want to believe it, especially after all that praying, fantasizing and not to mention, the bubble gum!

As I stood there devastated, it took all of me to not start crying. All of my dreams were thrown out of the window. I just stood there staring at the poster. As I looked longer and longer, I noticed some writing by my name. I looked closer and instantly got even more upset. Someone had written the word "faggot" next to my name. I continued to stare, thinking about everyone who saw that. Everybody is gonna think I'm like that. I kept thinking. I really couldn't move. It was like I was really frozen. It was shock I think. I didn't know who could have done something like this or why they did. I was never mean to anyone. Then after I got over all of that I got really mad. I got so mad that my head started to hurt. I wanted whoever did that to pay. As I began to slowly walk away from the poster this fool named d'Andre Willis walked by me and laughed right in my face and then called me a girl. I knew then who wrote that word by my name. I didn't even say anything to him. There was no time to ask questions or talk. I just socked him hard across the back of the head. When he turned around, I dived on him and we both were on the ground. He started scratching and clawing like a wild cat so I got up and started kicking him. Of course, by this time a big group of people was around us screaming and yelling. I was really getting into it when I was suddenly yanked by my arm. It was Mr.Albright, the meanest, ugliest man in the universe, also our principal. He snatched me around like I was a doll and dragged me and D'Andre to his office. By the time we got to his office, I noticed that D'Andre was crying and he had a little blood coming from his lip. I was proud of my work. I then had to explain to Mr. Albright what happened. All D'Andre said was that he didn't do it and that I had no proof. Mr. Albright was on his side. He had to call my mama and tell her what happened.

So that is why I'm here now: at home suspended for two days. My mother told me I couldn't go outside or watch cartoons. She wouldn't even listen to me. She told me to tell it to my father when he got home. He likes to hit first then ask questions. So right now I'm just a little scared. I know that if they'd just listen to me, they would understand. My mama thinks that just because I'm scared of what my father will do, that I'm really sorry for what I did. She's wrong. Since I'm not President, I don't care if I miss school for a few days. And besides, I got to show D'Andre and everyone else who wondered what a boy who plays with Barbie dolls fights like.

THE CRUELTY OF CHILDREN AND POLITICS

Questions

1.   Why did the author have such a hard time at school?

2.   Why did the author's mother tell him he could do anything even though she knew he had trouble at school?

3.   Discuss the cruelty of children and their words.

4.   What does the Barbie Doll represent?

Robert S. Hilton

LESSONS

ROBERT S. HILTON (b. 1943) lives in Altadena, California, near the San Gabriel Mountains. He makes and plays unique musical instruments, writes poems and stories, and teaches children's art classes. His other published works are "Embroidery Hoop" in *The Drumming Between Us* magazine and "Red Light Green Light (Arc of Stars)" in *Flash-BOPP Literary* Magazine.

A seven-year-old boy discovers his mother knows more than he does.

Funny how a child can crouch for hours. I try it now but my knees start complaining too soon and I'm forced to change position. But when I was small . . . . Mr. and Mrs. Simms were my Brooklyn neighbors. In front of their brownstone lived the most amazing tree. Everything about this old maple was fascinating to my seven-year-old senses. Leaves like hands, wonderful moth-wing whirly-bird seeds, coarse dark brown bark. I knew every line and crevice. It was a highway for the main attraction, the thing that had my little legs crouch/bent, eyes cross/focused, mind set/learning. I was there to study the big black carpenter ants. They marched up and down the giant twisted up trunk. It was as though they had a duty to touch every inch of bark before disappearing into a crevice. I can imagine them being held accountable by the record keeper, scolded in their chemical language, "The twisty branch on the far side was not examined today. Who knows what might be going on over there? Tomorrow, we must pay careful attention to the whole area."

The roots were a jumbled mess, heaped high, filling the narrow parkway, hinting at the hidden half of the massive tree concealed beneath the ground. The curb was broken, the sidewalk raised about six inches in a sharp cliff. It made an excellent ski jump for adventurous children on bicycles or metal clamp-on street skates when they sped past the tree toward my house. The thrill of being airborne for a fraction of a second was a constant attraction. I was too young to have those skills. I had the ants and the Simms' maple tree. "Just look at how their legs bend. Can't see that from a bicycle."

I was hungry for everything insect. On the opposite side of my house from the Simms' was my friend Roger. He lived in the brownstone where Big John used to live. Roger and I had begun to collect bugs. In my house I had a glass jar where I would deposit the day's catch.

My mother would never allow me to take the glass jar outside. "You could drop it and cut yourself."

"But Mommy, you can't see the bugs through plastic." She only let me use a Tupperware container to go out collecting. And it made it hard to let yesterday's bugs free. There was just too much transferring. Watching the old bugs crawl away was as much a thrill as catching them in the first place. My mother just didn't get it. If we had the glass jar outside with us, we could catch bugs for a while then watch them crawl, hop, or fly out. I wouldn't even need to ever bring them into the house. The watching was the whole purpose for the exercise. And there was no watching anything through Tupperware. Roger never complained, but I was constantly whining about not being trusted with the glass. "Please, please, pleeease, we'll put the jar in the dirt. We won't even pick it up. We'll just leave it down there, please." I was seven years old. I knew how to be careful.

My mother was never moved from her resolve. "Glass is too dangerous, You could cut yourselves."

In Roger's yard was a small tree, nothing like the big maple, but it provided our main hunting ground. Mostly, it gave up a constant supply of ladybugs. From the dirt and beneath rocks, black beetles were plucked. But we could never watch them once they were in the Tupperware. Well, for watching, at least I had the Simms' maple tree. I didn't share that pleasure with Roger or any one else. And I would never ever collect those big beautiful black ants.

One day another friend, Little John, came to my house. We never stopped calling him Little John, even though Big John had long since moved away.

Little John was excited, "R-o-b-e-r-t, R-o-b-e-r-t." I appeared. "There's a grasshopper in my backyard! Let's catch it!"

Oh boy, the two of us squealed with delight. A grasshopper in Brooklyn was really special. "You go back and make sure it doesn't get away. I'll get somethin' to put it in." I ran upstairs. There next to my bed were the Tupperware and the glass jar with the holes my father had poked in the top. I looked at the cloudy plastic Tupperware then at the jar with its ladybugs and rolly-pollys. There was no decision to be made. This was a grasshopper! It had to be seen. I sneaked the forbidden jar past my mother. I was outside. I made it. I had to run before she could put a stop to my adventure. I was elated. My feet were flying. I turned left to go past the Simms' house to Little John's and the waiting grasshopper. My friend the maple tree had been waiting too for this moment to teach me something important. The sidewalk cliff jumped up and stopped my racing feet. I went sprawling. I was holding the jar with both hands in an attempt at being careful. It hit the ground and broke just as my face slammed into it. The laceration followed my right jaw edge tearing in a straight line and splitting in a Y-shaped opening. I was more stunned and embarrassed than hurt. I looked at all of my precious bugs crawling amid the glass and dirt. I started re-collecting them. It seemed like the most urgent thing to be done at the time because I had no idea what I could possibly say when I got home. But now the blood was flowing. It ran down the front of my body, drenching my clothing. It ran down both arms caking up in the dirt and bugs I held in my hands. Still I stayed and collected until I couldn't find any more escapees. By the time I staggered back to the house, I was so soaked that I left bloody footprints down the sidewalk.

I knocked at the window and stood there rocking. "Mommy, Mommy, I think I'm hurt." I couldn't open the door without letting go of the bugs, so I waited. She was outside in a moment. My mother could move urgently without panic. She took in the situation and started to pull me into the house. I tried to tell her about my hands full of insects. "I need someplace to put my bugs," presenting my bloody fists. In two quick movements, she opened my hands and brushed out their contents of blood, dirt, and insects. I looked back at them as she pulled me inside.

I can't remember what she did next, if she washed me up or held a towel to my injured face. I do know that she called my father at his parents' house (my parents were already separated). He came and took me to a doctor to be stitched up. I remember the doctor had trouble getting me to shut up so he could sew my face. I was telling him the whole story about the bugs, the grasshopper, the tree, the sidewalk. The doctor looked to my father for support in quieting me. I looked too. Dad sat there grinning with pride that his son had not cried during this episode. For me it hadn't even been a consideration. That child's crying reflex had been conditioned and punished out of me. That exorcism was in large part why my parents were divorcing. Even now memories of my father are filtered through the still echoing phrase, "I'll give you something to cry about." My father never beat me, but he was such a big man and I was so small that a threat like that was like being hit by a car. My punishment was usually standing in the corner or having to sit by myself on the stairs.

I never did get in trouble for sneaking out with the glass. Mom never mentioned it. It would have been overkill. I learned more than about listening to her and not disobeying. The vision of the dead and dying insects being knocked out of my hands made me lose interest in collecting bugs again.

Besides, I would have been too embarrassed to ask my mother for another glass jar. I never did stop watching them though. I still do.

The carpenter ants continued their busy work on the maple tree. I didn't know at the time, and I never could have guessed that the growth of the colony in the tree would eventually kill it. It was still standing there as strong as ever a year later when we moved to California, still watching over me as my young bones stretched and grew. The broken sidewalk got worse but was never repaired. The scar on my jaw healed in thick cheloid ridges, like three worms crawling out of my face. Even though nobody ever teased me, or even mentioned it, I became self-conscious and wouldn't allow pictures to be taken of me. All through public school there was only one school picture of me and a few group pictures. Most of the yearbooks had that "missing student" silhouette. As I grew, the scar flattened out and became hardly noticeable, but I continued the no photo policy until I was a young adult. From age seven until the age of twenty, my family has only one photo of me, the one school picture I couldn't escape. I was at Los Angeles Airport saying goodbye to my family. I had been drafted and was being sent over seas. I listened to myself arguing with my grandmother about taking my picture when it dawned on me that I was only avoiding photos to keep up a record. It had become a personal tradition. Once she took the pictures, the gap ended.

After leaving New York, I stayed and grew up in California. L.A.'s semi-desert doesn't support maple trees, but there are plenty of ants. The West Coast ants are slender and reddish orange. They live in the ground. Their greatest feature is swiftness. They can run as fast as an object might fall, changing directions with no loss of speed. I still watch them. Almost every day I go out and check on the colony living in my backyard. This colony may not survive. They are attacked and invaded nightly by tiny brown ants. I can't do anything but watch. It's heartbreaking, but it's part of life. Lately, there's been new activity. Winged females appear in clusters around the openings. They look like larger winged versions of the workers. I've only seen the males with their smaller bodies, little heads, and black color on two occasions. They look like a completely different kind of flying insect. At those times there is a frenzy of activity. The workers run around in huge numbers. All of the ants climb the grass stalks moving up and down, but I've yet to see them take to the air. It's good to know that whatever happens to this colony, its seed will likely continue to flourish in new ground.

Sometimes when I have time to sit and think about my own life, I run my fingers over the right side of my jaw. It's flat outside but I can feel the knots of old scar tissue beneath the surface. It makes me remember the rough bark on Mr. Simms' maple tree with its moving lanes of big black carpenter ants, the giant snarl of roots disappearing into the earth, the raised sidewalk, and lessons I learned.

LESSONS

Facts

1. What was the author's favorite pastime?

2. What was the center of this activity?

3. Why couldn't the author use glass jars for his activity?

4. What was his mother's attitude toward the author's favorite activity?

Strategies

1. When does the author leave the voice of the adult and slip into the voice of the child?

2. What strategy does the author use to capture the child's voice?

3. What is the main point of the narrative?

Issues

1. Do mothers understand their male children?

2. What were the lessons learned?

3. Why didn't the author share the maple tree with his best friend? Shouldn't best friends share everything?

Writing Assignments

1. Think of a childhood adventure and the lessons learned and write the story from the child's perspective and voice.

2. Think about the things you liked and disliked about your childhood. Write a narrative using the child's voice about something you liked, disliked, or both.

Josef Pinckney (student)

BUTCH

JOSEF PINCKNEY was a student at Compton Community College when he wrote this essay. Currently, he attends the University of Nevada at Las Vegas majoring in Film Studies.

It's always hot in Fresno, even in the morning. Every weekday I walked back and forth to school by myself. I had to take certain streets in order to get to school in under 15 minutes. School started at 8:15. I always left at 8:00 to get there on time. Almost every street had dogs that barked very single time I walked by. Maple Street had a bulldog named Butch. This was the meanest dog I had ever seen in my life. Butch was about four feet tall, light brown and white hair with big teeth and the most vicious bark I ever heard in my short existence of eleven years. The owner of this monster would sometimes leave the gate open, but Butch would be chained up. The owner's house was very attractive; it was a two-story house with a nice big front yard that was always perfectly groomed with bushes that separated the yard from the driveway. It had two gates, one for the walkway and the other for the driveway. The scary thing about this dog was when I looked him in his dark green eyes they sent shivers down my spine every time. Sometimes I taunted the dog as I passed by just to feel safer. I threw rocks or sticks at him and called him names. For some reason he wasn't so scary if I was taunting him. I felt I had the power.

On one average sunny morning, when I woke up, I felt anything I did today was going to affect me for the rest of my life. I went through my normal morning ritual. I took my shower, got dressed and gathered my books in my backpack. I took my normal route to school. It was business as usual, as far as all the dogs barking at me. I turned on Maple, walking southbound. As I approached the house where Butch lived, something felt wrong. I didn't hear any barking. Usually he barked at me before he even saw me. I thought back to that premonition I woke up with that morning, so I stopped dead in my tracks. I looked around and saw nothing. Next I listened and heard nothing. It seemed to be a false alarm. I took slow steps toward the house where Butch stayed. I still didn't see or hear anything. I figured the coast was clear. Halfway past the house, I heard a noise. It was like the sound that claws make when they hit the cement. I made a dead stop. I looked to my left and saw him standing on all fours. I stood in the driveway looking at him and between us was an open gate and about ten feet. Right away I noticed that Butch wasn't chained up. He looked at me as if to say, "Oh yea brother, It's time for me and you to *RUMBLE!*"

Butch took two small steps toward me. He was breathing heavily through his mouth like he had just finished running a mile. I stood there frozen, but I was not scared. I was just waiting for the right time to start running. On some nature program the narrator said that when confronting a predator in a situation like this one, never look into his eyes or he will attack. That's supposed to be a sign of aggression. I stood there looking at Butch's mouth. It had a lot of sharp teeth and the jaws looked strong enough to bite through bone. At the same time I was thinking that I had to get to school in a few minutes. I interrupted my thoughts and decided to just survive this encounter with Butch. I reviewed my options. I could just run toward the school. I thought no because he would just chase me down and kill me. Or I could just stand here until the owner got back. I thought no again because he might just become impatient and attack anyway. So we just stood there looking at each other. Then all of a sudden a car going eastbound turned the corner. Butch and I both looked at that Toyota. I looked as if to cry out for help; it was just interrupting Butch. The car turned the corner heading southbound at about 15 miles per hour.

Suddenly a brilliant idea popped into my head. I told myself to run across the street before the car passed and that way I would create a barrier between the dog and me, or if I was to get lucky, he wouldn't notice the car and might get run over. I waited for the right time. Butch turned his head back toward me and focused on my chest like a guided missile locks onto a target. The car's speed accelerated to 25 mph. I thought to myself I need to compensate for the car's acceleration and everything will be all right. I looked back at Butch and he started to lick his chops as if he was about to enjoy a nice big juicy T-bone steak. As the car moved into the right position, I thought to myself, "I hope this works because I don't want to end up as Butch's breakfast."

All of a sudden, the car reached the spot. I shot out of my frozen state like a cannon. I didn't look back because I knew that killer dog was in pursuit. I reached the middle of the street and heard screeching tires. I hoped the car hit the dog. When I cleared the Toyota's path, I looked back. The car stopped where I had anticipated. I snapped my head back to look for the curb, so I wouldn't trip over it. I put my foot on the curb and started to slow down enough to make a direction change. Then I heard a kurr-pluck. I didn't look back because I knew what it was. Butch had jumped on the hood of the Toyota Corolla. I planted my right foot and cut to my left. As I was accelerating, I felt like I was cutting through the wind. Upon reaching full speed, running down the block, Butch started barking at me from behind. It was as if he was saying, "Where do you think you're going, you little *PUNK*?" The school gate was one block to my right, around the corner. When I looked back he was closer than I thought. So I looked for a parked car to jump on top of. To my left there was a parked brown car. I didn't notice what kind of car because I wasn't paying attention. The car was slippery with the morning dew on it. I slipped a little as I jumped on the car, but I recovered fast. Then I stepped onto the roof of the car, looked back, and saw Butch; he had also jumped on the car right after me. He came in so fast that he slipped on the same spot I did. He jumped over the windshield, leaping for me, but I side-stepped to the right. He over shot and fell off the car. I decided right then to make my final approach to the school.

I jumped off the roof and started to approach the corner. I cut over some groomed grass that looked like a football field. I slipped on the grass dew. I didn't want to risk breaking any bones so I tucked and rolled with form. I rolled and rolled until I was on all fours facing the way I came.

Then I saw him. He was four feet away from me growling viciously like a mad dog gone wild with a thirst for blood. He just stood there. I thought this was it. I couldn't get up because he would strike. I didn't want to move because he might attack. So we stood there again, staring each other down. It was a stand off, like two animals waiting for the other to make the first move. At this moment, I started to get scared. I thought it was all over, and I had lived a decent life. I faced him and looked him in his eyes.

Then it happened. Something happened that I never could have fathomed in my eleven years of living on this earth. I remembered all those stories about dogs attacking kids and the myth of the bulldogs and how they bite and never let go. Butch stopped growling and looked into my eyes. Suddenly, the fear went away. I stared into the eyes of my "Grim Reaper." I thought I was going to be another bite victim. Running through my head was the thought that I was going to die on some stranger's lawn, on a school day, at this particular time, on this earth. And he walked toward me. I stood motionless waiting for the worst to happen. During all this, I was still staring him in his eyes. He stopped at about one and a half feet in front of me. Then he just walked away.

"That's it," I said out loud. "That's all you're going to do to me, bark, stare, and chase me a half a block?"

I was relieved he didn't tear me limb from limb. But at the same time I was mad because after all of the taunting, spitting, throwing rocks, and yelling obscene profanity at him, he didn't do anything to me. I got up and dusted myself off. I felt good all day because I stood up and stared death in his eyes and won.

Now, looking back I thank Butch because he brought out emotions I never felt before, and he taught me the most valuable lesson of all—to always stand up for myself, and I learned I can perform under pressure. Everyday after that I would walk by just to see Butch and throw him a few treats. He would bark at everybody else, but he was always happy to see me.

BUTCH

Questions

1.   Why was it important for the author to stand up to Butch?

2.   Using the voice of the author, what kind of person do you think he was?

3.   Discuss the vivid images in the story and how the author creates these images.

Beverly S. Hill (student)

THE TOBACCO MARKET

BEVERLY S. HILL was a student at Los Angeles City College when she wrote this essay. She is currently pursuing a career in film with the goal of becoming a writer/director.

Ooooo, I am SO excited!! I can't sleep. I wonder if I'll be able to sleep at all tonight, I'm too excited, I just can't sleep. Okay, I'll just lie here until I hear Granddaddy get up. Uuup, there I hear him going to the bathroom; I hear Bigmamma in the kitchen. Okay, I'm ready to go. It's still dark out I wonder what time it is, ummmm 3:00 a.m. Okay, I got my clothes all ready last night. Let me go to the bathroom, pee, brush my teeth, wash my face, put on my clothes, OKAY I'M READY TO GO! Bigmamma, I'm ready, are we ready to go? Okay, I'll go wait in the truck. We gonna have breakfast first? Okay, we'll stop on the way. Cool! The truck's all loaded with the tobacco, we're ready to go. Bigmamma and Granddaddy are coming out of the house now. Oh no, it's startin' to rain! Granddaddy has to put somethin' over the tobacco so it won't get wet, we're almost ready, Okay they're gettin' in the truck now. OKAY—WE'RE READY TO GO! YEAH! We're pullin' out onto the road and *HERE WE GO!* Granddaddy, where's the tobacco market? Oh yea, Alabama, you told me before. How long will it take to get there? About two hours, Okay. I'm hungry, we gonna get some breakfast? Okay, maybe I'll go to sleep for a while. But I can't sleep! I'm too excited. It's still rainin'. The windshield wipers are movin' back and forth and back and forth and back and forth. I can't sleep, too excited. Oooooo, my head's fallin' on Bigmamma's shoulder.

The truck stopped. Oh are we there yet? It's still dark and rainin'. I guess I fell asleep. Oh, here we are to get breakfast! What is this place, a diner or somethin'? I wonder if Granddaddy has stopped here before or if this is the place he always stops. It's still rainin'. Ooooh, THIS IS SO MUCH FUN! I think I'm gonna get some pancakes. I love pancakes. Yes ma'am, I'll have some pancakes please and some orange juice. Umm, these are good. We always have ham and eggs and grits at Bigmamma's house. I love pancakes.

Okay, we're back on the road again. What time is it? It's still dark. I guess we'll be there soon. It's still rainin'. The windshield wipers are movin' back and forth and back and forth and back and forth. Mmmmmm, my head's fallin' on Bigmamma's shoulder.

The truck stopped. Are we there yet? Oh, it's daylight. Yea we're here! Oh Yippee! I can't wait, this is so exciting! Granddaddy, where we goin' first? Okay, I'll stay with you and Bigmamma. We goin' to the horse auction or the tobacco market? Okay, we'll go to the tobacco market first. Wow! This place is so big! All these giant stacks of tobacco everywhere. Mmmmmm, it smells so good in here. There's some other kids over there. I wonder if they wanna play with me? That auctioneer sounds so funny. How can he talk so fast? That's so funny. Bigmamma, can I go play with those kids? Okay, okay! I won't get lost I promise.

Hi, you wanna play? What's your name? My name's Beverly. I'm here with my Bigma and Granddaddy. My Granddaddy grows tobacco and we live in Florida. Where do you live? You wanna climb on top of those stacks of tobacco over there? There's horses over there, you wanna go see 'em. Isn't this fun? We had to get up at 3:00 this morning!! We stopped on the way and got pancakes. I love pancakes. I think my Granddaddy is gonna buy a horse today too. I live in Jacksonville, Florida, but I'm visiting my Bigma and Granddaddy for the summer. They live in Dellwood, Florida. Have you ever been there? My Granddaddy raises tobacco in the summer and butchers hogs in the winter. Bigma has chickens and she has a garden. She makes the best homemade biscuits! Wanna play paper or stone? Well, I gotta go now. It was nice to meet ya.

Granddaddy are you gonna buy a horse today? Okay, we just gonna go to the auction? Oooo that sounds fun. How does that guy talk so fast? Can you do that? OH GRANDDADDY YOU CAN DO THAT TOO!!! That's so cool Granddaddy I didn't know you could auction like that. Oh that is SO cool! Where'd you learn to do that? Granddaddy you're so funny.

We have to go now? Oh no, I don't wanna go yet! Can't we stay a little longer, this is so much fun! Can't we stay and watch the horses some more, please! I know, it's gettin' dark. Okay, can we stop at that place on the way back and get some more pancakes? I love pancakes! All right, maybe next time. Did you sell all your tobacco? Oh, that's good. I'm glad. Well, okay, lets go back to the truck. I met some kids from Mississippi and Tennessee. Their names are Debbie and Sue. Okay, we're back on the road again. I am kinda tired, but I can't sleep this has been too exciting, I really had fun today. Oh no, It's startin' to rain again, the windshield wipers are movin' back and forth and back and forth and back and forth. Mmmmmm, my head's falling on my Bigmamma's shoulder.

THE TOBACCO MARKET

Questions

1. The author uses internal dialogue to capture the child's voice. Do you think internal dialogue is as compelling as external dialogue? Explain.

2. Why is the author so excited about this trip? What does the tobacco market represent to the author?

Sandra Cisneros

THE HOUSE ON MANGO STREET

SANDRA CISNEROS (b. 1954) was born in Chicago, Illinois, and was at one time a high school teacher. Ms. Cisneros has published several books (including poetry): *Woman Hollering Creek and Other Stories* (1992), *My Wicked Wicked Ways* (1987), poetry, and *Loose Woman* (1994) poetry. The following vignettes are excerpts from *The House on Mango Street* published in 1984.

The narrator, Esperanza Cordero, is determined not to let the neighborhood nor ethnicity define her and her life.

The House on Mango Street

We didn't always live on Mango Street. Before that we lived on Loomis on the third floor, and before that we lived on Keeler. Before Keeler it was Paulina, and before that I can't remember. But what I remember most is moving a lot. Each time it seemed there'd be one more of us. By the time we got to Mango Street we were six—Mama, Papa, Carlos, Kiki, my sister Nenny, and me.

The house on Mango Street is ours, and we don't have to pay rent to anybody, or share the yard with the people downstairs, or be careful not to make too much noise, and there isn't a landlord banging on the ceiling with a broom. But even so, it's not the house we'd thought we'd get.

We had to leave the flat on Loomis quick. The water pipes broke and the landlord wouldn't fix them because the house was too old. We had to leave fast. We were using the washroom next door and carrying water over in empty milk gallons. That's why Mama and Papa looked for a house, and that's why we moved into the house on Mango Street, far away, on the other side of town.

They always told us that one day we would move into a house, a real house that would be ours for always so we wouldn't have to move each year. And our house would have running water and pipes that worked. And inside it would have real stairs, not hallway stairs, but stairs inside like the houses on T.V. And we'd have a basement and at least three washrooms so when we took a bath we wouldn't have to tell everybody. Our house would be white with trees around it, a great big yard and grass growing without a fence. This was the house Papa talked about when he held a lottery ticket and this was the house Mama dreamed up in the stories she told us before we went to bed.

But the house on Mango Street is not the way they told it at all. It's small and red with tight steps in front and windows so small you'd think they were holding their breath. Bricks are crumbling in places, and the front door is so swollen you have to push hard to get in. There is no front yard, only four little elms the city planted by the curb. Out back is a small garage for the car we don't own yet and a small yard that looks smaller between the two buildings on either side. There are stairs in our house, but they're ordinary hallway stairs, and the house has only one washroom. Everybody has to share a bedroom—Mama and Papa, Carlos and Kiki, me and Nenny.

Once when we were living on Loomis, a nun from my school passed by and saw me playing out front. The laundromat downstairs had been boarded up because it had been robbed two days before and the owner had painted on the wood YES WE'RE OPEN so as not to lose business.

Where do you live? she asked.

There, I said pointing up to the third floor.

You live *there*?

There. I had to look to where she pointed—the third floor, the paint peeling, wooden bars Papa had nailed on the windows so we wouldn't fall out. You live *there*? The way she said it made me feel like nothing. *There.* I lived *there.* I nodded.

I knew then I had to have a house. A real house. One I could point to. But this isn't it. The house on Mango Street isn't it. For the time being, Mama says. Temporary, says Papa. But I know how those things go.

Hairs

Everybody in our family had different hair. My Papa's hair is like a broom, all up in the air. And me, my hair is lazy. It never obeys barrettes or bands. Carlos' hair is thick and straight. He doesn't need to comb it. Nenny's hair is slippery—slides out of your hand. And Kiki, who is the youngest, has hair like fur.

But my mother's hair, my mother's hair, like little rosettes, like little candy circles all curly and pretty because she pinned it in pincurls all day, sweet to put your nose into when she is holding you, holding you and you feel safe, is the warm smell of bread before you bake it, is the smell when she makes room for you on her side of the bed still warm with her skin, and you sleep near her, the rain outside falling and Papa snoring. The snoring, the rain, and Mama's hair that smells like bread.

Boys & Girls

The boys and the girls live in separate worlds. The boys in their universe and we in ours. My brothers for example. They've got plenty to say to me and Nenny inside the house. But outside they can't be seen talking to girls. Carlos and Kiki are each other's best friend . . . not ours.

Nenny is too young to be my friend. She's just my sister and that was not my fault. You don't pick your sisters, you just get them and sometimes they come like Nenny.

She can't play with those Vargas kids or she'll turn out just like them. And since she comes right after me, she is my responsibility.

Someday I will have a best friend all my own. One I can tell my secrets to. One who will understand my jokes without my having to explain them. Until then I am a red balloon, a balloon tied to an anchor.

My Name

In English my name means hope. In Spanish it means too many letters. It means sadness, it means waiting. It is like the number nine. A muddy color. It is the Mexican records my father plays on Sunday mornings when he is shaving, songs like sobbing.

It was my great-grandmother's name and now it is mine. She was a horse woman too, born like me in the Chinese year of the horse—which is supposed to be bad luck if you're born female—but I think this is a Chinese lie because the Chinese, like the Mexicans, don't like their women strong.

My great-grandmother, I would've like to have known her, a wild horse of a woman, so wild she wouldn't marry. Until my great-grandfather threw a sack over her head and carried her off. Just like that, as if she were a fancy chandelier. That's the way he did it.

And the story goes she never forgave him. She looked out the window her whole life, the way so many women sit their sadness on an elbow. I wonder if she made the best with what she got or was she sorry because she couldn't be all the things she wanted to be. Esperanza. I have inherited her name, but I don't want to inherit her place by the window.

At school they say my name funny as if the syllables were made out of tin and hurt the roof of your mouth. But in Spanish my name is made out of a softer something, like silver, not quite as thick as sister's name—Magdalena—which is uglier than mine. Magdalena who at least can come home and become Nenny. But I am always Esperanza.

I would like to baptize myself under a new name, a name more like the real me, the one nobody sees. Esperanza as Lisandra or Maritza or Zeze the X. Yes. Something like Zeze the X will do.

Cathy
Queen of Cats

She says, I am the great great grand cousin of the queen of France. She lives upstairs, over there, next door to Joe the baby grabber. Keep away from him, she says. He is full of danger. Benny and Blanca own the corner store. They're okay except don't lean on the candy counter. Two girls raggedy as rats live across the street. You don't want to know them. Edna is the lady who owns the building next to you. She used to own a building big as a whale, but her brother sold it. Their mother said no, no, don't ever sell it. I won't. And then she closed her eyes and he sold it. Alicia is stuck-up ever since she went to college. She used to like me but now she doesn't.

Cathy who is queen of cats had cats and cats and cats. Baby cats, big cats, skinny cats, sick cats. Cats asleep like little donuts. Cats on top of the refrigerator. Cats taking a walk on the dinner table. Her house is like cat heaven.

You want a friend, she says. Okay, I'll be your friend. But only till next Tuesday. That's when we move away. Got to. Then as if she forgot I just moved in, she says the neighborhood is getting bad.

Cathy's father will have to fly to France one day and find her great great distant grand cousin on her father's side and inherit the family house. How do I know this is so? She told me so. In the meantime they'll just have to move a little farther north from Mango Street, a little farther away every time people like us keep moving in.

Our Good Day

If you give me five dollars I will be your friend forever. That's what the little one tells me.

Five dollars is cheap since I don't have any friends except Cathy who is only my friend till Tuesday.

Five dollars, five dollars.

She is trying to get somebody to chip in so they can buy a bicycle from this kid named Tito. They already have ten dollars and all they need is five more.

Only five dollars, she says.

Don't talk to them, says Cathy. Can't you see they smell like a broom.

But I like them. Their clothes are crooked and old. They are wearing shiny Sunday shoes without socks. It makes their bald ankles all red, but I like them. Especially the big one who laughs with all her teeth. I like her even though she lets the little one do all the talking.

Five dollars, the little one says, only five.

Cathy is tugging my arm and I know whatever I do next will make her mad forever.

Wait a minute, I say, and run inside to get the five dollars. I have three dollars saved and I take two of Nenny's. She's not home, but I'm sure she'll be glad when she finds out we own a bike. When I get back, Cathy is gone like I knew she would be, but I don't care. I have two new friends and a bike too.

My name is Lucy, the big one says. This here is Rachel my sister.

I'm her sister, says Rachel. Who are you?

And I wish my name was Cassandra or Alexis or Maritza—anything but Esperanza—but when I tell them my name they don't laugh.

We come from Texas, Lucy says and grins. Her was born here, but me I'm Texas.

You mean *she*, I say

No, I'm from Texas, and doesn't get it.

This bike is three ways ours, says Rachel who is thinking ahead already. Mine today, Lucy's tomorrow and yours day after.

But everybody wants to ride it today because the bike is new, so we decide to take turns *after* tomorrow. Today it belongs to all of us.

I don't tell them about Nenny just yet. It's too complicated. Especially since Rachel almost put out Lucy's eye about who was going to get to ride it first. But finally we agree to ride it together. Why not?

Because Lucy has long legs she pedals. I sit on the back seat and Rachel is skinny enough to get up on the handlebars which makes the bike all wobbly as if the wheels are spaghetti, but after a bit you get used to it.

We ride fast and faster. Past my house, sad and red and crumbly in places, past Mr. Benny's grocery on the corner, and down the avenue, which is dangerous. Laundromat, junk store, drugstore, windows and cars and more cars, and around the block back to Mango.

People on the bus wave. A very fat lady crossing the street says, You sure got quite a load there.

Rachel shouts, You got quite a load there too. She is very sassy.

Down, down Mango Street we go. Rachel, Lucy, me. Our new bicycle. Laughing the crooked ride back.

Laughter

Nenny and I don't look like sisters . . . not right away. Not the way you can tell with Rachel and Lucy who have the same fat popsicle lips like everybody else in their family. But me and Nenny, we are more alike than you would know. Our laughter for example. Not the shy ice cream bells giggle of Rachel and Lucy's family, but all of a sudden and surprised like a pile of dishes breaking. And other things I can't explain.

One day we were passing a house that looked, in my mind, like houses I had seen in Mexico. I don't know why. There was nothing about the house that looked exactly like the houses I remembered. I'm not even sure why I thought it, but it seemed to feel right.

Look at that house, I said, it looks like Mexico.

Rachel and Lucy look at me like I'm crazy, but before they can let out a laugh, Nenny says: Yes, that's Mexico all right. That's what I was thinking exactly.

Alicia & I
Talking
on
Edna's Steps

I like Alicia because once she gave me a little leather purse with the word GUADALAJARA stitched on it, which is home for Alicia, and one day she will

147

go back there. But today she is listening to my sadness because I don't have a house.

You live right here, 4006 Mango, Alicia says, and points to the house I am ashamed of.

No, this isn't my house I say and shake my head as if shaking could undo the year I've lived here. I don't belong. I don't ever want to come from here. You have a home, Alicia, and one day you'll go there, to a town you remember, but me I never had a house, not even a photograph . . . only one I dream of.

No, Alicia says. Like it or not you are Mango Street, and one day you'll come back too.

Not me. Not until somebody makes it better.

Who's going to do it? The mayor?

And the thought of the mayor coming to Mango Street makes me laugh out loud.

Who's going to do it? Not the mayor.

A
House
of
My Own

Not a flat. Not an apartment in back. Not a man's house. Not a daddy's. A house all my own. With my porch and my pillow, my pretty purple petunias. My books and my stories. My two shoes waiting beside the bed. Nobody to shake a stick at. Nobody's garbage to pick up after.

Only a house quiet as snow, a space for myself to go, clean as paper before the poem.

Mango
Says
Goodbye
Sometimes

I like to tell stories. I tell them inside my head. I tell them after the mailman says, Here's your mail. Here's your mail he said.

I make a story for my life, for each step my brown shoe takes. I say, "And so she trudged up the wooden stairs, her sad brown shoes taking her to the house she never liked."

I like to tell stories. I am going to tell you a story about a girl who didn't want to belong.

We didn't always live on Mango Street. Before that we lived on Loomis on the third floor, and before that we lived on Keeler. Before Keeler it was Paulina, but what I remember most is Mango Street, sad red house, the house I belong but do not belong to.

I put it down on paper and then the ghost does not ache so much. I write it down and Mango says goodbye sometimes. She does not hold me with both arms. She sets me free.

One day I will pack my bags of books and paper. One day I will say goodbye to Mango. I am too strong for her to keep me here forever. One day I will go away.

Friends and neighbors will say, What happened to that Esperanza? Where did she go with all those books and paper? Why did she march so far away?

They will not know I have gone away to come back. For the ones I left behind. For the ones who cannot out.

THE HOUSE ON MANGO STREET

Facts

1. The narrator moved several times. Why did she move so many times? Why was the move to Mango Street important?

2. Describe the physical characteristics of the house on Mango Street. Why didn't the narrator like the house?

3. What does the narrator's mother's hair symbolize?

4. Why doesn't Esperanza care what Cathy thinks?

Strategies

1. The author created short vignettes to tell Esperanza's story. Is this strategy effective? Why or why not?

2. In the vignette "Hair," the author starts the piece with short simple sentences; then, she creates one long repetitive sentence. Discuss the literary strategies of short sentences and repetition and how both enhance the child's voice.

3. Discuss the surface and underlying meanings of *The House on Mango Street*.

Issues

1. Discuss the meaning of "I have inherited her name, but I don't want to inherit her place by the window." Figuratively and literally, do women today still sit by the window?

2. In "Cathy, Queen of Cats," Cathy is moving out of the neighborhood. Discuss the reasons one nationality/ethnic group leaves a neighborhood when another moves in.

4. Why is the narrator ashamed of her house? What else is she ashamed of?

Writing Assignments

1. When we are children, there are everyday occurrences that make us feel safe and loved. Write an essay, using the child's voice, with safety and love as the focus. Use "Hair" as an example.

2. Write an essay using this literary style about your street and its surroundings.

Fannie Flagg

DAISY FAY AND THE MIRACLE MAN

FANNIE FLAGG (b. 1941) was born in Birmingham, Alabama as Patricia Neal and attended the University of Alabama. Ms. Flagg has had a varied career in television, theater and film as an actress, comedienne, producer, and writer. Her novels include *Fried Green Tomatoes at the Whistle Stop Cafe* (1987), *Daisy Fay and the Miracle Man* (1992), and her most recent book was published in 1998, *Welcome to the World Baby Girl!* The following story is an excerpt from *Daisy Fay and the Miracle Man.*

In her journal, a young girl, Daisy Fay Harper, describes the foibles of her mother and father and how their idiosyncrasies impact her life.

1952

April 1, 1952

Hello there . . . my name is Daisy Fay Harper and I was eleven years old yesterday. My Grandmother Pettibone won the jackpot at the VFW bingo game and bought me a typewriter for my birthday. She wants me to practice typing so when I grow up, I can be a secretary, but my cat, Felix, who is pregnant, threw up on it and ruined it, which is OK with me. I don't know what is the matter with Grandma. I have told her a hundred times I want to be a tree surgeon or a blacksmith.

I got a Red Ryder BB gun from Daddy and some Jantzen mix-and-match outfits Momma bought me at the Smart and Sassy Shop. Ugh! Grandma Harper sent me a pair of brown and white saddle shoes—Momma won't let me wear loafers, she says they will ruin my feet—and a blue cellophane windmill on a stick I am way too old for.

Momma took me downtown to see a movie called *His Kind of Woman* with Robert Mitchum and Jane Russell, billed as the hottest pair on the screen. I wanted to see *Pals of the Golden West* with Roy Rogers and Dale Evans, where Roy patrols the border for cattle-smuggling bandits. But Momma is mad at

Daddy for giving me a BB gun so I didn't push it. I'm not doing much except sitting around waiting for the sixth grade. My friend Peggy Box who is thirteen won't play with me anymore. All she wants to do is listen to Johnnie Ray sing "The Little White Cloud That Cried."

I am an only child. Momma didn't even know she was going to have a baby. Daddy was in bed with the flu, and when the doctor came to see Daddy, Momma said all of a sudden a big lump came up on her right side. She said, "Doctor look at this!" He told Daddy to get out of bed and for Momma to get in it. He said that lump was a baby, maybe even twins. Boy, was Momma surprised. But it wasn't twins, it was only me. Momma was in labor for a long time and Daddy got mad about it and choked the doctor. When I was being born, I kicked Momma so hard that now she can't have any more children. I don't remember kicking her at all. It wasn't my fault I was so fat and if Daddy hadn't choked the doctor and made him nervous, I would have been born better. Whenever she tells anybody the story about having me, her labor gets longer and longer. Daddy says I would have to have been a three-year-old child with hair and teeth and everything, to hear Momma tell it.

I was born in Jackson, Mississippi, and as far as me being a girl it was just fine because my daddy wanted a little girl. He said he knew I'd be a girl and he wrote a poem about me that was published in the newspaper in the Letters to the Editor section before I ever got here.

> We are expecting a blessed event in just a week or two
> And if my wife's cravings are to be a clue
> Then our daughter is going to be a little pig . . . it's true
> Because all her mother craves night and day is barbecue

I'm glad Daddy wanted a girl. Most men want boys. Daddy never wanted any old stinky boy who might grow up to have a big neck and play football. He feels those kind of people are dangerous. Baseball is our game. Jim Piersall is our favorite player. He screams and hollers and causes trouble and has a true understanding of the game.

Daddy says that everybody in history has a twin and that he and Mr. Harry Truman could be equals in history. Daddy and Mr. Truman both wear glasses, have a daughter, and are Democrats. I think that's why when it looked as though Thomas Dewey would win the election, Daddy jumped in the Pearl River and tried to drown himself. It took four of his friends to pull him out, one a member of the Elks Club.

Momma said he just did it to show off, besides, he had had eighteen Pabst Blue Ribbon beers. Momma says he isn't anything like Harry Truman at all. Mr.

Truman's little girl is named Margaret. I got stuck with Daisy Fay. Most people call me Little Fay because they call my Mother Big Fay, although I don't know why, she isn't all that big. Momma wanted to name me Mignon after her sister, but Daddy pitched a fit and said he didn't want his only daughter named after a steak. He was making such a commotion, and the woman with the birth certificate was tired of waiting, so Grandma Pettibone settled the whole thing by naming me Daisy, just because there happened to be a vase of daisies in the room. I sure would love to know who sent those rotten daisies anyway. Daddy and I hate that name because it sounds country and we are not country at all. Jackson is a big city and we live in an apartment. I prefer the name Dale or Olive, not after Olive Oyl but after the actress sister of Joan Fontaine, Olivia de Havilland.

Momma and Daddy are fighting all the time now. An Army Air Force buddy of Daddy's named Jimmy Snow called and told him that if he could get $500 Daddy could buy a half interest in a malt shop in Shell Beach, Mississippi, and make a fortune. The malt shop is right on a beach that looks just like Florida.

Jimmy won a half interest in the malt shop in a poker game and needs $500 to get the other half. He's a crop duster, so Daddy could run the whole thing and he would be a silent partner. Daddy has been crazy trying to get the money. He made Momma mad because he wanted to sell her diamond rings. She said they were not worth $500 and how dare he try to take the rings off her fingers! Besides, she wasn't going anywhere with him, him drinking so much. So, he invented a practical joke he was sure he could sell for $500. A friend of his has a filling station with an outhouse where he tried out his invention. He put a speaker under the outhouse and connected it to a microphone in the filling station. He made the mistake of trying it out on Momma. He waited until she went in and had time to sit down, then he disguised his voice and said, "Could you move over, lady, we're working down here!" Momma, who's very modest and says Daddy has never seen her fully undressed, screamed and ran out the door and cried for five hours. She said it was the most disgusting thing that ever happened to her.

This joke on Momma caused her to leave him and go visit her sister in Virginia to think about a divorce, something she does all the time. I had to go with her. The child always goes with the mother. My aunt has so many children that it made Momma nervous at dinnertime, so we came home.

I hope Daddy gets the money soon. If we move to Shell Beach, I can have a pony and go swimming every day. Daddy is busy working on his new invention. He has an English red worm bed in the backyard and as soon as they grow, he is going to freeze them and sell them all over the country.

A lot of people think Daddy is peculiar, including the members of his immediate family, but not me. His name is William Harper, Jr. Momma says that he got this idea to get out of Jackson when he was in the Army and learned to like Yankees. He still hates hunters, though. Whenever he reads in the paper where one of them shoots another, he laughs and chalks one up for our side. He loves all animals, cats in particular. He swears all dictators hate cats because they can't dominate them. Hitler would foam at the mouth at the sight of one, and I guess my daddy knows because he fought him in the war.

He was drafted in the Army Air Corps when I was only two years old. He cost them a lot of money because he is so skinny they had to make him special uniforms and special goggles with his own prescription so he could see.

But as Daddy says, "When you're at war, they'll take anything." Daddy didn't get out of the United States, but he did break his toe when he hit the ground before his parachute opened in Louisiana. The plane had already landed in the swamp when he jumped, so he could have just stayed in the plane, but Daddy lost his glasses and didn't see it had landed. That's where he met Jimmy Snow. Jimmy was a pilot and was always yelling bail out over the headset as a joke.

After Daddy left Louisiana, he was stationed in California and got Margaret O'Brien to sign the back of one of my pictures. He said she has false teeth just like Grandma. He also said that Red Skelton was a wonderful guy and told the boys dirty jokes to cheer them up. All of my Hollywood true-life stories come as a result of Daddy having been there during the war. Clark Gable is the best-looking man Daddy has ever seen, even though his mustache is uneven. Also, did you know that Dorothy Lamour has such ugly feet that they gave her rubber feet to wear every time she played a native? Momma says that's a lie, but I've never seen a picture of her with her shoes off unless she is in a movie. I wish he had met Audie Murphy, but he didn't. Daddy tells me when I grow up I am going to look just like Celeste Holm.

Daddy believes that if Momma had moved to Hollywood, California, after the war just like he had wanted to, we would be rich and I would probably be a star by now. I would love to meet Bomba the Jungle Boy and Judy Canova. But Momma wouldn't leave Jackson for anything.

Daddy hated being a soldier and was busted six times. Whenever he got a furlough, he wouldn't go back until the MPs came for him. One time when I was in the bathroom, they were banging on the door hollering for Daddy. Momma wanted me to hurry up and finish so I could say good-bye, but all that knocking made me nervous and Momma believes that is the reason I have to have so many enemas now. Momma blames the Military Police for ruining what had been a very successful toilet training period.

While Daddy was in the war, Momma and I lived in a big white house with my Grandmother and Grandfather Pettibone. We lived on one side and they lived on the other. Grandpa was sure funny. He stayed up all night once and planted a Victory garden that had forty-seven whiskey bottles lined up in a row. He loved whiskey and could put his leg over his head and do cartwheels. Grandma met him when she was in college. She was in a receiving line and when Granddaddy stopped in front of her, she laughed in his face, so they got married and moved to Virginia. He was very rich, and Grandma brought all her sisters but one to Virginia and married them off to rich men. But then Grandpa got to drinking too much and his family disowned him, and they had to move back to Jackson. Boy, was Grandma furious having to leave her rich sisters.

Grandpa became a pest control exterminator and raised chickens on the side. He was crazy about poultry of any kind and he used to play checkers on the kitchen table with this old rooster he had. Grandma says they weren't really playing checkers, but I think they were.

I had a good time living with Grandma and Grandpa, all except for the ducks and chickens in the backyard that used to peck my toes. They thought my toes were corn. Stupid things. I wasn't too crazy about Grandma wringing those chickens' necks either . . . one time one of them without a head chased me all over the backyard. It scared me so bad that I ran right through the screen door and ruined it.

Grandpa liked me a lot. He was always sneaking over to Momma's side of the back porch and stealing me out of my baby bed and carrying me down to the Social Grill and sitting me up on the bar. Once he took me to see a friend of his that was in jail. It made Momma and Grandma mad. They said I was too young to be visiting jails.

When Daddy came home from the Army for good, he brought me a rabbit fur coat from Hollywood and some Chiclets chewing gum and twenty Hershey bars. By then he had been busted down to private again, but he had a Good Conduct Medal. Momma says he must have bought it.

We didn't live with Grandma and Granddaddy too long, though. They didn't like Daddy and thought he was a little worm. Anyway, that's what Grandma called him. When Grandpa would get drunk, he would put chickens in Daddy's room. He also sent Momma a telegram that said there was a big rat living on the other side of the house. Then one night he got his pest control equipment and shot rat poison through our door, so we had to move. Right after that Grandpa went off to the Social Grill to have a drink and never came back. Somebody said they saw him driving a cab in Tupelo, Mississippi, but we don't know where he is. He left his chickens and everything. I sure do miss him. I have to go now. Felix is having kittens in the back of the refrigerator and Momma is having a fit. . . .

April 2, 1952

Guess what? I saw the kittens being born . . . I'm never going to have children. No wonder Momma was mad at me for weighing nine pounds.

I've told you a lot about my daddy, but the thing that makes him really special is that he is a motion picture operator and so is his daddy. I come from a show business family; even my mother once was a movie cashier. She was working in the theater because it was the Depression and because her daddy didn't worry about her if he could see her sitting in her glass cage.

Daddy running the movies makes me special. Some people call it cocky, but Daddy admires that in a person and told me that I don't have to say "Yes, sir" and "Yes, ma'am." He doesn't want his daughter sounding like a servant. I never do say it either, unless I am trying to be real sincere . . . or Momma is around.

Right after the Army, Daddy worked at the Woodlawn Theater. I spent every Saturday and Sunday in the projection booth in the balcony where colored people used to sit before they got smart and opened up their own movie houses. After that, white people wouldn't sit up there, which suited me fine because I had the whole balcony to myself. The theater had red seats and big green lights that looked like lilies going up the sides of the wall. I could hang over the rail and drop things on people I didn't like.

Momma says sitting in that balcony, looking down on people, has given me a superiority complex. Maybe so, but Daddy didn't want me downstairs where some child molester might sit down by me and then Daddy would have to kill him. However, I have my own instructions as far as that nonsense is concerned; if anybody gets funny with me, I am supposed to stand up and scream out loud, "This is a molester. Arrest him." Daddy told me that if everybody did that, there would be very few molesters.

He also gave me other useful information to protect me in the real world. If anyone hits me, I'm not to hit them back. I wait until their back is turned, then hit them in the head with a brick. I have a beautiful aristocratic nose and Daddy doesn't want it hurt. He himself has been saved from many a severe beating by bigger men by threatening to stab them in their sleep. The only bad time I ever had sitting in that balcony was while I was watching the movie *Mighty Joe Young* with Terry Moore. I was under the seat during the part of the picture where poor Mighty Joe Young was being hurt—I couldn't stand him being so unhappy. Some people see fit to stick their old gum under their seat. Daddy had to cut a lot of my hair off that night. I say that people should put their gum on the side of the popcorn box or else in a candy wrapper. Momma says I shouldn't sit under any more seats.

The Woodlawn Theater showed a lot of cheap movies. As I have gotten older, I am surprised to find out that Patricia Medina is not the star I thought she was. However, I still say that Mr. Goodbars and Raisinets are your best buy. Zeros, Zagnuts and Butterfingers are good, but a Bit-O-Honey lasts longer. I got a JuJu stuck in my ear once, so I stay away from them. Momma blames my cavities on eating all that candy, but I can pop gum better than anybody.

The Woodlawn Theater ran weekly serials: Buster Crabbe, the Green Hornet and Jungle Jim. My favorite is Nyoka, the Jungle Girl, who I like even better than Jungle Jim. Who cares about Johnny Weissmuller without Boy and Jane? Some people have no business sense. Nyoka could swing through the jungle faster than Tarzan any day.

Daddy would show me next week's serial at night when the theater closed. I was always the first to know that Nyoka hadn't been killed. I swear I never told, not once.

Nyoka has a lot to do with how I look in person. Daddy spent a whole day making me a swing rope on a tree in the backyard, but unfortunately he made an error in dynamics, as he put it. I grabbed ahold of the rope and he ran me back as far as he could and let go and it swung me right into the tree and now my right front tooth is chipped. Daddy thinks it makes me look different. Momma thinks it is awful.

Momma has a theory that Daddy has tried to kill me on several occasions. Once when I fell asleep in the living room, Daddy cracked my head carrying me into the bedroom. He also knocked me off the pier into the Pearl River when I was three and didn't come after me for a long time because he felt that young children, like young animals, could swim if they were scared enough. But I wasn't scared enough. You should have seen the trash I saw on the bottom of that river when I was waiting for him to come and get me . . . tin cans, an old RoiTan cigar box and an old Firestone tire. The Pearl River attracts a lower class of people if you ask me.

Then there was the time when he picked up a two-by-four on the side of the road and put it in the front seat by me and stuck it out the window. He told me to hold it, which I did, but when the wind hit the board, it turned around and hit me in the head and knocked me out. Another time, when a friend of Daddy's bought a brand new Buick, Daddy pressed the push-button window up on my neck. But that time I think it was just a matter of him not being familiar with the equipment.

The main thing Momma bases her theory on is once Daddy, who is very artistic, wanted to make a life mask of my face. He put plaster of paris on me but forgot the breathing holes. On top of that he also forgot to put Vaseline on my face. He had to crack the plaster off with a hammer. Momma didn't speak to him for a week on that one. I myself was sorry that it didn't turn out.

She also says he is going to ruin my nervous system because of the time he sneaked up on me when I was listening to *Inner Sanctum* on the radio. Just as the squeaking door opened, he grabbed me and yelled, "Got ya," real loud, which caused me to faint. She also didn't like him telling me Santa Claus had been killed in a bus accident and making me throw up.

The Pettibones have very delicate nervous systems. That's true. Momma is nervous all the time. She's worn a hole in the floor on the passenger's side of Daddy's car from putting on the brakes. Momma always looks like she is on the verge of a hissy fit, but that's mainly because when she was eighteen, she stuck her head in a gas oven looking at some biscuits and blew her eyebrows off. So she paints them on like little half-moons. People love to talk to her because she always looks interested, even if she isn't.

If Daddy is dangerous to my health, Momma's not much better. She nearly got us both killed in the street last winter. Momma had read the movie ad saying, "Every woman will want to see Joan Crawford as the woman who loves Johnny Guitar," and I guess she did. I wanted to see *Francis, the Talking Mule*, so I wasn't in a good mood anyway. When Momma takes me downtown, it is an all-day ordeal. She was crazy about mother-and-daughter dresses at the time and she made me wear some ratty dress I hated. Whenever we go downtown, she starts her window shopping. Look, look, look! It drives me crazy.

We always go to Morrison's Cafeteria to eat. That's OK because I can get three Jell-Os instead of vegetables. After the meal, Momma sits and smokes and drinks coffee. I have to watch her like a hawk. My job is getting up and pouring her more coffee. That goes on for hours. Then I have to pull her chair out and help her on with her coat. She is big on children having manners. This night I sat through eight cups of coffee and Joan Crawford, so to make me feel better she said I could pull the cord on the streetcar on the way home.

It wasn't my fault that there was a country woman on the streetcar that was crazy and talking into a paper sack. I was busy looking at her and missed our stop. Momma was mad because it was so cold and we had to walk two blocks back. She had on a big silver fox fur coat and she had her alligator purse, with the alligator head on it.

It was so dark we had to walk in the middle of the street. We'd gone about a block when she saw a car coming a mile away. She got hysterical and started running and screaming for me to get out of the street and jump up on the curb. I just stood there and watched her have a fit. She ran over to the side of the road and jumped up on the curb, but there wasn't even a curb on that side, just an embankment. She hit the side of it so hard that her high heels stuck in the mud and she bounced back out into the middle of the street. When she landed, her coat flew over her head and she skidded with her purse out in front of her.

By this time the car had come around the corner, and when its lights hit the eyes on her alligator purse, the man in the car ran off the side of the road. I hadn't moved because it was so interesting to see Momma having a running fit like that, and the man didn't get out for a long time. All he saw was an alligator head on a fur body in the middle of the winter in Jackson, Mississippi.

Finally, I went over and told him that it was only a woman in a coat that had jumped on the side of a hill. We helped her up, and I got her high heels out of the mud. Boy, was she mad. She wasn't hurt much, just skinned her knees and ruined her stockings and lost an earring.

Walking behind her the rest of the way home, I started to laugh and almost choked myself to death trying not to because I knew for sure she would kill me. I tried to pretend I was coughing. My face turned beet red and tears were streaming down my face. It's funny how when your life is in danger, you can't stop laughing, but when Momma turned around to beat me to death or worse, I was saved. She started to laugh. Then we both laughed so hard we had to sit down in the street and I ruined my mother-daughter dress.

But I'm in a lot of trouble with her now for a play I wrote. I thought it was real good. We put it on at school. It was called *The Devil-May-Care Girls*. Two beautiful career girls live in New York and wear evening gowns all the time. When the maid tells them Harry Truman is coming to dinner, they invite all their friends and hire a band and everything. It turns out that Mr. Truman is an insurance man with the same name. Ha-ha, boy, were they surprised!

I was the star, and my best friend, Jennifer May, was the other girl. Sara Jane Brady was the maid. I only cast her because she was so tall. She almost ruined the play by reading all of her lines right out of a notebook. Other than that, it went very well. We did it for the whole school. Momma is mad because I had the girls drink twenty-seven gin martinis.

I try hard to please her, but I think she is disappointed in me. Every time she gets mad at me she says I'm just like my daddy. I made her cry last Easter. She had bought me a pretty Easter outfit with a pink straw hat, white patent pumps and purse to match, but I got a black eye the day before Easter when Bill Shasa called my daddy a drunk. I tried to hit him in the back of the head with a brick, but I missed. I hate a boy who will hit a girl, don't you? We spoiled his Easter, too, though. Daddy gave me some Ex-Lax in a candy wrapper and Bill ate the whole thing.

Momma had her heart set on me playing the harp after someone once said I looked like a little angel. There wasn't anybody in Jackson who could teach harp music, so she settled on tap dancing. The Neva Jean School of Tap and Ballet promised to have your child on their toes in thirty days. The school was on top of the Whatley Drugstore, where they make the best banana splits in the whole world. I was a petal in the recital called "Springtime in Greentime" with a special number by the Gainer Triplets, who played a three-leaf clover. Skooter Olgerson was cast as a weed, but his momma didn't want him playing a weed and she yanked him out of the show. I didn't do too good in the recital. I was not in step but once.

Momma let me quit when I ruined all her hardwood floors practicing my shuffleball chain. Besides, Neva Jean said I was holding the whole class back. The only fun I ever had in that dance class was the day when Buster Sessions showed up in tap shoes that were too big for him. He is a real sissy and when his momma came to see him in the class, he got to tapping so fast, showing off, that one of his shoes flew off and hit the piano player, Mrs. Vella Fussel, in the back. Buster's mother wasn't even looking. She was sitting there in a fold-up chair, chewing a whole pack of Juicy Fruit gum and reading *Screen Secrets*.

Daddy and I bought a record of Mario Lanza singing "Because of You," as a surprise, and I learned the whole thing was for Momma's birthday. When she had some of her girlfriends over, Daddy put me on one of his jackets and a tie and painted a mustache on my face. He announced me and I came in the room and sang "Because of You" as loud as I could. Momma suggested maybe I should learn one of Patti Page's hits.

She was expecting a Mixmaster for her birthday, but Daddy got her a pair of expensive toenail clippers instead. I got her some Coty toilet water with sachet powder and two giant tubes of Colgate toothpaste and some Palmolive shaving cream for her legs. She tried to pretend she liked what I got her, but I know she didn't. I'm too young to buy a Mixmaster and I don't even know where they sell them.

What I can't figure out is, Felix is a calico cat and her kittens are black and white and real ugly.

April 12, 1952

Well, you are not going to believe what happened. Daddy froze five cartons of English red worms and when we thawed them out, they were all dead as door nails! Nobody is going to buy dead English red worms. Rats! The only other way Daddy could get that $500 is to ask his daddy to loan it to him, but

Grandfather Harper won't do it because he is mad at Daddy and is never going to speak to him again as long as he lives.

My granddaddy, Blondie Harper, is pretty well known around Jackson. When they used to have stage shows here, he ran the spotlight at the Pantages Theater. He was mean and if he didn't like someone's act, he would holler at them and turn the spotlight off. People used to come to the theater just to hear what he would yell at the Yankee comedians.

When Granddaddy first started the stagehands' union in Mississippi, he put stink bombs in theaters where they didn't want the unions, and that is why he is president of the stagehands' union to this day.

He never liked my daddy from the beginning. He thought Daddy was too little and skinny, and worse, he wore glasses and did bird imitations. Grandpa thinks he is a sissy, which he isn't.

Grandpa bought me a blue suede cowgirl outfit with white leather trim and boots to match, so he's all right in my book, but I feel sorry for Daddy. Grandpa calls Daddy a bad husband and father and all kinds of ugly things just because he happened to see him talking to a woman at Dr. Gus's Beer Joint. Daddy explained that he was simply talking union business. Grandpa said there weren't any women in the union. Daddy said that was exactly what he had been talking about at the time. If things weren't bad enough already, last week he had to go and put a whiz bomb in Grandpa's car.

I'll miss not seeing my Grandpa and Grandma Harper. I used to love to go see Momma Harper, because she and Aunt Helen would let me open their Miller High Life beers for them and have a sip.

My Aunt Helen is real pretty. As a little girl, she used to sleep with her arms folded like an angel, so if she died in the middle of the night, she would look beautiful. She doesn't like Daddy, either, because he put her boyfriend's picture on the back of the toilet seat once.

Momma still doesn't want to move to Shell Beach, but Daddy says that since nobody in her family or his family is speaking to him, we wouldn't be all that happy in Jackson anyway.

The only good thing that happened was that last night my dog, named Lassie, ate Momma's roast beef right off the table and we had to go out for supper so I got to see my Aunt Bess, who runs the Irondale Cafe´ across town. She's about sixty-five years old and has never been married. She told me that they may put "Miss" on her tombstone, but that she hasn't missed a thing.

She is Grandma Pettibone's sister. Her cafe´ is great. It is right by the railroad tracks and most of her customers are railroad men. The food is good, too. She has five colored ladies that work for her and they cook biscuits, turnip greens, and pork chops. Aunt Bess even has possum listed on her menu. Momma said it was only a joke or she hoped it was.

When Aunt Bess was twenty, her daddy looked at her and knew she was never going to get married like her other sisters, so he gave her enough money to start a business. She opened a barbershop, but sold that. Then she and her friend Sue Lovells started the Irondale Café. It is very successful.

All of the Pettibones are Methodist and hit the church every time the doors open. They get upset with Aunt Bess because she won't go with them. She loves to fish and one time when my grandmother was having one of her bingo parties at home, Aunt Bess, who was drinking, drove up to her house with a string of dead trout hanging out the side of the car. George, the colored man that she takes with her, was sitting right beside her in the front seat.

Aunt Bess is getting rich because all the old railroad men die and leave her their money. Most of them are bachelors and love Aunt Bess. But she gives it all away.

The café has gunshot holes all over the floor and ceiling from when Aunt Bess plays poker with the railroad men after she closes. They get to drinking and pretty soon there's a fight. Aunt Bess watches until she thinks it has gone on long enough, then she shoots off her gun.

Aunt Bess likes Daddy—thank goodness! The other night she kept slipping him Wild Turkey whiskey in a paper cup and it made Momma mad. Momma is real proper and hates it when Daddy has a good time. She put me in Catholic school because she thought it would make up for having Daddy for a daddy. Everybody says he is a bad influence on me.

Daddy won't let me be baptized a Catholic, but those nuns are having a good time trying. I have a lot of holy cards and get lots of attention because they think I'm going to hell. I like the nuns very much, all except Sister Plasida.

I have two boyfriends, Dwane Crawford and Luther Willis. Luther wears bow ties. When we had our fifth-grade dance, Luther and I were dancing to "The Tennessee Waltz" and Sister Plasida came over and took me into the hall and tried to wipe the lipstick and rouge off of me, which I wasn't even wearing. Momma, who was there in the PTA group, came in and told her not to do that because when I got excited, I had natural coloring.

I don't like catechism too much either. Daddy was the one that told me that the Epistles were the wives of the Apostles. That old priest went all funny when I asked him if Mary Magdalene was Jesus' girlfriend. He doesn't want you to ask questions at all.

I am a second-year Brownie. I got a first-aid badge that really comes in handy. One time after school, Jimmy Lee got hit by a car and was bleeding all over the place. I remembered what to do. I sat down and put my head between my knees to keep from fainting.

Once a colored man was in a wreck in front of my grandmother's house and had his ear cut off. When the ambulance came, they said to my grandmother, "We can't take him, you'll have to call a colored ambulance." Can you believe that they wouldn't help him with his ear? Boy, were we mad. Daddy said things were pretty bad when rednecks were in the medical profession.

I personally don't trust any of them as far as I can throw a gum wrapper, especially after the time Dr. Clyde told Momma that my tonsils would have to come out and that it would be a snap. He talked all about the ice cream I could eat and what fun it would be, and Momma took me to the Rexall and bought me a Sparkle Plenty doll.

When I got to the hospital, Dr. Clyde promised me my momma and daddy would be with me the whole time. Then they put me on this table and rolled me down the hall. I was OK until we got to these two big screen doors and my momma and daddy were told they would have to wait outside. I sat right up when I heard that. Momma and Daddy were looking scared, but those people at the hospital rolled me in the room alone and closed the doors.

Then some other people with masks started fooling around and even tried to take my Sparkle Plenty doll away. They asked if I was Catholic, which made me real nervous before an operation, and then they put this strainer on my face and tried to kill me with ether, one of the worst-smelling things I have ever smelled in my life.

When I heard a commotion outside the door, I tried to get up, but five against a little child is not fair. It was the worst experience of my life. I heard bells, sirens, and saw terrible things. I dreamed a story about a magician with a magic stick that scared me to death.

I found out later that as I was being rolled into the operating room Momma turned to say something to Daddy, but Daddy had run down to the end of the hall and shut himself into a telephone booth. Some doctors got him out and gave him a shot, he was so upset. I love him, but Daddy isn't much help in a real-life crisis.

Don't ever let them fool you with that ice cream stuff. I couldn't even taste it and didn't want it, to boot. After I got my strength back, I opened up the head of my Sparkle Plenty doll and pulled the eyes out.

Grandma Pettibone came over to the hospital and fanned me with a bingo card and I got to miss school, but other than that, the hospital was the pits.

DAISY FAY AND THE MIRACLE MAN

Facts

1.   How old is the narrator and what grade is she in?

2.   How did Daisy Fay get her name?

3.   Who is Felix? Describe its condition.

4.   Where did Daisy Fay's daddy serve in the army?

5.   Only one person in the combined Harper and Pettibone families likes Daisy Fay's daddy. Who is that person?

6.   Where did Daisy Fay's daddy want to move? Why?

7.   Name the schemes Daddy Harper invented to raise money for the move.

8.   Why does Daisy Fay refer to her family as being in "show business"?

9.   The narrator says, "Momma has a theory that Daddy has tried to kill me on several different occasions." Name those occasions.

Strategies

1.   The narrator uses several cliches, such as, "hizzy fit," "pitched a fit," and "dead as door nails." Discuss and analyze the author's strategy of using adult cliches in a child's voice.

2.   Daisy Fay tells a story about her birth, but it does not coincide with the actions of her parents. The author uses this technique to highlight the innocence of the child. Discuss the effectiveness of this technique.

3.   The narrator paints a clear picture of her mother and father. Which rhetorical mode(s) does the author use to accomplish this?

4.   Describe and discuss the narrator's voice. Is it consistently the voice of a child? Is there an adult perspective?

5. To whom is the narrator telling her story?

Issues

1. Do you think the narrator is a Daddy's girl or a Momma's darling? Support your answer with readings from the text.

2. The narrator points out that colored people bought their own theater because they had to sit in the balcony at the white theater. However, she also says, "Momma says sitting in that balcony, looking down on people, has given me a superiority complex." Discuss this apparent contradiction.

3. Discuss the differences between Mother and Father Harper's personality.

4. In 1952, why was it inappropriate and surprising to take an injured colored person to the hospital in a white ambulance and to have a colored person sitting in the front seat of a car? What was the narrator's attitude toward these events?

Writing Assignments

1. Use one or more of your journal entries to write a narrative essay in the child's voice.

2. Analyze the diaries of Daisy Fay in *Daisy Fay and the Miracle Man* and Esperanza in *The House on Mango Street*, then compare and/or contrast the narrators in each essay.

3. Write an essay analyzing Fannie Flagg's creation of the child's voice in *Daisy Fay and the Miracle Man*.

William A. LaVallee (student)

"DEAR FRIEND . . ."

WILLIAM A. LaVALLEE was a student at Los Angeles City College when he wrote this essay. Currently, he attends Antioch University studying psychology.

From where I was sitting to the left of my mother—my sister, Jude, flanked her on the right—I could see my father's profile barely peeking over the top edge of the coffin across the room. Occasionally, one of the line of mourners would block my view as they approached the coffin and, in their religious homage, knelt briefly as they genuflected on the kneeling stool to pay their respects. Each time he was blocked, I sort of leaned to the left and then to the right, whichever continued to give me the best view, to see if he were still there.

Yep. No doubt about it. My father was dead, embalmed and lying in state in the living room of the Rabenhorst Funeral Home. But there *was* doubt about it. My mind still refused to totally accept the fact that he was gone. I was told he was gone by the hospital authorities the night we rushed from my family's home to his room in the Lady of the Lake Hospital in nearby Baton Rouge. It had been proven to me by the fact when I watched as his body was taken away to the embalming studio. I heard it on the evening news on all the radio and television stations during the Sports News of the day, and there he was now. All spruced up, but in a coffin. But my mind still seemed to want to reject the idea entirely.

I was nineteen and not ready to lose my father. We weren't finished. In fact, in the day since he had died, in retrospect of our lives together, it somehow seemed we had hardly even begun. There was so much I didn't know about him. So much he didn't know about me. There were so many questions I had forgotten—neglected to ask . . . answers I would never get because there was no one else who could give them. And now, he was dead.

After what seemed endless hours of craning my neck, accepting the tearful condolences, the crowd of mourners, consisting of family, friends and strangers, thinned out. At last, there was no one left in the mourning room but Mother, Jude and me.

"Would you like one more moment of visitation before we close for the night?" The voice of the mortician was deep, resonating in an echo.

My mother nodded and the three of us rose slowly and cautiously made our way across the room toward Daddy's body. I know I felt horrid. My mother's deep sobs and flowing tears told of a love she had had for over twenty years with my father. A fleeting thought crossed my mind wondering what Jude in her Down Syndrome view of the world *really* thought and what did she *really* feel? At fourteen she had had him in even less time than I had and they adored one another. She looked very sad, but who knew? She had been his favorite. We all knew that, but it didn't matter—Jude was everybody's favorite.

We stared down at my father and my mother gripped my arm. She looked up at me and smiled, "Your father loved you so!" she said.

I nodded, unable to speak because of the huge lump that suddenly was choking me. I knew.

Her smile grew wider and warmer, "You remember the elf?"

I did a double-take. Of *course*, I remembered the elf. Why *wouldn't* I remember the elf? What an odd thing for Mother to bring up at this moment. What*ever* made her say that, of all things? And how the hell did she *know* about the elf? I had never told her or Daddy.

. . .

Sittin' on the back steps, I put the book down. "The Shoemaker and the Elves." What a great idea! I wanted one. Nobody really played with me, so I'd get me a elf. All year, all fourth grade, dunno why, maybe 'cause I was the new boy, but I was always left back when the other kids ran an' played in Bogan's field. An' when I came home, too. Nobody but me to play with.

I had to hurry before Mother an' Daddy got home from work. I dug around in the grimy inside of my booksack an' pulled out the stub of a chewed yellow pencil an' a Blue Horse notebook.

"Dear Elf," I scribbled, *"I want a friend. Love, William."*

Rippin' the page from the notebook, I slammed through the back porch's screen door an' slapped the note down on the worn wooden kitchen table. He'd want somethin' to eat. Fixin' shoes, prob'ly at my Uncle Sam's shoeshop all night, was hard work. I'd run errands for Uncle Sam, so I knew how he made work. So, the elf'd prob'ly be hungry.

Peter Pan Peanut Butter with globs of real butter mixed in. That's the kinda samich he'd like. Climbin' on Mother's restin' stool, I hiked myself onto the kitchen counter an' creaked opened the rusty-hinged bread box. A big black roach jumped out, but not fast enough. With bare hand I squashed it an' grabbed two slices of white bread from the opened loaf. Gettin' the top kitchen cab'net open almost made me fall, but I got the jar of peanut butter, took the bread an' slid back off the counter. An' Ova'tine. I *loved* Ova'tine. My elf'd like Ova'tine, too. I grabbed the milk an' Ova'tine from the fridge. The smudgy glass from my after-school snack was still on the table. I twisted open the bottle top, poured the milk into the glass. Mother always put two of the big spoons of Ova'tine. Scoopin' it, I dumped four.

I hid the feast behind the washin' machine next to my bed on the back porch until late that night, until I heard the steady breathin' of Mother an' Daddy's snorin' from their bedroom. Slidin' outta my bed, I got the treat, I tiptoed to the kitchen, carryin' the tray an' placed it all in the middle of the table, an' proppin' up the letter against the glass, I lit it with my father's flashlight I had sneaked from his workbox.

I climbed back into my bed an' stared through the screen at the deep black sky, with its too-late-to-wish-on twinklin' stars an' big smile of the yellow Man In The Moon. A dog barked somewhere down the road an' my hammerin' heart was the last thing I heard before the Sandman sprinkled dust in my eyes.

I was only half-asleep most of the night an' tried to listen for sounds from the kitchen of the elf comin' in, findin' my note an' gift, an' eatin', an' maybe he'd come out to the porch, see me, an' we could talk. But I couldn't make it an' kept driftin' off.

The sunup was like a big Roman candle goin' off in my face an' the moment it peeped over the garage, I bolted from bed an' listened closely at the kitchen door. No sound. No one was up yet, but me. Cautiously, I opened the door, tryin' hard not to creek it and wake everybody. I stopped dead in the doorway. What I saw made my mouth drop open an' my eyes almos' bugged right outta my head. The samich was gone. My note was gone. The glass stood all alone on the table, sparkly clean, glistenin' in the mornin' light from the window and against it the torn top from a cakebox was propped.

I crossed the room, circled the table and gawked at the piece of cardboard. There was writin' on it. My eyes were so jumpin' in my head, I couldn't read and so I reached out with shaky fingers and picked it up. From somewhere in the house, there was a noise an' so, clutchin' my note, I scurried back onto the porch, climbin' into my bed. I pulled the covers up over my head, but left enough of a tent so that the mornin' light could shine on my letter.

"Dear William. Thank you for such a nice meal. After a hard night of working repairing shoes, I was really hungry. How did you know I liked Ovaltine and Peter Pan Peanut Butter sandwiches with butter smeared on? I guess you knew because that's what friends do, they know what their friends like. Love to you. Your elfin friend."

I din't tell no one about what had happened for me. And that night I lay awake until after everyone was sleep, then I slid out of bed and reachin' under my bed I took out the now almost stale samich I had made in the afternoon. The Ova'tine was kinda lumpy and the milk was kinda curdly, but hidin' it until the middle of the night was the best I could do without givin' it all away. The note under my pillow I had writ before goin' to bed; I told my elf that I liked him an' hoped he liked me an' maybe we could meet sometime an' play. I crept into the kitchen, without no lights an' put everythin' on the table.

I slept real good that night. The next mornin' again I was up before anyone else . . . he had come back. Everythin' was gone, 'cept the new note. He told me we could be friends. I had a friend. I finally had a real friend.

That's how it had begun. Note after note, I poured out my heart, no secrets withheld, all fears told, love expressed. Night after night, I prepared feast after feast. Morning after morning there were answers to my notes—filled with encouragement, with advice, with love. I learned how to be and to have a friend. I never told anyone about my elf—except for once.

"How come you never play with us?" the boy asked.

"Y'all never useta ask me."

"Well, we did, we started, but you never would," said another boy. "Don'tcha wanna have a friend?"

"I got a friend," I smiled, pullin' out a most recent note an' showin' them. With a rush of words, I tol' them everythin' from readin' about elves, to the first night, through to that day. I was excited. They'd like me, too, an' be my friends. They'd want to meet him, too.

"You are a crazy!" one of them said, crumpling and tossing my note onto the ground.

"Yeah! Yeah!"

"I'm not! I'm not! It's true, it's true, it's true!"

I got pushed down into the mud, as I stooped to pick up my precious note an' they laughed, an' poked at me, an' called me names as I ran away, tears streaming down my face.

That night I poured my heart out to my elfin friend and told him how much I loved him, how much he was my friend and how from that day on, I'd never, ever, ever, ever play with those ugly kids again.

And so, I kept up my letter an' all with my elf. How long it went on is up for grabs.

One mornin' was a shocker.

"Dear William. I was so sorry that time when you told me your little schoolmates didn't believe you about me. I love you very much, and the last thing I'd want to do is hurt you or help anyone else hurt you. But I have been thinking about us. I can never come out and play with you and you're always asleep when I come to visit. You should have friends you can play with. Real little friends. And William, there's a little girl who lives far away who needs a friend right now. She needs a friend as badly as

you did when we first started visiting. So, I have to say goodbye to you. You're a big boy and know how to be a good friend to other boys, I know because you've been a good friend to me. I know you understand why I have to go now. I love you. Your elfin friend."

I *din't* understand. I *din't* want to understand. And I couldn't make the tears stop. That night, the next, the next and the next, I made the food, wrote the note. Every mornin' it was all on the table just as I had left it.

After a while, I stopped doing it and I knew the elf was gone, had gone to help someone else and was never coming back. I began to play with other boys and girls and soon I wasn't the new kid on the block.

"How'd you know about my elf?" I was finally able to ask.
"Your daddy told me."
"He *knew*?"
She smiled, "He loved being your elf."
It's hard to believe I said it, but I did: "You mean, there wasn't any *real* elf?" Not the brightest question for a nineteen-year-old man.

Guiding Jude, Mother walked back to the row of chairs where we had been sitting, and as she gathered up her purse and other belongings she told me, "We knew it was hard for you, moving, changing schools and all, but we didn't know how lonely you were. Then, you wrote that first note to the elf and during the night, daddy heard a noise and got up to check. He saw your note, sat down and read it by the light from the flashlight. That night and every night after that, your daddy would get up after you were asleep and creep into the kitchen. He'd eat that dry peanut butter sandwich and drink the Ovaltine you left for him while he read your letter and wrote an answer. You know, he was left-handed . . . " She took a breath and I numbly nodded my head. "So, he would laboriously write the notes with his right hand. He didn't want you to suspect it was him."

We started down the aisle of the mortuary for the door.

"After a while, he thought that maybe he was harming you more than helping you, by keeping you from making new friends. So, he wrote you the last note, so that you could go out and make some real friends."

My ears were hearing this story from Mother faster than my heart could beat and take it all in.

"That night he cried himself to sleep, and for a long time after that, when you would still leave the food and the notes, he would tell me that his heart was breaking, but he knew it was the right thing to do."

"And he never told me!" I croaked.

"Of course not! He didn't want you to lose that childlike innocence and belief you had." Mother patted me on the cheek. "You know, you never have."

We left the mortuary and got into our car, leaving behind the remains of my father, a man who had given me so much love, had protected me, had helped me in ways I never imagined. I had thought there was so much he didn't know about me, but he had known more of my childhood secrets than anyone else. There was so much I thought I didn't know about him, and yet—through the loving guidance in his letters—he taught me lessons that serve me even today. He had answered all of my childhood questions . . . . I don't remember a lot of them, I don't remember a lot of the answers, but I know somewhere deep inside me, I live by the principles my father instilled in me.

"DEAR FRIEND . . ."

Questions

1. Why did the author's father become his elfin friend? What did the father accomplish? Explain.

2. Why did the mother tell the author his father's secret at the funeral?

3. Why is this act of love so important to the author?

4. When you listen to the author's voice, what do you hear?

5. Discuss any unique friendships you had as a child.

Langston Hughes

SALVATION

LANGSTON HUGHES (b. 1902-d. 1967) was born in Joplin, Missouri. He is the writer of numerous poems ("I, Too, Sing America," "Mother to Son," "The Negro Speaks of Rivers"), short stories, novels (*Not Without Laughter*), and plays (*Simply Heavenly*). Mr. Hughes also wrote a column for the black-owned newspaper *Chicago Defender* highlighting the wise and humorous character of Jesse B. Simple. (To review a collection of Simple stories see *Simple Speaks His Mind, The Best of Simple,* and *Simple's Uncle Sam.*) A premier writer during the Harlem Renaissance movement, Mr. Hughes wrote two autobiographies, *The Big Sea* and *I Wonder as I Wander.* "Salvation" is an excerpt from *The Big Sea*, published in 1940.

A twelve-year-old boy is told that he will see Jesus and be saved, but instead he discovers the perils of religion.

I was saved from sin when I was going on thirteen. But not really saved. It happened like this. There was a big revival at my Auntie Reed's church. Every night for weeks there had been much preaching, singing, praying, and shouting, and some very hardened sinners had been brought to Christ, and the membership of the church had grown by leaps and bounds. Then just before the revival ended, they held a special meeting for children, "to bring the young lambs to the fold." My aunt spoke of it for days ahead. The night I was escorted to the front row and placed on the mourners' bench with all the other young sinners, who had not yet been brought to Jesus.

My aunt told me that when you were saved you saw a light, and something happened to you inside! And Jesus came into your life! And God was with you from then on! She said you could see and hear and feel Jesus in your soul. I believed her. I had heard a great many old people say the same thing and it seemed to me they ought to know. So I sat there calmly in the hot, crowded church, waiting for Jesus to come to me.

The preacher preached a wonderful rhythmical sermon, all moans and shouts and lonely cries and dire pictures of hell, and then he sang a song about the ninety and nine safe in the fold, but one little lamb was left out in the cold.

Then he said: "Won't you come? Won't you come to Jesus? Young lambs, won't you come?" And he held out his arms to all us young sinners there on the mourners' bench. And the little girls cried. And some of them jumped up and went to Jesus right away. But most of us just sat there.

A great many old people came and knelt around us and prayed, old women with jet-black faces and braided hair, old men with work-gnarled hands. And the church sang a song about the lower lights are burning, some poor sinners to be saved. And the whole building rocked with prayer and song.

Still I kept waiting to *see* Jesus.

Finally all the young people had gone to the altar and were saved, but one boy and me. He was a rounder's son named Westley. Westley and I were surrounded by sisters and deacons praying. It was very hot in the church, and getting late now. Finally Westley said to me in a whisper: "God damn! I'm tired o' sitting here. Let's get up and be saved." So he got up and was saved.

Then I was left all alone on the mourners' bench. My aunt came and knelt at my knees and cried, while prayers and songs swirled all around me in the little church. The whole congregation prayed for me alone, in a mighty wail of moans and voices. And I kept waiting serenely for Jesus, waiting, waiting—but he didn't come. I wanted to see him, but nothing happened to me. Nothing! I wanted something to happen to me, but nothing happened.

I heard the songs and the minister saying: "Why don't you come? My dear child, why don't you come to Jesus? Jesus is waiting for you. He wants you. Why don't you come? Sister Reed, what is this child's name?"

"Langston," my aunt sobbed.

"Langston, why don't you come? Why don't you come and be saved? Oh, Lamb of God! Why don't you come?"

Now it was really getting late. I began to be ashamed of myself, holding everything up so long. I began to wonder what God thought about Westley, who certainly hadn't seen Jesus either, but who was now sitting proudly on the platform, swinging his knickerbockered legs and grinning down at me, surrounded by deacons and old women on their knees praying. God had not struck Westley dead for taking his name in vain or for lying in the temple. So I decided that maybe to save further trouble, I'd better lie, too, and say that Jesus had come, and get up and be saved.

So I got up.

Suddenly the whole room broke into a sea of shouting, as they saw me rise. Waves of rejoicing swept the place. Women leaped in the air. My aunt threw her arms around me. The minister took me by the hand and led me to the platform.

175

When things quieted down, in a hushed silence, punctuated by a few ecstatic "Amens," all the new young lambs were blessed in the name of God. Then joyous singing filled the room.

That night, for the last time in my life but one—for I was a big boy twelve years old—I cried. I cried, in bed alone, and couldn't stop. I buried my head under the quilts, but my aunt heard me. She woke up and told my uncle I was crying because the Holy Ghost had come into my life, and because I had seen Jesus. But I was really crying because I couldn't bear to tell her that I had lied, that I had deceived everybody in the church, that I hadn't seen Jesus, and that now I didn't believe there was a Jesus any more, since he didn't come to help me.

SALVATION

Facts

1.   What does Aunt Reed say about being saved?

2.   How does young Hughes interpret what his Aunt Reed said about salvation?

3.   Why does Hughes finally stand up to get saved?

4.   Why does he cry about it later?

Strategies

1.   What makes the event Hughes relates easy to visualize?

2.   There are two voices in this essay—adult and child. In the prose portion of the essay, select one sentence that captures the adult's voice and one sentence that captures the child' voice. Do the same with the dialogue.

3.   Why does the author describe Wesley's salvation?

4.   Hughes combines two rhetorical modes in his essay. What are they?

5.   What is the author's conflict?

6.   What is the main point?

Issues

1.   Was Hughes saved? Explain your answer.

2.   Is Hughes criticizing religion in this essay? If so, why and what aspect of religion is he criticizing?

3.   What is salvation?

Writing Assignments

1.   Write a narrative relating an incident involving religion using the child's voice.

2.   Write a documented essay on the effects of religion during a particular era.

Charles Dubois Rucker (student)

A GREAT MAN

CHARLES DuBOIS RUCKER is a student at Los Angeles City College studying English. He plans to become a lawyer.

"Now I lay me down to sleep, I pray the Lord my soul to keep; before I die if I should sleep, I pray the Lord let me be. God bless my Mommy, my Daddy, my brothers, my dog, Morris, and his babies, my Auntie Alice and Uncle Bill, the man at the store, myself, you God, and everybody in the world. Amen."

I like to pray because everybody can get blessed, that's what my grandma say and I would be a great man. I don't know what she mean but it sound good, so I will keep on praying. "A great man. Yeah, I'm gonna be a great man." I really love my grandma, she so pretty and nice. She give me everything I want, gets me out of trouble when I'm being bad, she sing to me all the time. She always sing about God. I stay at her house on Saturday and Sunday and we have so much fun. We play, we go to the park, sing, eat ice-cream, and go to church on Sunday morning and sometimes we stay all day long in church. I go to sleep, wake up and we still in church and grandma still singing with her pretty smile. She dress so nice and I get to wear nice shoes and a nice suit. I feel like a big boy, "A great man," just like grandma would say.

Sunday was my time to be a great man. One day, grandma, grandpa, and me sat at the dinner table to eat dinner, just like everyday when I was at they house. I heard grandma say to grandpa I was gonna get baptism. I say, "Grandma, what you say baptism?" And grandad say, "Don't worry, you gonna really like baptism. There is a pool right by the big picture behind Preacher Jones. You gonna take a short swim." I thought, "swim in church by the Preacher Jones?" I really like the preacher. He jumps, sings, dances, yells, make the people sing and run around, fall on the floor, cry, cry harder and harder. Music plays when Preacher Jones raises his hands. Miss Jones, Mr. Wilson, Aunt Alice, grandma, my friend James' mama sing, and they all wear dresses that look just alike, the men and the women. Everybody, all of them move side to side when they sing my favorite song. We all sing at the same time, "I'm coming up on the rough side of the mountain." I love that song.

One day my mommy took me to grandma's house after school. It was Friday. No school for two days just like most Fridays. Mama took me to grandma's house and my two brothers, Anthony and Ali, to Uncle Bill's house. I could not stop smiling. I was so happy my insides in my body felt so good, like when Christmas comes, but it was not Christmas time. I got out of the car and run to grandma's door. She opened it and I ran in. I say, "Grandma, I'm so happy, really happy." And grandma say, "You got a big weekend. You about to give yourself to the Lord. You have every right to be happy. So go in the house and tell your grandpa how you feel." I ran to grandpa and told him all about my good feelings. He looked like he got happy just like me.

That Sunday I put on my suit and this time my suit is brand new. My shoes was brand new and my shirt and my tie, everything brand new. This made me even happier like grandpa looked when I told him about me being happy. Grandma and grandpa got dressed and went to church. I felt even more happy. In church, we sing my favorite song then everything stops. It got quiet. Then Preacher Jones started to call names. He called my friend, James, and Crystal, and Frederick, then he called my name, "Charles Dubois Rucker." My grandma say to me, "Get up and go to Preacher Jones." I did quickly because I like Preacher Jones. He was a great man like grandma say I will be someday. Preacher Jones made all of us stand in line. I was second in line, Crystal was first. Some of the people in the dresses that sang every time Preacher Jones raised his hand put a white bed cover on Crystal and took her behind the big picture. When I saw her again she was wet everywhere, her hair and arms and legs. I was scared after seeing her. Preacher Jones took my hand next and the men and women that sang put the same white cover on me. I was scared, but I could not stop smiling.

I went behind the picture and just like grandma say it was a little swimming pool. They took me into the pool with the cover on and Preacher Jones say some word to God, then push me backward in the water and pulled me up fast. I got wet so fast and then it was the next person's turn.

Grandma say to me, "How you like getting baptized?" I say, "That was baptism?" She say, "Yes." I say, "I like that Grandma, can I get in line again?" She say, "No, you cannot but you are now truly a great man," and I looked at myself and at the people in the church, then I looked back at grandma and say, "I feel like a great man, grandma, just like the man on the picture behind Preacher Jones." She gave me a hug and say, "I'm proud of you, Charles Dubois Rucker, and yes, you are a great man just like that man on the picture behind Preacher Jones." Amen.

A GREAT MAN

Questions

1.   What is a great man according to the author?

2.   Why does the author want to be a great man?

3.   How does the author portray his voice of innocence? Explain.

Esmeralda Santiago

WHEN I WAS PUERTO RICAN

ESMERALDA SANTIAGO (b. 1948) was born on the island of Puerto Rico where she spent the beginning of her childhood. A few years later, along with six brothers and sisters, she moved with her family to New York. Ms. Santiago overcame language and culture differences and went on to Harvard University where she graduated with highest honors. Her first memoir, *When I Was Puerto Rican*, was published in 1993, and *Almost a Woman*, her second memoir, was published in 1998. The following excerpts are from Ms. Santiago's first book, *When I Was Puerto Rican*.

These excerpts capture the vulnerability of a curious, bright child who is loved and nurtured by her family and friends.

Jibara

We children slept in hammocks strung across the room, tied to the beams in sturdy knots that were done and undone daily. A curtain separated our side of the room from the end where my parents slept in a four-poster bed veiled with mosquito netting. On the days he worked, Papi left the house before dawn and sometimes joked that he woke the roosters to sing the *barrio* awake. We wouldn't see him again until dusk, dragging down the dirt road, his wooden toolbox pulling on his arm, making his body list sideways. When he didn't work, he and Mami rustled behind the flowered curtain, creaked the springs under their mattress, their voices a murmur that I strained to hear but couldn't.

I was an early riser but was not allowed out until the sun shot in through the crack near Mami's sewing machine and swept a glistening stripe of gold across the dirt floor.

The next morning, I turned out of the hammock and ran outside as soon as the sun streaked in. Mami and Papi sat by the kitchen shed sipping coffee. My arms and belly were pimpled with red dots. The night before, Mami had bathed me in *alcoholado*, which soothed my skin and cooled the hot itch.

"*Ay bendito*," Mami said, "here's our spotty early riser. Come here, let me look." She turned me around, rubbing the spots. "Are you itchy?"

"No, it doesn't itch at all."

"Stay out of the sun today so the spots don't scar."

Papi hummed along with the battery-operated radio. He never went anywhere without it. When he worked around the house, he propped it on a rock, or the nearest fence post, and tuned it to his favorite station, which played romantic ballads, *chachachas,* and a reading of the news every half hour. He delighted in stories from faraway places like Russia, Madagascar, and Istanbul. Whenever the newscaster mentioned a country with a particularly musical name, he'd repeat it or make a rhyme of it. *"Pakista´n. Sacrista´n. ?Do´nde esta´n?"* he sang as he mixed cement or hammered nails, his voice echoing against the walls.

Early each morning the radio brought us a program called "The Day Breaker's Club," which played the traditional music and poetry of the Puerto Rican country dweller, the *jibaro.* Although the songs and poems chronicled a life of struggle and hardship, their message was that *jibaros* were rewarded by a life of independence and contemplation, a closeness to nature coupled with a respect for its intractability, and a deeply rooted and proud nationalism. I wanted to be a *jibara* more than anything in the world, but Mami said I couldn't because I was born in the city, where *jibaros* were mocked for their unsophisticated customs and peculiar dialect.

"Don't be a *jibara*," she scolded, rapping her knuckles on my skull, as if to waken the intelligence she said was there.

I ducked away, my scalp smarting, and scrambled into the oregano bushes. In the fragrant shade, I fretted. If we were not *jibaros*, why did we live like them? Our house, a box squatting on low stilts, was shaped like a *bohio*, the kind of house *jibaros* lived in. Our favorite program, "The Day Breaker's Club," played the traditional music of rural Puerto Rico and gave information about crops, husbandry, and the weather. Our neighbor Dona Lola was a *jibara*, although Mami had warned us never to call her that. Poems and stories about the hardships and joys of the Puerto Rican *jibaro* were required reading at every grade level in school. My own grandparents, whom I was to respect as well as love, were said to be *jibaros.* But I couldn't be one, nor was I to call anyone a *jibaro*, lest they be offended. Even at the tender age when I didn't yet know my real name, I was puzzled by the hypocrisy of celebrating a people everyone looked down on. But there was no arguing with Mami, who, in those days, was always right.

On the radio, the newscaster talked about submarines, torpedoes, and a place called Korea, where Puerto Rican men went to die. His voice faded as Papi carried him into the house just as Delsa and Norma came out for their oatmeal.

Delsa's black curly hair framed a heart-shaped face with tiny pouty lips and round eyes thick with lashes. Mami called her *Munequita*, Little Doll. Norma's hair was the color of clay, her yellow eyes slanted at the corners, and her skin glowed the same color as the inside of a yam. Mami called her La Colora´, the red girl. I thought I had no nickname until she told me my name wasn't Negi but Esmeralda.

"You're named after your father's sister, who is also your godmother. You know her as Titi Merín."

"Why does everyone call me Negi?"

"Because when you were little you were so black, my mother said you were a *negrita*. And we all called you *Negrita*, and it got shortened to Negi."

Delsa was darker than I was, nutty brown, but not as sun ripened as Papi. Norma was lighter, rust colored, and not as pale as Mami, whose skin was pink. Norma's yellow eyes with black pupils looked like sunflowers. Delsa had black eyes. I'd never seen my eyes, because the only mirror in the house was hung up too high for me to reach. I touched my hair, which was not curly like Delsa's, nor *pasita*, raisined, like Papi's. Mami cut it short whenever it grew into my eyes, but I'd seen dark brown wisps by my cheeks and near my temples.

"So *Negi* means I'm black?"

"It's a sweet name because we love you, *Negrita*." She hugged and kissed me.

"Does anyone call Titi Merín Esmeralda?"

"Oh, sure. People who don't know her well—the government, her boss. We all have our official names, and then our nicknames, which are like secrets that only the people who love us use."

"How come you don't have a nickname?"

"I do. Everyone calls me Monín. That's my nickname."

"What's your real name?"

"Ramona."

"Papi doesn't have a nickname."

"Yes he does. Some people call him Pablito."

It seemed too complicated, as if each one of us were really two people, one who was loved and the official one who, I assumed, was not.

Someone
Is
Coming
To Take
Your Lap

"Papi, what's a sin?" I was collecting grass for the camels of the Three Magi, who were coming that night with presents for all the children. The only grass to be had in the *barrio* grew in the alley, along the edges of fences that kept chickens and scrawny dogs separated from one another.

"A sin is when you do something that makes God angry."

"Like what?"

"Well, let's see. There's the first commandment, 'Honor thy father and mother.' "

"What's a commandment?"

"It's actually commandments. God wrote ten of them so people would know what to do."

"What do the others say?"

"Thou shalt not take the Lord's name in vain."

"What does that mean?"

"It means you shouldn't mention God except in prayers."

"You can't say '*Ay Dios Mío*'?"

"Not technically."

"But everyone says it."

"Very religious people don't."

"We don't go to church, but we believe in God."

"Is it a sin not to go to church?"

"If you're a Catholic."

"Are we Catholic?"

"Yes. But not very good ones."

I finished collecting grass for the camels, while Papi told me more about the commandments. We never got through all ten, because I kept interrupting him for explanations of what murder was, and what adultery meant.

. . .

Papi was to lead the novenas for Don Berto. After dinner he washed and put on a clean white shirt, pulled a rosary and a Bible from his dresser, and started out the door.

"Do you want to come?" he asked me.

"*¡Si!* I would! *¡Si!*"

"Only if you bring a long-sleeve shirt," Mami said. "I don't want you sick from the night air."

We walked on the pebbled road as the sun set behind the mountains. Toads hopped out of our way, their dark brown bodies bottom heavy. The air smelled green, the scents of peppermint, rosemary, and verbena wafting up from the ground like fog.

"Papi, what's a soul?"

"The soul is that part of us that never dies."

"What do you mean?"

"When people die, it's just the body that dies. The soul goes up to the sky."

"I know. Mami told me that already."

He laughed. "Okay, so what more do you want to know?"

"What does the soul do?"

"It goes to live with Papa Dios in Paradise."

"When people are alive . . . what does the soul do?"

He stopped and stared at the tip of his work shoes. "Let's see, what does it do?" He massaged his forehead as if that would make the answer come out quicker. "Well, it is the soul of a person that writes poetry."

"How?"

He pinched his lower lip with his thumb and index finger, and pulled it back and forth in small tugs. He dropped his hand and took mine in his then began walking again.

"The soul lives inside a person when she's alive. It's the part of a person that feels. A poet's soul feels more than regular people's souls. And that's what makes him write poetry."

Clouds had formed above the mountains in streaks, like clumps of dough that had been stretched too thin.

"What does the soul look like?"

He let out a breath. "Well, it looks like the person."

"So my soul looks like me and your soul looks like you?"

"Right!" He sounded relieved.

"And it lives inside our bodies?"

"Yes, that's right."

"Does it ever come out?"

"When we die . . ."

"But when we're alive . . . does it every come out?"

"No, I don't think so." The doubt in his voice let me know that I knew something he didn't, because my soul travelled all the time, and it appeared that his never did. Now I knew what happened to me when I walked beside myself. It was my soul wandering.

The sun dipped behind the mountains, leaving flecks of orange, pink, and turquoise. In the foreground, the landscape had become flat, without shadow, distanceless.

"Papi, what happens to the body when it's buried?"

"It decomposes," he said. "It becomes dust."

We were joined by a group of mourners on their way to the Marin house. They wished us all a good evening, and the rest of the way we walked in dreadful silence.

Papi settled into his place in front of the house, next to an altar with a picture of Don Berto holding his machete. I wondered if his soul had already gone to live with Papa Dios, or if he was floating around watching to see if his daughters and sons were paying him the proper respect now that his body was rotting under the ground. I tried to send my soul up, to meet him halfway between heaven and earth, but I couldn't get out, held by the fear that if he saw my soul he might try to take it with him.

"Someone is coming to take your lap, freckles," Doña Lola cuddled Alicia. We sat in her kitchen, sipping coffee from blue enamel tin cups. Mami had told me to take the baby when I brought a bag of pigeon peas to Doña Lola, who would give us coffee in return. She grew it in the crags that rose behind her kitchen, up the hill from the latrine. I had helped her pick the red, swollen fruit, and she had roasted them in a giant frying pan on her fogón then laid the blackened beans out to cool before storing them in an odd assortment of cans and jars.

"Papi said by the time the new baby is born we will have electricity."

"Ah, yes," Doña Lola sighed, "electricity. Pretty soon they'll bring water, too, and then they'll pave the road and bring cars, buses maybe. Ah, yes."

"Buses, Doña Lola?"

"Trucks and buses. And then the *Americanos* will come looking for *artesanías*." She spit into the yard and chuckled as if remembering a private joke. "Those *Americanos* are really something . . . ."

"Do you know any?"

"Oh, I've known a few. Yes. A few. You know, it's an *Americano* that owns the *finca* back there."

"Lalao's *finca*?"

"Bah! A *otro perro con ese hueso*. That *finca* doesn't belong to Lalao. That man doesn't own the hole to lay his corpse in."

"But everyone says . . ."

"*Del dicho al hecho hay un gran trecho*."

"What does that mean?"

"It means there's a long way between what people say and what is. That *finca* belongs to Rockefela."

"Who's he?"

"An *Americano* from the *Nueva Yores*. He's going to build a hotel back there." The *finca* stretched across the road to the horizon, the tall grass broken now and then by groves of lemon, orange, and grapefruit trees, herds of cattle, and, in the distance, a line of coconut palms.

"What will they do with all those cows?"

"Doña Lola guffawed. "You're worried about the cows? What about us?"

"Well, we don't live on the *finca* . . ."

"Do you think they will let us stay here if they build a hotel?"

"Why not?"

"*Yo conozco al buey que faja y a la víbora que pica*." She swallowed the last drop of coffee and got up from her stool brusquely, startling Alicia, who reached her arms out to me and clung to my neck the minute she was close enough.

I loved Doña Lola's *refranes*, the sayings she came up with in conversation that were sometimes as mysterious as the things Papi kept in his special dresser. "I know the bull that charges and the serpent that stings" could only mean that she distrusted Americans, and that this mistrust had come from experience.

But in the time I'd lived in Macu'n I'd never seen an American, nor had I ever heard mention of a Rockefela, nor plans for a hotel in what everyone called Lalao's *finca*.

When I came home, Alicia on my hip, a can of freshly roasted coffee in my hand, Mami was peeling *ñame* and *yautía* tubers for that night's supper.

"Mami, is it true that they're going to build a hotel on Lalao's *finca*?"

"That will be the day!"

"Doña Lola said they'll make us all move."

"They've been talking about bringing electricity here since before you were born. And the rumor about a hotel in Lalao's *finca* is older than the hopes of the poor. Your granddaughters will be *señorita* before anything like that happens around here."

I was relieved we wouldn't have to move and helped Mami peel the sweet potatoes.

"Where are *los Nueva Yores*?" I asked later as I tore the fish bones out of the soaking salted codfish.

"That's where Tata lives." Tata was my mother's mother, who had left Puerto Rico while I was still a toddler. Every so often Mami received a letter from her with a money order, or a package with the clothes my cousins in the United States had outgrown. "It's really called *Nueva Yor*, but it's so big and spread out people sometimes call it *los Nueva Yores*."

"Have you ever been there?"

"No, I haven't . . . . Maybe someday . . . ," she mused as she set a pot of water to boil on the fire. "Maybe."

Why Women Remain Jamona

Sunday morning before breakfast Abuela handed me my piqué dress, washed and ironed.

"We're going to Mass," she said, pulling out a small white *mantilla*, which I was to wear during the service.

"Can we have breakfast first, Abuela? I'm hungry."

"No. We have to fast before church. Don't ask why. It's too complicated to explain."

I dressed and combed my hair, and she helped me pin the *mantilla* to the top of my head.

"All the way there and back," she said, "you should have nothing but good thoughts, because we're going to the house of God."

I'd never been to church and had never stopped to classify my thoughts into good ones and bad ones. But when she said that, I knew what she meant and also knew bad thoughts would be the only things on my mind all the way there and back.

I tried to look as holy as possible, but the white *mantilla* tickled my neck and the sides of my face. I wished I didn't have to wear it, and that was a bad thought, since all the women and girls walking in front of us wore theirs without any complaints.

I love my mother, my father, all my sisters and brothers, my *abuela* and *abuelo*, all my cousins, the governor of Puerto Rico, Doña Lola, my teacher. A boy went by too fast and bumped into me, so I bumped him back, and that was bad, because Jesus said we should turn the other cheek, which seemed stupid, and there went another bad thought.

I counted all the squares on the sidewalk up to the steps of the church, then I counted the steps, twenty-seven. No bad thoughts.

The church was cool, dark, and sweet smelling. Abuela dipped her fingers into a bowl at the entrance and crossed herself. I dipped my fingers, and there was nothing but water. I tasted it, and she gave me a horrified look and crossed herself. She took my hand and walked me down the aisle lined with pews. When we came to the front, she half knelt, looking up to the altar, and crossed herself again before sliding in to take her seat. I did the same thing.

We were early. Music came from somewhere behind us. When I turned around to see, Abuela leaned down and whispered, "Face forward. You should never look behind you in church." I was about to ask why, but Abuela put her fingers to her lips and shushed me as everyone stood up. I couldn't see anything except the back of the man in front of me. He wore a wrinkled brown suit that stretched into folds around his waist because he was so fat. That must have been a bad thought.

The church's windows were of colored glass, each window a scene with Jesus and his cross. The two I could see without turning my head were beautiful, even though Jesus looked like He was in a lot of pain. The priest said something, and everyone knelt. The altar had an enormous Jesus on his cross at the center, the disciples at his feet. Tall candles burned in steps from the rear of the altar to the front, where the priest, dressed in purple and yellow robes, moved his hands up and down and recited poetry that everyone in the church repeated after him. Two boys wearing white lace tunics helped him, and I was jealous, because their job seemed very important. Envy, I knew, was a bad thought.

I counted the times people stood up, knelt down, stood up. That didn't seem right. I shouldn't be in church counting things. I should feel holy, blessed. But I got an itch in the space between my little toe and the sole of my foot. I scraped my shoe against the kneeling bench on the floor. The itch got worse. We knelt again, so I leaned back and took the shoe off to scratch my foot. But I had to get up, because the person next to me wanted to get through. And other people in the same pew got up and squeezed past me, kicking my shoe toward the aisle in the process. Abuela leaned down. "I'm going to take communion. You wait right here."

As soon as she was gone, I slid over to the end of the pew and looked up the aisle. No shoe. I felt for it with my foot all along under the pew but couldn't find it. It was wrong to look back in church, so it seemed that it would be worse to look down. But I didn't want Abuela to come back and find me with one shoe missing.

The people who went up to the altar knelt in front of the priest so he could put something into their mouths. As soon as Abuela knelt, I dove under the pew and looked for my shoe. It was under the pew behind us so I crawled under ours, over the kneeling bench, and stretched to get the shoe. I crawled up just as Abuela came down the aisle. I knelt piously, my hands in prayer, and stared in front of me, trying to look like I was having nothing but the very best thoughts. Abuela went into the pew in front of me, looked over, seemed confused, got out, then knelt next to me. "How foolish. I thought we were one pew up," she whispered.

When everyone had come back, I realized the man with the wrinkled brown suit was two pews up, and I looked up at Jesus on his cross and prayed, "Please, Jesus, don't let her find out I moved during the service." Which I knew was a bad thought.

WHEN I WAS PUERTO RICAN

Facts

1.   What name is the Puerto Rican country dweller called? Is this perceived as a good or bad name by the author?

2.   What is the author's nickname and what does it mean?

3.   What does "someone is coming to take your lap" mean? Who is going to take whose lap?

4.   What does the author know about the soul that her father doesn't know?

5.   List some of the author's bad thoughts.

Strategies

1.   In the beginning of the chapter "Someone Is Coming To Take Your Lap," the author has a meaningful discussion with her father about sin. Discuss how the author captures the innocence of childhood and the patience and love of her father through dialogue.

2.   How do the author's questions help emphasize the child's voice and perspective?

3.   When the author begins to count her bad thoughts, does this trigger any of your memories regarding church and religion?

4.   The author uses the rhetorical modes of definition, description, and persuasion with regard to "bad thoughts." Is using mixed strategies effective? Why?

Issues

1.   Discuss the all too real need of one group of people to look down on another group even though each group belongs to the same nationality. For instance, the author's mother looked down on the Jibara.

2.   The author's father says when describing the soul, "... it's the part of a person that feels." Can an author's voice come from his or her soul?

3.   Children ask questions all the time, and therefore, get information from different sources. Who do they tend to believe and why?

Writing Assignments

1.   Write a narrative essay mixing different rhetorical modes, using the child's voice about prejudice within the same nationality or racial group.

2.   Write an essay analyzing the religious perceptions of Langston Hughes in "Salvation" and Esmeralda Santiago in *When I Was Puerto Rican*.

Anne Moody

WHAT IS WHITE?

ANNE MOODY (b. 1940) was born in Mississippi. She graduated from a historically Black college, Tougaloo College, in 1964. Ms. Moody was an organizer and fundraiser for the Congress of Racial Equality (CORE) during the civil rights movement (1961-1964). The excerpts "What is White?" and "A Dollar a Day" are from Ms. Moody's 1969 autobiography *Coming of Age in Mississippi*.

The author struggles with how to deal with racism and the hypocrisy of both blacks and whites regarding racism.

That white lady Mama was working for worked her so hard that she always came home griping about backaches. Every night she'd have to put a red rubber bottle filled with hot water under her back. It got so bad that she finally quit. The white lady was so mad she couldn't get Mama to stay that the next day she told Mama to leave to make room for the new maid.

This time we moved two miles up the same road. Mama had another domestic job. Now she worked from breakfast to supper and still made five dollars a week. But these people didn't work Mama too hard and she wasn't as tired as before when she came home. The people she worked for were nice to us. Mrs. Johnson was a schoolteacher. Mr. Johnson was a rancher who bought and sold cattle. Mr. Johnson's mother, an old lady named Miss Ola, lived with them.

Our house, which was separated from the Johnsons' by a field of clover, was the best two-room house we had been in yet. It was made out of big new planks and it even had a new toilet. We were also once again on paved streets. We just did make those paved streets, though. A few yards past the Johnsons' house was the beginning of the old rock road we had just moved off.

We were the only Negroes in that section, which seemed like some sort of honor. All the whites living around there were well-to-do. They ranged from schoolteachers to doctors and prosperous businessmen. The white family living across the street from us owned a funeral home and the only furniture store in Centerville. They had two children, a boy and a girl. There was another white family living about a quarter of a mile in back of the Johnsons who also had a boy and a girl. The two white girls were about my age and the boys a bit younger. They often rode their bikes or skated down the little hill just in front of our house. Adline, Junior and I would sit and watch them. How we wished Mama could buy us a bike or even a pair of skates to share.

There was a wide trench running from the street alongside our house. It separated our house and the Johnsons' place from a big two-story house up on the hill. A big pecan tree grew on our side of the trench, and we made our playhouse under it so we could sit in the trench and watch those white children without their knowing we were actually out there staring at them. Our playhouse consisted of two apple crates and a tin can that we sat on.

One day when the white children were riding up and down the street on their bikes, we were sitting on the apple crates making Indian noises and beating the tin can with sticks. We sounded so much like Indians that they came over to ask if that was what we were. This was the beginning of our friendship. We taught them how to make sounds and dance like Indians and they showed us how to ride their bikes and skate. Actually, I was the only one who learned. Adline and Junior were too small and too scared, although they got a kick out of watching us. I was seven, Adline five, and Junior three, and this was the first time we had ever had other children to play with. Sometimes, they would take us over to their playhouse. Katie and Bill, the children of the whites that owned the furniture store, had a model playhouse at the side of their parents' house. That little house was just like the big house, painted snow white on the outside, with real furniture in it. I envied their playhouse more than I did their bikes and skates. Here they were playing in a house that was nicer than any house I could have dreamed of living in. They had all this to offer me and I had nothing to offer them but the field of clover in summer and the apple crates under the pecan tree.

The Christmas after we moved there, I thought sure Mama would get us some skates. But she didn't. We didn't get anything but a couple of apples and oranges. I cried a week for those skates, I remember.

Every Saturday evening Mama would take us to the movies. The Negroes sat upstairs in the balcony and the whites sat downstairs. One Saturday we arrived at the movies at the same time as the white children. When we saw each other, we ran and met. Katie walked straight into the downstairs lobby and Adline, Junior, and I followed. Mama was talking to one of the white women and didn't notice that we had walked into the white lobby. I think she thought we were at the side entrance we had always used which led to the balcony. We were standing in the white lobby with our friends, when Mama came in and saw us. "C'mon! C'mon!" she yelled, pushing Adline face on into the door. "Essie Mae, um gonna try my best to kill you when I get you home. I told you 'bout running up in these stores and things like you own 'em!" she shouted, dragging me through the door. When we got outside, we stood there crying, and we could hear the white children crying inside the white lobby. After that, Mama didn't even let us stay at the movies. She carried us right home.

All the way back to our house, Mama kept telling us that we couldn't sit downstairs, we couldn't do this or that with white children. Up until that time I had never really thought about it. After all, we were playing together. I knew that we were going to separate schools and all, but I never knew why.

After the movie incident, the white children stopped playing in front of our house. For about two weeks we didn't see them at all. Then one day they were there again and we started playing. But things were not the same. I had never really thought of them as white before. Now all of a sudden they were white, and their whiteness made them better than me. I now realized that not only were they better than me because they were white, but everything they owned and everything connected with them was better than what was available to me. I hadn't realized before that downstairs in the movies was any better than upstairs. But now I saw that it was. Their whiteness provided them with a pass to downstairs in that nice section and my blackness sent me to the balcony.

Now that I was thinking about it, their schools, homes, and streets were better than mine. They had a large red brick school and nice sidewalks connecting the buildings. Their homes were large and beautiful with indoor toilets and every other convenience that I knew of at the time. Every house I had ever lived in was a one- or two-room shack with an outdoor toilet. It really bothered me that they had all these nice things and we had nothing. "There is a secret to it besides being white," I thought. Then my mind got all wrapped up in trying to uncover that secret.

One day when we were all playing in our playhouse in the ditch under the pecan tree, I got a crazy idea. I thought the secret was their "privates." I had seen everything they had but their privates and it wasn't any different than mine. So I made up a game called "The Doctor." I had never been to a doctor myself. However, Mama had told us that a doctor was the only person that could look at children's naked bodies besides their parents. Then I remembered the time my Grandma Winnie was sick. When I asked her what the doctor had done to her she said, "He examined me." Then I asked her about "examined" and she told me he looked at her teeth, in her ears, checked her heart, blood and privates. Now I was going to be the doctor. I had all of them, Katie, Bill, Sandra, and Paul plus Adline and Junior take off their clothes and stand in line as I sat on one of the apple crates and examined them. I looked in their mouths and ears, put my ear to their hearts to listen for their heartbeats. Then I had them lie down on the leaves and I looked at their privates. I examined each of them about three times, but I didn't see any differences. I still hadn't found that secret.

That night when I was taking my bath, soaping myself all over, I thought about it again. I remembered the day I had seen my two uncles Sam and Walter. They were just as white as Katie them. But Grandma Winnie was darker than Mama, so how could Sam and Walter be white? I must have been thinking about it for a long time because Mama finally called out, "Essie Mae! Stop using up all that soap! And hurry up so Adline and Junior can bathe 'fore that water gits cold."

"Mama," I said, "why ain't Sam and Walter white?"

" 'Cause they mama ain't white," she answered.

"But you say a long time ago they daddy is white."

"If the daddy is white and the mama is colored, then that don't make the children white."

"But they got the same hair and color like Bill and Katie them got," I said.

"That still don't make them white! Now git out of that tub!" she snapped.

Every time I tried to talk to Mama about white people she got mad. Now I was more confused than before. If it wasn't the straight hair and the white skin that made you white, then what was it?

A DOLLAR A DAY

I was fifteen years old when I began to hate people. I hated the white men who murdered Emmett Till and I hated all the other whites who were responsible for the countless murders Mrs. Rice had told me about and those I vaguely remembered from childhood. But I also hated Negroes. I hated them for not standing up and doing something about the murders. In fact, I think I had a stronger resentment toward Negroes for letting the whites kill them than toward the whites. Anyway, it was at this stage in my life that I began to look upon Negro men as cowards. I could not respect them for smiling in a white man's face, addressing him as Mr. So-and-So, saying yessuh and nossuh when after they were home behind closed doors that same white man was a son of a bitch, a bastard, or any other name more suitable than mister.

Emmett Till's murder provoked a lot of anger and excitement among whites in Centreville. Now just about every evening when I go to work, Mrs. Burke had to attend a guild meeting. She had more women coming over now than ever. She and her friends had organized canvassing teams and a telephone campaign, to solicit for new members. Within a couple of months most of the whites in Centreville were taking part in the Guild. The meetings were initially held in the various houses. There were lawn parties and church gatherings. Then when it began to get cold, they were held in the high school auditorium.

After the Guild had organized about two-thirds of the whites in Centreville, all kinds of happenings were unveiled. The talk was on. White housewives began firing their maids and scolding their husbands and the Negro communities were full of whispered gossip.

The most talked-about subject was a love affair Mr. Fox, the deputy sheriff, and one of my classmates were carrying on. Bess was one of the oldest girls in my class. She was a shapely, high brown girl of about seventeen. She did general housekeeping and nursing for Fox and his wife.

It was general policy that most young white couples in Centreville hired only older Negro women as helpers. However, when there were two or more children in the family, it was more advantageous to hire a young Negro girl. That way, they always had someone to baby-sit when there was a need for a baby-sitter. My job with Linda Jean had been this kind. I kept Donna and Johnny on Sundays and baby-sat at night when they needed me.

Even though the teen-age Negro girls were more desirable for such jobs, very few, if any, were trusted in the homes of the young couples. The young white housewife didn't dare leave one alone in the house with her loyal and obedient husband. She was afraid that the Negro girl would seduce him, never the contrary.

There had been whispering in the Negro communities about Bess and Fox for some time. Just about every young white man in Centreville had a Negro lover. Therefore Fox, even though he was the deputy sheriff, wasn't doing anything worse than the rest of the men. At least that's the way the Negroes looked at the situation. Fox wasn't anyone special to them. But the whites didn't see it that way. The sheriff and all of his deputies were, in the eyes of their white compatriots, honorable men. And these honorable men were not put into office because they loved Negroes. So when the white community caught on about Fox and Bess, naturally they were out to expose the affair. Such exposure would discourage other officers from similar misbehavior.

Mrs. Fox was completely devoted to her husband. She too thought he was an honest man and she was willing to do anything that would prove him innocent. Soon a scheme was under way. Mrs. Fox was to leave home every so often. It had been reported that every time she was out and Bess was left there alone, Fox found his way home for one reason or another. Mrs. Fox left home purposely a couple of times while the neighbors kept watch. They confirmed the report that Fox would always return home. So one day Mrs. Fox decided to take the children and visit her mother—but she only went as far as the house next door. Bess was to come and give the house a thorough cleaning on the same day.

Mrs. Fox waited almost an hour at her neighbors' and nothing happened. It was said she was ready to go home and apologize to Bess and call her husband and do likewise. But just as she was about to do so, Fox drove up and went inside. She waited about thirty minutes more, then went home.

When she walked into her bedroom there they were, her husband and Bess, lying in her bed all curled up together. Poor Bess was so frightened that she ran out of the house clothed only in her slip with her panties in her hands. She never set foot in Mrs. Fox's house again. Neither did she return to school afterward. She took a job in the quarters where she lived, in a Negro café. It was said that she didn't need the job, though. Because after her embarrassing episode with Fox, her reputation was beyond repair, and he felt obligated to take care of her. Last I heard of Bess, she was still in Centreville, wearing fine clothes and carrying on as usual. Fox is no longer deputy, I understand, but he and his wife are still together.

It appeared after a while that the much talked about maids raids were only a means of diverting attention from what was really taking place in those guild meetings. In the midst of all the talk about what white man was screwing which Negro woman, new gossip emerged—about what Negro man was screwing which white woman. This gossip created so much tension, every

Negro man in Centreville became afraid to walk the streets. They knew too well that they would not get off as easily as the white man who was caught screwing a Negro woman. They had only to look at a white woman and be hanged for it. Emmett Till's murder had proved it was a crime, punishable by death, for a Negro man to even whistle at a white woman in Mississippi.

I had never heard of a single affair in Centreville between a Negro man and a white woman. It was almost impossible for such an affair to take place. Negro men did not have access to white women. Whereas almost every white man in town had a Negro woman in his kitchen or nursing his babies.

The tension lasted for about a month before anything happened. Then one day, a rumor was spread throughout town that a Negro had been making telephone calls to a white operator and threatening to molest her. It was also said that the calls had been traced to a certain phone that was now under watch.

Next thing we heard in the Negro community was that they had caught and nearly beaten to death a boy who, they said, had made the calls to the white operator. All the Negroes went around saying, "Y'all know that boy didn't do that." "That boy" was my classmate Jerry. A few months later I got a chance to talk to him and he told me what happened.

He said he had used the telephone at Billups and Fillups service station and was on his way home when Sheriff Ed Cassidy came along in his pickup truck.

"Hey, buddy," Cassidy called, "you on your way home?"

"Yes," Jerry answered.

"Jump in, I'm goin' your way, I'll give you a lift."

Then Jerry told me that when they got out there by the scales where the big trucks weigh at the old camp intersection, Cassidy let him out, telling him that he had forgotten something in town and had to go back and pick it up. At that point, Jerry told me, he didn't suspect anything. He just got out of the truck and told Cassidy thanks. But as soon as the sheriff pulled away, a car came along and stopped. There were four men in it. A deep voice ordered Jerry to get into the car. When he saw that two of the men were Jim Dixon and Nat Withers, whom he had often seen hanging around town with Cassidy, he started to run. But the two in the back jumped out and grabbed him. They forced him into the car and drove out into the camp area. When they got about five miles out, they turned down a little dark dirt road, heavily shaded with trees. They pushed Jerry out of the car onto the ground. He got up and dashed into the woods but they caught up with him and dragged him farther into the woods. Then they tied him to a tree and beat him with a big thick leather strap and a piece of hose pipe.

I asked him if they told him why they were beating him.

"No, not at first," Jerry said, "but when I started screamin' and cryin' and askin' them why they were beatin' me Dixon told me I was tryin' to be smart and they just kept on beatin' me. Then one of the men I didn't know asked me, 'Did you make that phone call, boy?' I said no. I think he kinda believed me 'cause he stopped beatin' me but the others didn't. The rest of them beat me until I passed out. When I came out of it I was lying on the ground, untied, naked and bleeding. I tried to get up but I was hurtin' all over and it was hard to move. Finally I got my clothes on that them sonofabitches had tore offa me and I made it out to the main highway, but I fainted again. When I woke up I was home in bed.

"Daddy then was scared to take me to the hospital in Centreville. I didn't even see a doctor 'cause they were scared to take me to them white doctors. Wasn't any bones or anything broken. I was swollen all over, though. And you can see I still have bruises and cuts from the strap, but otherwise I guess I'm O.K."

When I asked him whether they were going to do anything about it, he said that his daddy had gotten a white lawyer from Baton Rouge. But after the lawyer pried around in Centreville for a few days, he suddenly disappeared.

Jerry's beating shook up all the Negroes in town. But the most shocking and unjust crime of all occurred a few months later, about two weeks before school ended.

One night, about one o'clock, I was awakened by what I thought was a terrible nightmare. It was an empty dream that consisted only of hollering and screaming voices. It seemed as though I was in an empty valley screaming. And the sounds of my voice were reflected in a million echoes that were so loud I was being lifted in mid-air by the sound waves. I found myself standing trembling in the middle of the floor reaching for the light string. Then I saw Mama running to the kitchen, in her nightgown.

"Mama! Mama! What's all them voices? Where're all those people? What's happening?"

"I don't know," she said, coming to my bedroom door.

"Listen! Listen!" I said, almost screaming.

"Stop all that loud talking fo' you wake up the rest of them chaps. It must be a house on fire or somethin' 'cause of all the screamin'. Somebody must be hurt in it or somethin' too. Ray is getting the car, we gonna go see what it is," she said and headed for the back door.

"You going in your gown?" I asked her.

"We ain't gonna git out of the car. Come on, you can go," she said. "But don't slam the door and wake them chaps up."

I followed her out of the back door in my pajamas. Raymond was just backing the car out of the driveway.

When we turned the corner leaving the quarters, Raymond drove slowly alongside hundreds of people running down the road. They were all headed in the direction of the blaze that reddened the sky.

The crowd of people began to swell until driving was utterly impossible. Finally the long line of cars stopped. We were about two blocks away from the burning house now. The air was so hot that water was running down the faces of the people who ran past the car. The burning house was on the rock road, leading to the school, adjacent to the street we stopped on. So we couldn't tell which house it was. From where we sat, it seemed as though it could have been two or three of them burning. I knew every Negro living in the houses that lined that rock road. I passed them every day on my way to and from school.

I sat there in my pajamas, wishing I had thrown on a dress or something so I could get out of the car.

"Ray, ask somebody who house it is," Mama said to Raymond.

"Hi! Excuse me." Raymond leaned out of the car and spoke to a Negro man. "Do you know who house is on fire?"

"I heard it was the Taplin family. They say the whole family is still in the house. Look like they are done for, so they say."

Didn't any one of us say anything after that. We just sat in the car silently. I couldn't believe what the man had just said. "A whole family burned to death—impossible!" I thought.

"What you think happened, Ray?" Mama finally said to Raymond.

"I don't know. You never kin tell," Raymond said. "It seems mighty strange, though."

Soon people started walking back down the road. The screams and hollering had stopped. People were almost whispering now. They were all Negroes, although I was almost sure I had seen some whites pass before, "I guess not," I thought, sitting there sick inside. Some of the ladies passing the car had tears running down their faces, as they whispered to each other.

"Didn't you smell that gasoline?" I heard a lady who live in the quarters say.

"That house didn't just catch on fire. And just think them bastards burned up a whole family," another lady said. Then they were quiet again.

Soon their husbands neared the car.

"Heh, Jones," Raymond said to one of the men. "How many was killed?"

"About eight or nine of them, Ray. They say the old lady and one of the children got out. I didn't see her nowhere, though."

"You think the house was set on fire?" Raymond asked.

"It sho' looks like it, Ray. It burned down like nothing. When I got there that house was burning on every side. If it had started on the inside of the house at some one place then it wouldn't burn down like it did. All the walls fell in together. Too many strange things are happening round here these days."

Now most of the people and cars were gone, Raymond drove up to the little rock road and parked. I almost vomited when I caught a whiff of the odor of burned bodies mixed with the gasoline. The wooden frame house had been burned to ashes. All that was left were some iron bedposts and springs, a blackened refrigerator, a stove, and some kitchen equipment.

We sat in the car for about an hour, silently looking at this debris and the ashes that covered the nine charcoal-burned bodies. A hundred or more also stood around—Negroes from the neighborhood in their pajamas, nightgowns, and housecoats and even a few whites, with their eyes fixed on that dreadful scene. I shall never forget the expressions on the faces of the Negroes. There was almost unanimous hopelessness in them. The still, sad faces watched the smoke rising from the remains until the smoke died down to practically nothing. There was something strange about that smoke. It was the thickest and blackest smoke I had ever seen.

Raymond finally drove away, but it was impossible for him to take me away from that nightmare. Those screams, those faces, that smoke, would never leave me.

The next day I took the long, roundabout way to school. I didn't want to go by the scene that was so fixed in my mind. I tried to convince myself that nothing had happened in the night. And I wanted so much to believe that, to believe anything but the dream itself. However, at school, everybody was talking about it. All during each class there was whispering from student to student. Hadn't many of my classmates witnessed the burning last night. I wished they had. If so, they wouldn't be talking so much, I thought. Because I had seen it, and *I* couldn't talk about it. I just couldn't.

I was so glad when the bell sounded for the lunch hour. I picked up my books and headed home. I couldn't endure another minute of that torture. I was in such a hurry to get away from the talk at school I forgot to take the roundabout way home. Before I realized it, I was standing there where the Taplins' house had been. It looked quite different by day than it had at night. The ashes and junk had been scattered as if someone had looked for the remains of the bodies. The heavy black smoke had disappeared completely. But I stood there looking at the spot where I had seen it rising and I saw it again, slowly drifting away, disappearing before my eyes. I tore myself away and ran almost all the way home.

When I walked in the house Mama didn't even ask me why I came home. She just looked at me. And for the first time I realized she understood what was going on within me, or was trying to anyway. I took two aspirins and went to bed. I stayed there all afternoon. When it was time for me to go to work after school, Mama didn't come in. She must have known I wasn't in the mood for Mrs. Burke that evening. I wasn't in the mood for anything. I was just there inside of myself, inflicting pain with every thought that ran through my mind.

That night Centreville was like a ghost town. It was so quiet and still. The quietness almost drove me crazy. It was too quiet for sleeping that night, yet it was too restless for dreams and too dry for weeping.

A few days later, it was reported that the fire had started from the kerosene lamp used by Mrs. Taplin as a light for the new baby. Nobody bought that story. At least one of those who witnessed that fire and smelled that gasoline. They were sure that more than a lampful of kerosene caused that house to burn that fast.

There was so much doubt and dissension about the Taplin burning that finally FBI agents arrived on the scene and quietly conducted an investigation. But as usual in this sort of case, the investigation was dropped as soon as public interest died down.

Months later the story behind the burning was whispered throughout the Negro community. Some of the Taplins' neighbors who had been questioned put their scraps of information together and came up with an answer that made sense:

Living next door to the Taplin family was a Mr. Banks, a high yellow mulatto man of much wealth. He was a bachelor with land and cattle galore. He had for some time discreetly taken care of a white woman, the mother of three whose husband had deserted her, leaving her to care for the children the best way she knew how. She lived in a bottom where a few other poor whites lived. The Guild during one of its investigations discovered the children at home alone one night—and many other nights after that. Naturally, they wondered where the mother was spending her nights. A few days' observation of the bottom proved she was leaving home, after putting the children to bed, and being picked up by Mr. Banks in inconspicuous places.

When the Taplin family was burned, Mr. Banks escaped his punishment. Very soon afterward he locked his house and disappeared. And so did the white lady from the bottom.

I could barely wait until school was out. I was so sick of Centreville. I made up my mind to tell Mama I had to get away, if only for the summer. I had thought of going to Baton Rouge to live with my Uncle Ed who was now married and living there with his family.

A few days before school ended I sat in the midst of about six of my classmates who insisted on discussing the Taplin family. By the time I got home, my nerves were in shreds from thinking of some of the things they had said. I put my books down, took two aspirins, and got into bed. I didn't think I could go to work that evening because I was too nervous to be around Mrs. Burke. I had not been myself at work since the Emmett Till murder, especially after the way Mrs. Burke had talked to me about the Taplin family. But she had become more observant of my reactions.

"What's wrong with you? Is you sick?" Mama asked me. I didn't answer her.

"Take your shoes off that spread. You better git up and go to work. Mrs. Burke gonna fire you."

"I got a headache and I don't feel like going," I said.

"What's wrong with you, getting so many headaches around here?"

I decided not to wait any longer to tell Mama my plan.

"Mama, I am gonna write Ed and see can I stay with him this summer and get a job in Baton Rouge. I am just tired of working for Mrs. Burke for a dollar a day. I can make five dollars a day in Baton Rouge and I make only six dollars a week here."

"Ed them ain't got enough room for you to live with them. Take your shoes off," Mama said, and left me lying in bed.

As soon as she left, I got up and wrote my letter. About five days later I received an answer from Ed. He said I was welcome, so I started packing to leave the next day. Mama looked at me as if she didn't want me to go. But she knew better than to ask me.

I was fifteen years old and leaving home for the first time. I wasn't even sure I could get a job at that age. But I had to go anyway, if only to breathe a slightly different atmosphere. I was choking to death in Centreville. I couldn't go on working for Mrs. Burke pretending I was dumb and innocent, pretending I didn't know what was going on in all her guild meetings, or about Jerry's beating, or about the Taplin burning, and everything else that was going on. I was sick of pretending, sick of selling my feelings for a dollar a day.

WHAT IS WHITE?
A DOLLAR A DAY

Facts

1.   How did the Moody children make their Indian sounds?

2.   The Moody children were satisfied with their play things until they saw the play things of the white children. What did the black children want that the white children had?

3.   Why was Ms. Moody angry with her children for following their playmates into the theater lobby?

4.   In "What is White?," why was the author confused about the issue of whiteness?

5.   What was the Guild, its activities and its purpose?

6.   Why was Jerry, the author's classmate, beaten?

7.   Why was the Taplins' house torched?

8.   Why did the author leave Centreville?

Strategies

1.   In "What is White?" several rhetorical modes are used to explore the meaning of white. What are they?

2.   The author lends an adult perspective to the incident at the movies; she thinks about being white and what that means. Is this change in perspective and voice needed to illuminate the author's feelings or is the disruption too abrupt?

3.   The teenage voice of Moody is tinged with cynicism in "A Dollar a Day." In which paragraphs is this cynical teenage voice clearly heard?

4.   Which adjectives would you use to describe the other emotions of the teenage Moody?

Issues

1.   In "What is White?" success is compared to the people who are the neighbors of the author. Discuss whether or not black people measure success by comparing themselves to white people today. If they do, why?

2.   Why did things change among the friends after the movie incident? Discuss this incident in the framework of shaping all the children's thoughts regarding race.

3.   The author says in the beginning of the chapter, "A Dollar a Day," that she hates Negroes more than whites. Explain why?

4.   In "A Dollar a Day" the author brings up the murder of Emmett Till. Discuss Till's murder and its meaning then and now.

5.   In order to get along in the white world in Centreville, the Negro wore a mask. Discuss the reasons for wearing a mask and whether or not a mask is worn today.

6.   Do all cultures create a facade to deal with other cultures? Or is this done only when one group considers itself either superior or inferior?

7.   Why did the author think Centreville was choking her? Is that a common feeling among teenagers?

Writing Assignments

1.   Research the Emmett Till incident in 1954 and a recent (1990s) incident of racial brutality. Analyze the comparisons and the contrasts and write a compare and/or contrast essay on your findings.

2.   Write an essay, using the child's voice mixed with the adult perspective, about an event when you were between eight and twelve years old that caused you to run away—physically and/or mentally.

ACKNOWLEDGMENTS

From *Daisy Fay and the Miracle Man* Copyright © 1981 by Fannie Flagg. Reprinted by permission of The Wendy Weil Agency, Inc.

"The Sky is Gray," copyright © 1963 by Ernest J. Gaines, from BLOODLINE by Ernest J. Gaines. Used by permission of Doubleday, a division of Random House, Inc.

From COMING OF AGE IN MISSISSIPPI by Anne Moody. Copyright © 1968 by Anne Moody. Used by permission of Doubleday, a division of Random House, Inc.

From I KNOW WHY THE CAGED BIRD SINGS by Maya Angelou. Copyright © 1969 and renewed 1997 by Maya Angelou. Reprinted by permission of Random House, Inc.

Copyright © 1990 by Gish Jen. First published in The Atlantic Monthly. Reprinted by permission of the author.

"Pat and Pan" by Sui Sin Far. From *Mrs. Spring Fragrance*. Copyright © 1912 by A.C. McClurg & Co.

"Toussaint," from CHINA BOY by Gus Lee. Copyright © 1991 Augustus S. M. S. Lee. Used by permission of Dutton, a division of Penguin Putnam Inc.

Reprinted with the permission of Simon & Schuster, Inc., from FAMOUS ALL OVER TOWN by Danny Santiago. Copyright © 1983 by Danny Santiago.

"Impressions of an Indian Childhood" by Zitkala-Sa was originally published in The Atlantic Monthly in 1900. It was also included in *Old Indian Legends* copyright © 1901.

AUTHOR INDEX

TITLE INDEX